Praise for *Smarter Pricing, Smarter Profit*

"People often ask me what is the one thing I suggest they read in order to understand all of the changes in the [legal] market and how their firms can best adapt. I now have an answer for them: Read this book." –Toby Brown, Chief Practice Officer, Akin Gump Strauss Hauer & Feld LLP and Chair of the LMA's Client Value Special Interest Group

"*Smarter Pricing, Smarter Profit* is soup to nuts the most comprehensive and forward-looking resource I have seen yet. It covers market conditions, both historical business of law practices and those needed for the future, and a framework to manage all stages of pricing and managing work to profitable conclusions. This book should be required reading for anyone involved in pricing or managing legal work. I will need many copies of this book as I plan to distribute it widely within my firm." –Chris Emerson, Director, Practice Economics Group, Bryan Cave LLP and Vice President of ILTA's Business & Financial Management Peer Group

"Pricing can be regarded as both an art and a science. Too often within the legal sector this has been translated into using a combination of budgeting and gut-feel, practices that more closely resemble a dark art than genuine pricing enlightenment. But now there's an alternative. In *Smarter Pricing, Smarter Profit*, Stuart Dodds integrates so much material into a single, logical framework. It provides a step-by-step guide for improving pricing performance and, ultimately, profitability.

It's easy to read, packed with practical ideas for improving results within firms and is presented by one of the world's leading practitioners in the field. I recommend this book to anyone charged with responsibility for improving their firm's pricing performance." –Colin Jasper, Director, Jasper Consulting

SMARTER PRICING, SMARTER PROFIT

Cover design by ElMarie Jara/ABA Publishing.

Printed in the United States of America.

18 17 16 15 14 5 4 3 2 1

Library of Congress Cataloging-in-Publication Data

Dodds, Stuart J.T., author.
Smarter pricing, smarter profit / Stuart JT Dodds.
pages cm
Includes bibliographical references and index.
ISBN 978-1-61438-984-2 (alk. paper)
1. Practice of law--Economic aspects--United States. 2. Lawyers--Fees--United States. I. Title.
KF315.D63 2014
340.068'8--dc23

2014008457

Discounts are available for books ordered in bulk. Special consideration is given to state bars, CLE programs, and other bar-related organizations. Inquire at Book Publishing, ABA Publishing, American Bar Association, 321 N. Clark Street, Chicago, Illinois 60654-7598.

www.ShopABA.org

Stuart J. T. Dodds

SMARTER PRICING, SMARTER PROFIT

A GUIDE FOR THE LAW FIRM OF THE FUTURE

Defending Liberty
Pursuing Justice

For Ophelia and Isla, both of whom make the ride worthwhile

Contents

Foreword

Much has been written about the need for the legal market to adapt to change. Most lawyers and firms know they need to embrace change on some level, but what these people are really craving is a simple, practical guide on how to get started and how to move their practices successfully into this new world of competition. Enter Stuart Dodds and this book.

The book's title, *Smarter Pricing, Smarter Profit*, reflects the simple yet compelling approach taken. Stuart sets the stage, lays out the path, and then leads the reader on an understandable and highly valuable journey.

His "Set, Get, Manage, and Review the Price" approach lays out the plan for lawyers and firms that want to successfully navigate their way into a 21st-century practice. To bring the reader down this path, he takes a wide range of topics and connects them into a coherent whole. His suggestions for how to take each step and implement them are highly practical.

Expect to find suggestions and techniques that are easily understood and very reasonable to implement for any firm. Even those who are knowledgeable on one or many of the topics he covers will find plenty of gems among his suggestions (as I did).

People often ask me what is the one thing I suggest they read in order to understand all of the changes in the market and how their firms can best adapt. I now have an answer for them: read this book.

Toby Brown
Chief Practice Officer,
Akin Gump Strauss Hauer & Feld LLP
and Chair of the LMA's Client Value Special Interest Group

Chapter 1

Introducing Our Framework

Set, Get, Manage, Review

This book seeks to provide you with an easy-to-read roadmap, guiding you through how you can drive improvements to your law firm's existing pricing and legal project management capability and also to the overall profit contribution made in this ever-changing legal environment.

When reading this book, you may come across some similar content and ideas you have seen in other publications (some of which are included in the bibliography at the end of this book), and indeed I continue to be indebted to a number of key individuals who have helped challenge my thinking on these topics.

However, what this book seeks to do that I believe existing publications do not is to provide you with a very simple framework to get from A to Z, covering four fundamental and integrated processes related to pricing, negotiation, effective project management, and, ultimately, improved profitability.

I have referred to these as

- **Setting the Price** (i.e., the "art and science" behind defining the "right" price),
- **Getting the Price** (i.e., communicating *and* negotiating the value of your proposition),
- **Managing to Price** (i.e., delivering efficiently and to an appropriate quality on your proposal), and

- **Reviewing the Price** (i.e., providing the basis to get even better next time).

From my reading around this topic over a number of years, existing materials seem to focus on one, two, or perhaps even three of these processes, but not all four together. This book seeks to address this gap.

Therefore, during the course of this book, I'll introduce you to a framework that is both simple and intuitive.

This is a framework I have developed over a number of years working for a couple of well-known international law firms, but is one I believe is equally applicable to any law firm regardless of size or geographic reach.

Let's have a look at each key stage in a bit more detail.

The first stage focuses on what I call "**Set the Price.**" This is where you look to identify the most appropriate *pricing option* to adopt, conduct the appropriate analysis (including past performance using similar approaches but with the potential client in mind), and also conduct the necessary approvals within your own organization prior to communicating your proposed pricing approach to the client.

The second stage is one that is often given less attention. I call this "**Get the Price.**" This covers both the communication of *our value proposition* to the client and also the *commercial negotiation* with the client (an area often overlooked by many lawyers).

The third stage is "**Manage to Price.**" This section focuses on *how we deliver* our services to our clients in a cost-effective and efficient manner and to the agreed price. Whereas the first two sections focus primarily on price, this section focuses more on the concept of legal project management.

The fourth and final stage is "**Review the Price.**" This is the section often skipped by many who seek to move on to the next matter or engagement, and yet the value of conducting some of the approaches outlined in this section well can be extremely significant. It is here we can identify further improvements to our pricing and processes to become even more efficient and effective. It is here that we would incorporate feedback from the client and the client team on both our pricing and delivery approaches and where we can identify process improvement to support future matters. Figure 1.1 on the next page provides a quick overview of the overall process.

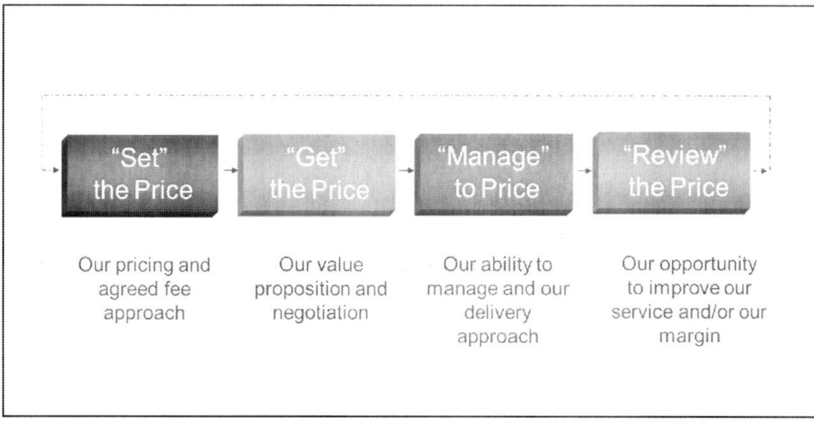

Figure 1.1
Introducing Our Framework

The overall intent is to build greater commercial confidence both when pricing our services for clients and when seeking to identify ways to further improve the delivery of those services to clients through effective matter management, enhanced through process improvement.

In my experience to date, law firm focus has traditionally been spent (especially in recent years) on the first stage, set the price. An increasing focus is now being given to the third stage, manage to price (although this is an area where currently there is arguably more hype than action). However, very little focus has been given (in my opinion) to the remaining two sections: those of get the price and review the price. And yet both these areas, when done well, will also deliver significant value to both law firm and client alike.

This book has been structured around each of the four key themes outlined above, bookended by some introductory chapters to help establish the current market context and challenges at the front (Chapters 2 and 3) and a couple of chapters looking forward to what developments in this area may mean in the future, specifically around the changing role of technology (Chapter 22) and the changing nature of law firm professional and business support (Chapter 23).

As part of the Set the Price section, we will take a quick look at pricing theory (Chapter 4), before looking at how we should start pricing a matter, and why it is important to do this with the end goal clearly in mind (Chapter 5). We will then conduct a quick review of the different types of pricing approaches that are increasingly being adopted (which I prefer to call *appropriate* fee agreements), and then round off this section with a look at how conducting some very simple pricing analysis can add significant value to your bottom line in Chapters 6 and 7, respectively.

In the Get the Price section, the focus changes toward how to more effectively communicate our value proposition to clients (Chapter 8). We then move on to a couple of chapters dedicated to how to best prepare for a pitch (Chapter 9) and engage with clients' procurement teams, a group becoming increasingly influential in law firm selection (Chapter 10). The remainder of this part of the book provides some pointers as to how to best prepare for and then conduct commercial negotiations with our clients (Chapters 11 and 12, respectively)—an area still given very little attention in the majority of law firms today.

The next section, Manage to Price, provides an overview on the rise and importance of legal project management (Chapter 13) and how to get started or reinvigorate current initiatives in this area (Chapter 14). The remainder of this section then provides you with some guidance on what I recommend you do at the start of any matter (Chapters 15 and 16), how to maintain momentum during the matter (Chapter 17), and, finally, how to successfully close a matter (Chapter 18).

The final key section, Review the Price, seeks to bring together many of the themes already discussed. Many of the activities introduced in this section are often overlooked, yet the value of doing them is immense. First, we will look at why gathering client and client team feedback is important (Chapter 19). We will then look at a number of recommended ways to measure performance (Chapter 20), before closing with a chapter on why legal process improvement really is where the "gold dust" is in helping deliver more cost-effective, profitable, and compelling client value and service (Chapter 21).

Much of what I will cover in the book may be similar to approaches you are already taking within your own firms. However, approaching the area of law firm pricing and delivery using the simple integrated framework outlined here will hopefully provide you with a much more solid footing to drive benefit to your own firm and to your clients, and will also position you well for the inevitable changes our industry will experience.

Along the way, I also hope that some of these chapters raise a number of interesting concepts for you, and perhaps even some questions, as we go through the Set, Get, Manage, Review framework itself.

As a minimum, this will ideally help reinforce and validate the path you are already on. Best case: you will hopefully gather an additional number of suggested approaches to try, or gain further facts to help you promote the need for change within your own firm.

Some of you may choose to jump straight to the section that is most appropriate to you at the time, whereas some of you may wish to read from beginning to end. There is no right or wrong method. Whatever your approach, I hope that this provides you with a number of helpful hints and tips, while also encouraging some of your own ideas as to how best to successfully navigate this environment for yourself and your firm.

But before diving into the first of our four key stages, it is useful to have a brief look at some context that sets the backdrop to our discussion. This context looks at two key areas—firstly, the "rise of the new normal" in the legal environment, and secondly, some basic information about law firm economics or the "business of law."

As we shall see subsequently, each of the four major areas outlined above play a key role in impacting profitability positively or negatively depending upon the path chosen. Even *very small* changes in one of these areas can contribute to more *significant improvements* overall.

This book aims to be your guide or roadmap to help you to select the right path.

Now to begin our journey.

Chapter 2

The Rise of the New Normal

2012 wasn't a good year for law firms. Okay, I admit, it wasn't a bad year (unless you were unfortunate enough to be caught up in one of the high-profile law firm collapses). What it was, was a normal year. At least "normal" as of now.

It was a year in which law firm profits in the United States increased by 4.3 percent, revenues grew by 3.6 percent (in part due to an increased focus on getting collections in during the fourth quarter), and demand grew by 0.2 percent. What demand growth there was primarily driven by the Am Law 1–50 and smaller firms.

The Citi Private Bank Law Firm Survey summarized growth as follows: "[W]hen we look at the full year 2012 results, the Am Law 1–50 still finished 2012 flat to the prior year, and smaller firms still saw a decline vs. 2011."[1]

In effect, it was a *flat market* with capacity creeping ahead of demand and overall fee-earner productivity declining. To paraphrase the conclusion of the article slightly, this could be viewed as "*the new definition of a good year for the legal industry*."

This picture is also not just limited to those operating in the United States. Similar patterns are being experienced in both the United Kingdom and continental Europe, where there remains sluggish market demand. Only in Asia and Latin America has there been a slightly more positive outlook,

---

1. Dan DiPietro & Gretta Rusanow, *Citi: Firms Posted 4.3 Percent Rise in 2012 Profits*, Am Law Daily (Feb. 7, 2013).

with a number of high-growth economies driving demand for legal services, and even this, according to some commentators, is now beginning to slow (for example, in China and Brazil).

This has brought even more acute focus on pricing, fee approaches, the means of matter delivery, and the means by which law firms are seeking to address these issues within the legal press, legal commentators, law firm clients, and law firms themselves.

Given the need for most firms to chase a relatively static level of demand and therefore differentiate themselves in terms of matter efficiency and client satisfaction, it is "unlikely that companies will want to revert to the more casual and costly pricing of earlier days."[2] From a law firm's perspective, meaningful growth is only likely to come from clearly identifying and exploiting opportunities as they come along, rather than relying solely on growth of the overall market.

Whether one agrees with the phrase "the new normal," which is often used to summarize the current market situation and was reportedly first used in a legal context by Paul Lippe in a thought-provoking article in March 2010,[3] it is clear that the more traditional approach to law firm pricing has significantly shifted over the last few years, and has accelerated since the global financial crisis.

It is also clear that there is *no* return to the unchallenged fee estimate or indeed the double-digit profit per equity partner increases that some firms annually achieved. In April 2012, as part of a survey conducted by Thomson Reuters of leaders of 52 of the world's largest firms, "64 percent of respondents predicted that their firms' profit per equity partner growth in 2012 would be in the 1 to 5 percent range."[4]

---

2. ALM LEGAL INTELLIGENCE, THINKING LIKE YOUR CLIENT: LAW FIRM STRATEGIC PLANNING 13 (2012), *available at* http://www.lexisnexis.com/pdf/intelligence/ALM-Report-Strategic-Planning-in-Law-Firms.pdf.

3. Paul Lippe, *Welcome to the Future: Embracing the New Normal*, AM LAW DAILY (Mar. 19, 2010), *available at* http://amlawdaily.typepad.com/amlawdaily/2010/03/0319future.html.

4. Thomson Reuters Peer Monitor/Georgetown Law Ctr. for the Study of the Legal Profession, 2013: Report on the State of the Legal Market 7 n.11 (2013), *available at* https://www.law.georgetown.edu/continuing-legal-education/executive-education/upload/2013-report.pdf.

As Paul identified in his article, the change at the time was being driven by six underlying key themes:

- **alternative staffing**, that is, using the right resource for the right task (and that may *not* be from the same firm)—not just staffing that has either traditionally been used or is "visible"
- **predictable pricing**, where there is a *shared* view on what is *reasonable* in terms of price and *value*
- **defined quality**, where the work "product" is clearly assessed against explicit, outcome-based criteria
- **client intimacy**, which Paul defined as "firms [doing] a better job of enabling success and preventing risk"[5] through being more knowledgeable of, and integrated with, their clients
- **technology**, where this is being used to enable lawyers to work "smarter," whether through collaboration tools or similar
- **process innovation**, where both firm and client find ways to work "better, faster, and cheaper"

What was true back in March 2010 is even more true and firmly entrenched now—as are the consequences to law firms of getting it "wrong." Although some in the profession still cling to the hope that the world will go back to the pre-2008 days where demand for legal service was vibrant and pricing pressure (relatively) nonexistent, the population of this group continues to dwindle and are beginning to more closely resemble a legal equivalent of the "Flat Earth Society."

The financial crisis in 2008 may have dramatically accelerated the pace of change (or indeed been the catalyst), but change was going to come. Given that in the decade prior to 2008 law firms in the United States increased their rates 6 to 8 percent per annum on average (often double the prevailing rate of inflation), something was going to give—and it did.

There is a greater need for law firms to be pragmatic and "nimble" in responding to clients' collective requests, and this frequently challenges

5. Lippe, *supra* note 3.

some long-held traditions and models around firm profitability, the traditional partnership model, "appropriate" quality of work product, hiring, and retention, to name a few.

As some members of our collective client base seem increasingly focused on securing bigger and bigger discounts and greater certainty of outcome, seeking to implement agreements that can often last multiple years, and looking to transfer more commercial risk to their selected law firm provider, it can often feel a daunting prospect to be a practicing lawyer and, even more so, to be a *profitable* practicing lawyer.

Each of the themes outlined in this chapter has contributed to the rise in importance of pricing and project management disciplines generally, and alternative fee arrangements specifically, as now essential skills within the arsenal of today's lawyer. This trend, and those similar, is going to continue. In a recent survey, 60 percent of law firm leaders agreed that the pace of change is only going to increase in the future,[6] and although not all will be related to pricing or project management, the themes of commerciality, efficiency, and client satisfaction will remain constant.

Don't forget *(a summary of the key points):*

- A "flat" market is likely to become the definition of a good year for the legal industry
- Any meaningful growth is likely to come from clearly identifying and exploiting approaches as they come along and not via "organic" growth
- Pricing and delivery expectations have permanently changed
- Becoming a profitable practicing lawyer (and law firm) is now essential

6. Thomas S. Clay & Eric A. Seeger, Law Firms in Transition 2012: An Altman Weil Flash Survey 3 (2012), *available at* http://www.altmanweil.com/LFiT2012/.

Chapter 3

Law Firm Economics 101: How Law Firms Make Money

(Or the Business of Law)

Law firms exist to make money.

There, I said it. Although some lawyers are in practice due to a love of the law, associated intellectual challenge, and a desire to help people through its application, fundamentally, law firms and lawyers are there to make money. There is nothing wrong in that. All other professional services businesses, such as management consulting (my previous background), are there to do likewise.

But are we really aware of what key factors influence how these firms *make* money, and, as importantly (as we shall see later on in this book), how not to *lose* money? From experience, firms often tend to focus on the potential revenue line, but seldom pay much attention to the expenses when it comes to winning a piece of work from an existing or (especially) a new client, or in trying to mitigate the "silly mistakes" that can impact profitability.

This chapter provides a quick overview of the key drivers of law firm profitability and some current (as of mid-2013) market context. As we shall see as we discuss the key themes of this book in more detail, an awareness and understanding of each of these drivers is vital to ensure that we, in our respective law firms, can continue to price and perform client matters cost-effectively whilst delivering to the now expected levels of client value and client service.

But why does profitability matter? Apart from the obvious compensation element, strong profitability is critical in having a strong market profile, strong league table rankings (for those who need to worry about these things), overall competitive positioning, lateral recruitment, attorney retention, and finally, future investment (for example, new office openings or major infrastructure projects). Therefore, achieving a competitive level of profitability is regarded as being fundamental in a firm's ability to sustaining its overall competitiveness.

What is becoming more apparent is that there is a critical need now to *actively* manage profitability on a number of dimensions—at a firm, practice, and individual level, by work type, and by client. By their very nature, some of the themes are "macro" or "micro."

In today's environment, the need to pay attention to profitability is no longer a temporary area of focus, reviewed *in extremis* when we "sense" things are taking a turn for the worse. Instead, this needs to be one of the top law firm management priorities and remain so.

How a Law Firm Makes Money

Let's start at the very beginning.

The ability of a firm to deliver revenue is driven by the markets in which it operates (which will include current and potentially new clients), the nature of the services it seeks to provide, and the relative value placed on these services by the end client.

A firm's ability to generate fees (or "fee capacity") is therefore, by definition, a proportion or a subset of the overall revenue potential.

Fee capacity is linked to the number, seniority, and expertise of timekeepers; (historically) the number of hours they would expect to work for their clients; and the rate at which they would typically conduct this work (recognizing, as we will discuss later, that this may vary by client, period, or matter).

External factors also play a key role. The volume of matters conducted, the nature of these matters, and the competitive pricing pressure from other firms all play a role in either limiting this fee capacity potential or increasing it. Similarly, as clients are beginning to explore and adopt non-hourly-fee approaches, this more traditional approach to determining fee capacity potential is being, in my view, appropriately challenged.

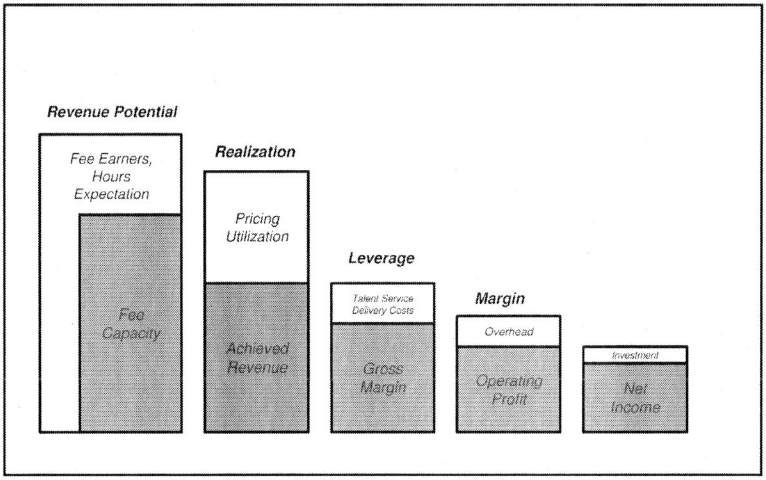

Figure 3.1
The Law Firm's Business Model
Source: Adapted from MICHAEL ROCH, PRICING & PROFITABILITY FOR LAW FIRMS/BUSINESS MODEL FOR A LAW FIRM 12 (2011).

What this traditional approach does is reinforce the view that revenue is based on *hours worked for the client*, rather than the fundamental tenet of pricing—that is, that the price should reflect the *appropriate value to the client*. It therefore places a *false limit* on the potential fee capacity for those partners willing to be more flexible in the fee approaches adopted and level of risk shared with their clients (for example, through pricing on a contingent- or fixed-fee basis). Figure 3.1 above shows this in graphic form.

The Basics of Law Firm Profitability

Most law firms are currently experiencing a "twin squeeze" on their profitability. A declining, or relatively static, revenue base coupled with the need to manage expenses (the resultant "gap" between the two, the revenue *not* expended, being "profit").

The first theme, that of declining or static revenue, is being driven by the *downward pressure on fees.*

This, in some areas, can be very significant as new entrants seek to aggressively price to take market share, coupled with a reduction in certain types of work. As an illustration, when looking at the United States for 2012, only Labor/Employment and Corporate work had a positive growth rate in overall billings, and even then low—1 to 3 percent, respectively.[1]

The second theme, managing expenses, is being impacted by the *upward pressure on costs.*

Although many firms went through some very difficult times during the latter part of 2008 through to 2010, with a high number of redundancies within both legal and nonlegal staff costs ("direct expenses") and associated reduction in "indirect expenses" (for example, occupancy costs, information technology, and administrative support), the softening of current demand has meant that similar reviews of staffing continue in most jurisdictions. Even in those jurisdictions that were relatively insulated from the global financial crisis, and have benefited from significant inward investment by Chinese, Indian, and Brazilian corporations, a number of firms have needed to reduce staffing during 2012, such as in Australia.

Expense "cuts" being made were, however, only temporary, with many significant investment projects (for example, in new IT systems) being deferred rather than abandoning specific programs or activities. As such, there remains a key need to manage expenses, with recent data indicating that expenses are running about 3–5 percent higher year on year as of 2010.[2]

Expense costs are also being impacted by the ongoing intense competition for the "best" laterals in the market, which in turn is driving associated compensation costs higher in the hope that these "stars" bring in significant additional revenues once in situ. (I would imagine that no one needs

1. Thomson Reuters Peer Monitor/Georgetown Law Ctr. for the Study of the Legal Profession, 2013: Report on the State of the Legal Market 3 (2013).

2. *Id.* at 7.

to be reminded what happens when this goes awry, such as with Dewey & LeBoeuf.)

"Growth Is Dead"

Prior to 2008, demand grew on average by 3.9 percent each year (with "demand" here being defined as the growth in billable hours).

Current demand growth is, however, much more limited. It has been estimated that the U.S. legal market grew by as little as 0.5 percent in 2012, and the signs in 2013 are little better, with even optimists sensing that the status quo is perhaps the best they can hope for.

What little growth law firms have managed to secure has therefore primarily been at the expense of other firms (often due to "loss leader" pricing), despite the anticipated growth in areas such as regulatory and compliance. It is this (among other factors) that has prompted one well-respected legal commentator, Bruce MacEwen (of Adam Smith, Esq.), when looking at the legal industry in the United States, to declare "growth is dead."

As can be seen from figure 3.2 on the next page, although demand is certainly better than in 2009, it continues to remain soft, even when compared with more recent "lean" years. Nor is this picture only relevant to those in the United States, with a similar pattern being evident elsewhere. Although the volume of matters may be increasing in some practice areas, the level of overall spend is not—or at the very least, not keeping step.

When looking at a more granular level, the demand picture is mixed, however. During 2012, the growth experienced by *midsize U.S. firms* was relatively strong, with demand rising by 2.6 percent, compared with the Am Law 100 firms (at 0.2 percent) and Am Law 100–200 firms (at 0.6 percent). This, in part, may be due to clients looking to engage with more cost-effective firms on certain matters (for example, litigation).[3] Again, a pattern not uncommon in the other major legal markets. What is certainly easier to

3. Corey Brandon, Russ Schmidt & Marcos Ramirez, Peer Monitor: Monthly Client Report (December 2012).

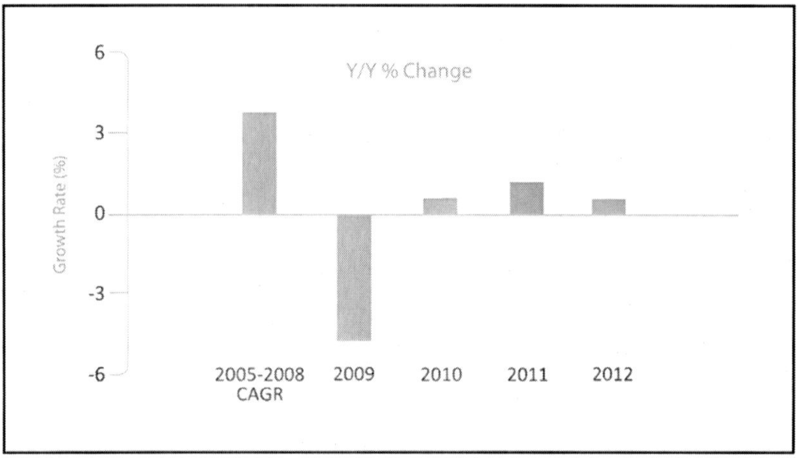

Figure 3.2
The Change in Demand for Legal Services
Source: REUTERS PEER MONITOR/GEORGETOWN LAW CTR. FOR THE STUDY OF THE LEGAL PROFESSION, 2013: REPORT ON THE STATE OF THE LEGAL MARKET 2 (2013).

predict is that the waters ahead are going to remain choppy, and there is no room for complacency. A proverbial life jacket may be a wise investment.

Watching the Revenue Line

If growth really is dead, what can a law firm realistically do to stay afloat (apart from buy life jackets in bulk)?

One immediate response is to focus on, and conduct *better and smarter management* of, the revenue line itself.

In a law firm, and indeed many other professional services firms that "sell expertise" rather than a product, revenue is impacted by four key drivers:

- the rate a firm is able to charge clients
- overall realization
- the firm's productivity
- the number of lawyers present (and "how well" they are used)

Let's take a look at each in turn.

Rates

Of the four key drivers, this is probably the one best understood.

Until the global financial crisis, law firms were typically able to increase their standard rates by anywhere from 6 percent to 10 percent per annum (depending upon jurisdiction). Given that their underlying costs were probably rising at a significantly more modest level (2 percent to 4 percent depending upon jurisdiction), the resulting difference between the two numbers was pure profit.

It was this difference that drove the rapid increase in many firms' level of partner profit, and that has set the unrealistic compensation expectations today as partners compare current levels of profit to the "golden days" pre-2008.

But, as we are aware, the world changed. Many law firms are now lucky if they are able to pass a much more modest 3–4 percent increase in rates through to their clients. Coupled with a similar, if not higher, level of rising costs, and the current (and I would predict more likely going forward) level of rate increases at best keep many firms "cost and revenue neutral." In other words, rising rates merely compensate for rising costs. And remember, just because you raise rates, there is no guarantee a client will accept this increase.

Many clients, particularly since late 2008, have begun to institute rate freezes for two, sometimes three, years (as an aside, this is an approach adopted by many French banks, although they are certainly not alone in doing so). Based on pure math alone in this scenario, unless a law firm proactively seeks to move away from hourly based billing *and* also improve their overall efficiency, they will experience declining profitability from these clients year on year.

Therefore increasing rates is no longer a viable solution in trying to address, or at least "mask," the more inherent challenges within our industry.

Realization

The realization rate can be defined a number of ways.

The most commonly used definition is the percentage of the firm's standard billing rate (sometimes referred to as the "rack rate") actually collected. It is a metric that converts the "time value" into cash receipts (with time value being the product of demand—that is, billable hours—and pricing—that is, hourly rates).

Although it is very much an internal measure, monitoring realization is vital to any law firm for one reason above all others. It is what I call the "1-3-4" Rule™ (which we will return to later), which basically states that a 1 percent increase in realization can drive approximately a 3 percent improvement in profitability (depending upon the underlying cost base), *but the converse is also true*! (The "4" part of the 1-3-4 Rule™ states that if discounting by 1 percent, we would need to bill 4 percent *more time* to get back to the original level of profit *before* applying the discount. Given the focus on greater efficiency, we all know that is no longer an option.)

As such, it provides a useful indicator of where management attention needs to be focused at either a client- or matter-specific level, if reviewed at an appropriate level of detail (see sidebar: Realization: A Multidimensional Metric?).

The realization rate is primarily impacted by three main factors, reflecting

- any agreed-upon discounts you may give a client;
- any write-*downs*, which are reductions you make to the bill *before* sending (for example, where a partner identifies work that has been duplicated elsewhere, or is of the view it has not delivered any value to the client); and finally,
- any write-*offs*, which are reductions made *after* the bill has been sent (for example, where the client has challenged a specific charge, or even sometimes when a client refuses to pay for services rendered, such as when a matter fails to complete satisfactorily).

As a metric, it is commonly looked at as a *matter* level, *client* level, and *firm* level.

For most firms, alarm bells *should* start ringing when realization gets to *about the 65 percent mark*, as the impact of declining realization on profitability after this point becomes much more significant (as the impact is not truly linear). *But the metric, if viewed in isolation, can be misleading.* Take the following two scenarios.

Firm A achieves very high realization but has done so due to very low rates. In this example, Firm A has potentially left some money on the table.

Firm B, on the other hand, has relatively low realization, but against higher rates. They have done so intentionally due to their pricing and discounting policy. Firm B has lower realization but higher overall revenue. This discounting approach is often adopted by accountancy firms, and indeed some in the legal world too—especially in emerging jurisdictions where offering higher discounts against higher rates is commonplace. Unless you understand what is driving the number, you may come to an incorrect conclusion about how your firm is performing.

Realization: A Multidimensional Metric?

It is useful to examine realization at its *component* level. Although the usual definition of realization is the percentage of the firm's standard billing rate actually collected, there are a number of other approaches that can be as, and often be *more*, useful. A short report by James Cotterman (published in 2012) expanded upon this in a bit more detail.[4]

In the article, James argues that it is important to understand more fully the various components of realization, and how these impact realization. There are seven potential components, outlined below:

- where *timekeepers discount* their time at point of timesheet entry (either intentionally or otherwise) impacting potential revenue capture
- *write-downs of unbilled time* (most common, and in part due to a nervousness of the partner that the client will not perceive the *value* of work conducted)
- client adjustments that result in write-offs to receivables, through more active client monitoring of billing
- *pricing variance.* Although firms typically measure realization against the respective timekeeper's standard (rack) rate, this can also be done against the agreed client rate (if, for example, discounts are given). The variance can be a useful measure to determine how effective the discounting approach has been. Whereas standard rate realization reflects not only the impact of any pricing decisions, but also the impact of matter management,

Continued

4. JAMES D. COTTERMAN, ALTMAN WEIL, ISSUES IN REALIZATION (2012), *available at* http://www.altmanweil.com/index.cfm/fa/r.resource_detail/oid/31e47129-d73e-4e08-97ce-5b6f1d4419a0/resource/Issues_in_Realization.cfm.

Realization: A Multidimensional Metric? *Continued*

staffing, and service efficiency, actual rate realization removes the pricing element, allowing more granular analysis.

- *efficiency variance* looks at the non-pricing issues that impact realization, such as staffing decisions and overall process efficiency. Another part of this component is the speed of collections, with slower collections and/or longer billing cycles leading to less money being collected, lower realization, and also higher working capital requirements.
- *turnover of unbilled time*. In other words, what have we worked but not yet billed? For most firms this is typically 1.5–2.5 months. Depending upon the type of fee arrangements adopted by your firm, up to 0.5 months may be driven by contingent fee matters.
- *turnover of accounts receivable (AR)*. In other words, how many months of revenue are sitting in fees receivable. This is also typically one and a half to two and a half months (for most), which in turn impacts a firm's working capital requirements.

Therefore, if we were to just look at realization through the more traditional lens, we would not be able to identify, and therefore appropriately address, some of the underlying root causes of potentially poor performance. As the article concludes, "(t)he appropriate remedy will vary based on the cause" and "(t)he only way to get to the cause is to get into the details."[5] To make this metric meaningful, that is exactly what we need to do. A number of the tips outlined in this book will give you some potential approaches on how to do this.

Productivity Matters (But Perhaps Not as Much as You Think!)

Productivity is defined as the total number of *billable* hours recorded, divided by the number of lawyers at a law firm.

It is a key indicator of how successful a firm is using its available fee-earning resources, and underlying demand for its services. We, in law, don't particularly like the term "productivity," though (perhaps it makes us sound like we work in manufacturing), so prefer to call it *utilization*. For the purposes of this chapter, though, I am going to stick with productivity, as that is fundamentally what it is.

5. *Id.* at 6.

When looking at the United States for 2012, productivity was down slightly from the previous year by around 1–2 percent. This was driven by two key factors: the relatively static demand, as already mentioned above, coupled with an increase in the number of lawyers joining the profession (estimated by some at around 2 percent per annum).

Again, slight differences driven by law firm size emerge. Only those firms classified as midsize (that is, outside the Am Law 200) fared relatively well, with a reduction in productivity of only 0.2 percent, despite more significant headcount growth than other areas (of 2.7 percent).[6]

Indeed, when taking a broader view, over the last three years productivity has been relatively flat.

This is particularly concerning when recognizing that during this time a number of firms implemented significant staffing reductions, especially during 2009 and 2010. Again, the issue of overcapacity is one that many firms continue to grapple with today: for example, Weil Gotshal's redundancy program in June 2013—also coupled with a reduction in partner remuneration for 30 partners[7]—and similar activity by a raft of mid-tier U.K. firms during the early part of 2013, despite trainee retention levels in the United Kingdom remaining around the mid-80 percent mark.[8]

As illustrated above, this is not just specific to the United States but in other major markets too, nor is this solely a consequence of the global financial crisis—but is more symptomatic of the profession.

There has been a similar picture of flat (or declining) productivity evident even prior to 2008. One frightening statistic is that less than 50 percent of all law firm graduates from U.S.-based law schools in 2011 had obtained jobs in law firms.[9] You do not need to look too far to hear of other, similarly disturbing, examples.

---

6. BRANDON, *supra* note 3.

7. Matt Byrne, *Weil Gotshal Lays off More Than 150 in Latest U.S. Cuts*, THE LAWYER (June 24, 2013), *available at* http://www.thelawyer.com/news/people/cuts-and-redundancies/weil-gotshal-lays-off-more-than-150-in-latest-us-cuts/3006366.article.

8. *Linklaters Retention Rate Edges Up*, THE LAWYER (Aug. 1, 2013), *available at* http://www.thelawyer.com/solicitor/training-contract/linklaters-retention-rate-edges-up-to-87-per-cent/3008087.article.

9. Thomson Reuters Peer Monitor/Georgetown Law Ctr. for the Study of the Legal Profession, *supra* note 1, at 9.

Undeniably in "harder times," the first area to be looked at is the underlying costs, with cost cutting seen to be a relatively quick means of improving overall profitability. Whilst some judicious pruning of costs is never a bad idea, this often seems to take on the realms of extremes within the legal practice with associate and professional support staff being the first to be invited to explore pastures new, and then onto the (perceived underperforming) partners themselves, as in 2009 and 2010.

Put bluntly, valuable experience is being shown the door. How many other industries get rid of the more highly skilled individuals, only to "panic recruit" when the market begins to pick up (often, at a *higher* cost)? In addition, many of the other cost elements (for example, rent, information technology, salaries, etc.) do not tend to fluctuate much year on year, so any reduction here (unless you no longer need the resource or service) is temporary at best. *A much better focus is on the revenue line, and by association, pricing.*

Getting better at pricing, and aligning that price to the value important to the client, is key. We still tend to price our services based on the actual costs of production (the "inputs"), rather than in the value we are generating for our clients (the "outputs"), nowhere moreso than with the perpetuation of the billable hour, and it is a habit we need to get rid of. Not making silly mistakes that impact revenue through ineffective project management is another.

(By adopting some of the recommendations outlined in this book, this will hopefully allow you to focus more on the revenue part of the equation—and you can still do your "pruning" as required, but hopefully need to do so less frequently.)

The Magic Ingredient to Better Profitability and Happier Clients: Leverage

The fourth and final driver is leverage (sometimes referred to as "gearing").

It is *the* magic ingredient to better profitability, and is a key focus of our clients as they seek better value for their money. This, in their view, typically means "pushing work down" to the lowest level, something that is not always the case as it needs to be the lowest *appropriate* level to do the work efficiently, which may mean a partner in some instances. The intent of what our clients are trying to achieve is correct, however—removing the temptation by some to staff at a higher rate if they could.

It is the amount of non-equity partner work done per equity partner, often expressed in the form of 1:[insert number]. For example, if leverage was shown as being 1:5, this would indicate one equity partner hour worked for each five hours of non-equity partner time worked (regardless of level). It is this that is the most powerful lever in improving profit. (Note: Some firms do not make the distinction between the equity status of partners when adopting this metric. In these cases, leverage would be determined as the proportion of *partner* time vs. *non-partner* time.) Figure 3.3 highlights this in simple terms.

Taking this concept to the logical extreme, this then drives better resourcing at a lower overall cost (that is, lower client fees), but improves the overall profitability of the matter for the law firm. Very seldom in life do two mutually desired objectives present themselves in one simple solution. *Better leverage* is that solution.

The other great thing about this driver is that *it is one we, as law firms, can directly control*, one that is not dependent upon market forces. If only for this reason alone, law firms should embrace the basics of legal project management and, perhaps more pertinently here, legal *process* improvement.

Profitability: A Meaningful Measure?

Most law firms will have wrestled with how best to express their respective profitability in a meaningful way. Some have used measures based on the effective financial contribution per partner hour; others may have more or less sophisticated metrics. Coupled with this, there are a myriad of ways to also allocate cost, each based on firm preference (or ignorance of other methods).

Profitability is driven by the allocation of direct and indirect expenses to the firm. This is done for each matter (as appropriate), with these costs then being deducted from the matter fees received. At the aggregate, firm-wide level, this then is divided across all equity partners to give an average, the (in)famous PEP, or profit per equity partner (also known as PPP, profit per partner).

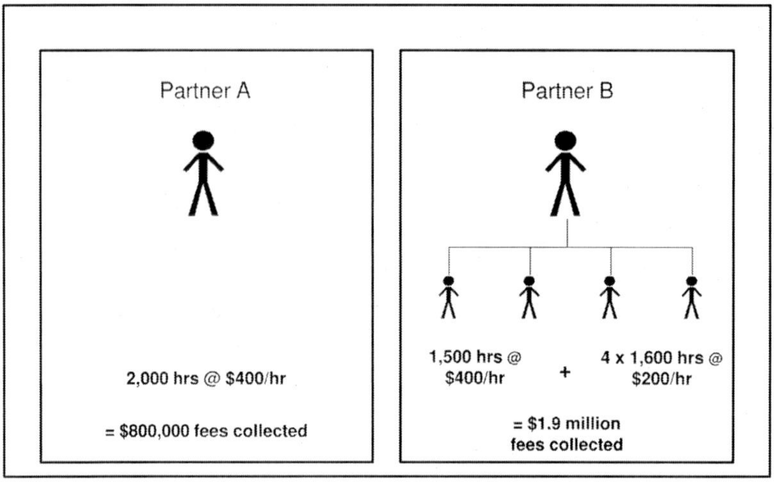

Figure 3.3
An Illustration of the Impact of Leverage: Just Add Leverage and Stir

This has become *the key reporting metric* for most law firms, giving those with higher PEP bragging rights in the lawyer playground of the pages of the *American Lawyer* (which was instrumental in developing the metric and promotion of its usage years ago through its annual league tables, since adopted in other jurisdictions).

But the outlook is far from rosy. According to *The Lawyer*, as of the end of July 2013, the average PEP for those U.K. firms that had reported earnings for 2012–2013 (86 in total), 48 percent (41 firms) had seen their PEP decline from the previous 12-month period, and 25 percent (10) of those had seen it fall by more than 15 percent.[10] Although many of the firms experiencing the decline in PEP have either merged (and therefore incurred costs and potentially expanded the ranks of equity partners) or had invested in long-delayed programs (for example, renewing their IT infrastructure), this decline will become more acute given the rising costs in the industry.

But fundamental issues with the actual PEP/PPP metric itself remain.

10. Joanne Harris, *Profitability Plummets at Growing Number of U.K. Firms*, The Lawyer (July 29, 2013), *available at* http://www.thelawyer.com/analysis/the-lawyer-management/financial-news/profitability-plummets-at-growing-number-of-uk-firms/3007921.article.

It can drive short-term behavior in a pursuit of immediate revenue. It ignores a range of other determinants of law firm "health" such as client retention, client satisfaction, law firm retention and morale, and, indeed, firm-wide profitability. It does not account for any pro bono or corporate social responsibility initiatives undertaken by a firm. And most crucially for us, it does not attempt to reflect the value we have (hopefully) added for our clients.

Its method of calculation is also open to interpretation. It is determined by the average of firm-wide profit divided by all equity partners, yet a number of articles focused on law firm profitability note that the equity spread from the highest to lowest earning partners in some firms may be as high as 9-to-1 throughout the Am Law 100 (so where is the average there?). Oh, and it is "self-reported" by the firms, with them providing details of firm revenue, profit, and number of "eligible" partners—this in turn leading to a broader question around how it is calculated and whether it really is an apples-for-apples comparison (even if the apples happen to be green or red).

But it gives a focus. Although there is not necessarily anything better on the immediate horizon, we would be well served to recognize the dangers of slavishly adhering to the mantra of PEP/PPP in this new world while the search for a more meaningful metric continues.

The challenge of any profitability metric is that it can become divisive as partners begin to compare themselves with others and then enter the managing partner's office and demand higher compensation based on their higher profitability number.

It is also critical to view profitability in the longer (or at least mid-) term. Looking at profitability on a specific matter may be helpful as means to redirect a matter veering off its intended course, but greater value is looking at this measure at a client or practice area/service level to see how this compares against the relative peer group. (There is another consideration when looking at profitability at a matter basis, and that is the role played by productivity. In quieter times, if you have lawyers who are not being fully engaged on matters—through no fault of their own—it is unfair to have this impact the matter-specific profit.)

Therefore, view profitability at a more aggregate and comprehensive level rather than via a single metric. This allows more-informed decisions to be taken—not only at an immediate pricing level but also in how these matters are being managed and staffed (themes we'll return to later).

It perhaps goes without saying that you need to make sure your partners are *aware* of what drives law firm profitability. Many (frighteningly) are not. Also, you need to make sure your partners *understand* what these various metrics mean and how they work in tandem.

If used well, these measures should help drive the pursuit of the *right revenue*. Not just any revenue, but revenue that delivers an appropriate level of profit to the law firm at an acceptable cost to the client (when aligned to the value being delivered).

But these metrics need some interpretation. This in turn requires a different skill from, and complementary to, that possessed by a large number of lawyers: financial analysis. Step forward those in finance and (increasingly) pricing roles to become the advisors to the business you have always wanted to be.

It may be a development that some of us may wish had never materialized, but the fundamental issue is that we now clearly need to embrace the *business of law*.

Don't forget *(a summary of the key points):*

- Understanding how a law firm makes money, and more importantly how they can stop losing money, is the key premise of this book.
- Active management of profitability is no longer a "nice to have."
- The law firm traditional pricing model (hourly rates) is now under legitimate challenge.
- Organic growth is dead—at least for now. Delivering more compelling commercial propositions is the key to driving profitable revenue.
- Better and smarter awareness, understanding, *and* control of the revenue line is essential—better pricing and project management have a critical role to play.
- Leverage is the magic ingredient to improve profitability—and is one that lawyers (not the market) can directly control.
- We need to view traditional law firm metrics more comprehensively, which means adding a few more.

Step One: Set the Price

Chapter 4

Pricing and the Question of Value: An Introduction

The disciplines of business development and marketing have become accepted in the vast majority of law firms today.

For those fulfilling these roles, they will hopefully be aware of the four Ps of marketing: product, placement, promotion, and last—but certainly not least for the purposes of our book—pricing.

Of these four key elements, pricing is the only one that produces revenue rather than cost, and yet—until relatively recently in the legal profession—it has not been given much attention. This is perhaps surprising, as this is what ultimately determines a firm's profitability.

Pricing has a key role to play in helping any organization achieve its strategic business goals. However, the pricing practices within law firms—namely, cost-plus pricing, customer-driven pricing, and competitive pricing—can severely limit a law firm's ability to drive and sustain profitable growth.

The Limitations of Traditional Pricing Models

Let's have a brief look at each of these approaches in turn, and how they limit pricing potential:

- Cost-plus pricing:

  - This is perhaps the most common pricing approach, where you set your price based on an agreed level of markup, or increase from your estimated costs of providing your product or service, which allows you to realize an acceptable level of profit. However, this approach inevitably suffers from the assumption that you *can* determine cost before you set price, and then that the price does not then impact the ultimate demand for your product or service.
  - What this approach does do is limit the potential level of profitability through inaccurate pricing, and yet this remains the dominant form of pricing within the legal industry.
- Customer-driven pricing:
  - This approach is based on the end customer's willingness to pay. However, this approach, too, has its own limitations, as this assumes you understand and know what the customer is prepared to pay for your service or product.
  - One of the fundamental concepts advocated by the Professional Pricing Society (the main professional body for those in the pricing field, and therefore the authority on all things pricing) is the need to effectively communicate the ultimate value of a product to the customer, rather than creating a pricing structure based on primarily what they *say* they are willing to pay (a concept we will return to when we talk about Getting the Price).
- Competitive pricing:
  - This is driven by the competitive environment and is one that many of us reading this book will be extremely familiar with.
  - However, once again there is a limitation to this approach—this time in that it tends to drive an unhealthy focus on gaining market share at the expense of seeking to maintain or enhance profitability. This can also create the proverbial "race to the bottom."

Whilst each of these approaches may have its place if used sparingly, pricing as a discipline encourages us to be slightly more strategic in our approach. This is achieved through adopting the three guiding principles of strategic pricing—being value based, proactive, and profit driven.[1] Thinking about our own respective situations, each of these principles is equally applicable to how we approach pricing within our own firms.

The Concept of "Price"

We hear the term every day, but what does "price" actually mean?

To paraphrase the Professional Pricing Society's definition, price is defined as the amount of resources (normally understood as money, products, or services) that need to be "sacrificed" in order to acquire some other resource. Price ought to reflect the value of the desired resource or its relative worth, merit, or importance.[2]

There are two main ways in which price can therefore be determined—from a cost-based perspective or a value-based perspective. Figure 4.1 highlights the key differences in approach.

In the value-based approach, you start with what the customer is willing to pay, determine the actual value for the customer, and then try to control your cost as much as possible to meet the price that most accurately reflects the value you will deliver and is in line with what customers require. (Note: this is not the same as customer-driven pricing, which does not recognize the key element of value generation.)

Ron Baker, one of the prime advocates of value pricing within professional services, notes the following:

The word value has a specific meaning in economics: "the maximum amount that a consumer would be willing to pay for an item." Therefore value pricing can be defined as the maximum amount a given customer is willing to pay for a particular service, before the work begins. This is

1. Thomas T. Nagle, John E. Hogan & Joseph Zale, *The Strategy and Tactics of Pricing: A Guide to Growing More Profitably* 6 (Prentice Hall 5th ed. 2010).

2. Professional Pricing Society, Certified Pricing Professional Programme Study Guide, 3 (2008).

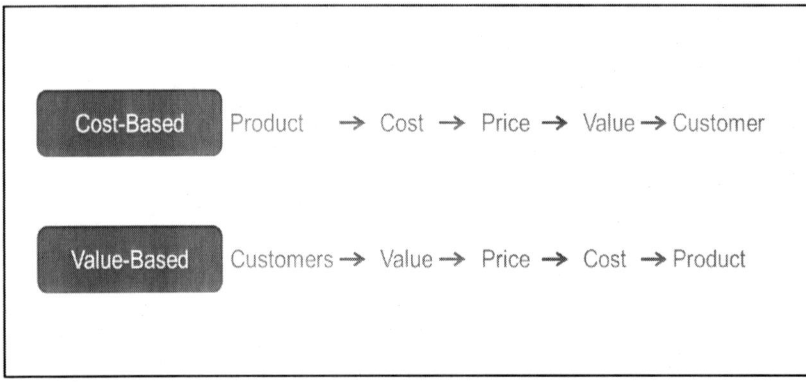

Figure 4.1
The Difference Between Cost- and Value-Based Pricing Approaches
Source: Diagram based on Exhibit 1.2, "Alternative approaches to value creation"; Nagle, *supra* note 1, at 8.

not to suggest we can capture 100 percent of maximum value, but rather that we have the potential to access some of it utilizing strategic pricing.[3]

Here it is also useful to acknowledge that although profits are certainly important, making satisfactory profits is a much more common and realistic objective than maximizing profits.[4] For many of us, if we were able to replicate this across all our product and service lines within our firms, this would be a great start. One way that we as an industry can do this is by moving away, where appropriate, from the still-dominant hourly based (and typically therefore cost-plus) approach used in law firms today.

The Steps to Implementing Value Pricing

Ron Baker outlined his recommended eight steps to implementing value pricing in his book of the same name.[5] As he states, it is important not to skip any of the steps, as all are necessary to developing a score competency in pricing—but I would add to this.

3. Ronald J. Baker, *Implementing Value Pricing: A Radical Business Model for Professional Firms* 233 (2010).
4. Kent B. Monroe, *Pricing: Making Profitable Decisions* (McGraw-Hill 3d ed. 2003).
5. BAKER, *supra* note 3, at 229–318.

These eight steps, summarized in table 4.1, clearly align with the key themes we will be addressing throughout the remainder of this book. It is certainly true that each of the eight steps identified are critical and they act as a wonderful starting point, but I believe there are a few more, which we will also address as we go. (Although, even if you were to adopt only these eight steps, you would still make massive strides in your efforts to practice "smarter pricing" and deliver "smarter profit" when compared with many in our industry.)

Table 4.1: Value Pricing and Our Framework

	Ron Baker's steps to implementing value pricing	Where in our framework
1	Conversation—that is, determining your client's wants and needs on the engagement	Set the Price
2	Pricing the customer—that is, developing your pricing options for your client	Set the Price
3	Developing and pricing options—that is, determining your pricing options for your client (note that it says "options" not "option"—provide a choice)	Set the Price
4	Presenting options to the customer	Get the Price
5	Customer selection codified into the Fixed Price Agreement—that is, agreeing on the engagement scope, objectives, and pricing basis	Manage to Price
6	Proper project management—that is, planning the work	Manage to Price
7	Scope creep and change orders—that is, managing to scope	Manage to Price
8	Pricing after action reviews—that is, taking time to review, reflect, and improve	Review the Price

Source: Baker, *supra* note 3, at 233–234.

Types of Price

When talking about price, it is also helpful to understand the three basic types of price that exist.

- List price: This is basically the quoted price for a good service. In a law firm, this is typically the standard hourly rate for a specific level of expertise, although it may be a fixed price for a specific service.
- Invoice price: This is the price after any volume or relationship discount has been applied. From a law firm perspective, this is sometimes known as the "billed" price (which is not necessarily what we ultimately collect from our clients).
- Pocket price: This is the price after all allowances, refunds, and discounts are applied. In law firms, my sense is that we do not look at this one enough, so we'll return to this concept in Chapter 7.

There is one other term that you may have come across that I also think is worthy of a mention, the term "reference price."

This is the price that clients develop based on a comparative evaluation of competing offers in the marketplace. This may be through their previous experience of having to pay for the service product in question, what they perceive to be the average market price for the product or service in question, what they perceive to be a fair price, and also what they expect the price to be.

This concept is important for two reasons: The first is that this reference price for many matters forms the basis of what the client expects to pay from the outset, especially for more routine or "business as usual" type of work in which there are many more providers for them to choose from. The second is that this can also inform a client's negotiation position, which we will return to when we discuss how to best prepare for and conduct a client negotiation.

The "Right" Price

Trying to determine the right price can be very difficult, regardless of industry, but this can be made significantly easier by understanding the basic rules of pricing. These rules require knowledge in five complementary areas: your firm's objectives, your firm's customers, your firm's competition, our industry, and your firm's underlying costs.

One way to visualize this is to imagine a house.

Our imaginary house has a floor, which here represents our cost—or, more precisely, the cost-plus model of pricing. It has a roof, the height of which will depend upon the value of the product or service delivered to the client. And in the middle (that is, the gap between the floor and the roof) is the price driven by the market, with this in turn being driven by whether your product or service is seen to be one in the premium market, mid-market, or other. The basic concept is shown in figure 4.2.

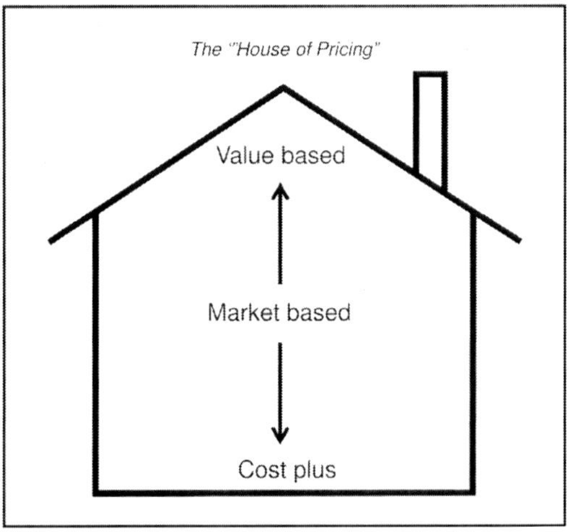

Figure 4.2
Constructing Your Pricing

Much as the original construction of a house can be seen from a different view (for example, the builder or carpenter), each part of our house is also driven from a slightly different viewpoint or perspective.

The "floor" is more an accounting- or finance-based perspective, looking to ensure that we would recover cost with some level of markup as appropriate. The "interior" is more of a sales-focused perspective, conscious of what it will take to be competitive within the market. The "roof," our third view, is more value driven, and is probably akin to the architect's view in how high they were able to build the house whilst keeping all the key features intact.

This third view is one we have more typically seen adopted within professional services firms by management consultants. For example, McKinsey (for one) often seeks to align its fee commensurate to 5 percent to 10 percent of the overall value delivered to its clients for the engagement they are directly supporting (based on an agreed business case). Similarly, while I worked as a procurement consultant, we often tied our remuneration directly to the level of tangible savings we were able to deliver for our clients.

From our pricing perspective, the price could be anywhere within the house's interior, but it is impacted by the basic rules of pricing outlined above.

(Note of thanks: I am extremely grateful to Colin Jasper who has allowed me to reproduce his analogy here with his kind permission).

Our next chapter will go into a bit more detail about how you can go about setting the right price.

The Impact of Price

But nowhere so far have we talked about the actual impact of price, except in relatively vague terms. It is now time to correct that omission. I am not going to talk here about the complex mathematical formula of pricing, but will merely highlight one or two themes that can be applied for all.

The 1-3-4 Rule™

One of the themes I typically address when presenting internally within my firm or at conferences is what I have called the 1-3-4 Rule™.

Simply put, the 1-3-4 Rule™ states that for every 1 percent improvement in price, the potential increase to profitability is 3 percent. To get the same level of improvement in profitability without increasing price you would need to work 4 percent more billable time. This is also shown in figure 4.3.

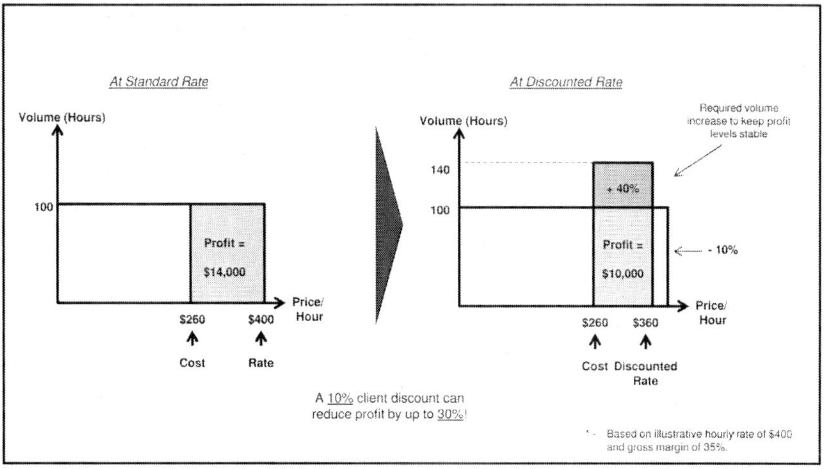

Figure 4.3
The 1-3-4 Rule™

As we know, in today's legal environment not only are we seeing pressure on the traditional hourly rate model, but we're also seeing greater pressure to do more with less time and clearly demonstrate value and efficiency. Therefore the opportunity to work more time as a means to improving profitability is probably fast disappearing (rightly so). This leaves us with the other part of the equation—that is, having a closer look at our pricing. Interestingly, having done this in a number of firms, this rule in the main holds true, although I remember when doing this once in Asia, the numbers actually became 1-2-3 (which is perhaps easier to remember!), driven by the differing cost structure.

This is further exemplified in table 4.2 on the next page, which shows the impact of client discounting (the main way that law firms have sought to control price) on profit.

Given that most law firms have a margin of somewhere between 20 percent and 45 percent (with only a lucky handful above that top figure), I have used the representative values in the range below so that it is easier for you to find out where you may sit. Unsurprisingly, the lower the margin your firm has, the greater sensitivity to changes in price your firm becomes, and therefore in the face of further pricing pressure would require a greater number of billable hours to enable you to effectively "stand still."

Table 4.2: Discounting and Margin

The Impact on Margin (revised margin shown)

Impact of extra discount \ Current margin	20%	25%	30%	35%	40%	45%	50%
20%	0.0%	6.3%	12.5%	18.7%	25.0%	31.2%	37.5%
15%	5.9%	11.8%	17.6%	23.5%	29.4%	35.2%	41.2%
10%	11.1%	16.7%	22.2%	27.8%	33.3%	38.8%	44.4%
5%	15.8%	21.1%	26.3%	31.6%	36.8%	42.1%	47.4%
1%	19.2%	24.2%	29.3%	34.3%	39.4%	44.4%	49.5%

A Common Phenomenon

Nor is this phenomenon specific to our own industry. In one of the very earliest articles to address how better management of pricing could contribute to profit (by Michael Marn and Robert Rosiello), the authors determined that "improvements in price typically have 3 to 4 times the effect on profitability than proportionate increases in volume."[6]

As part of their study, they compared the difference to profit of implementing a 1 percent increase in volume versus implementing a 1 percent increase in price. They estimated that for a company with average economic performance, improving the company's respective unit volume by 1 percent gave a 3.3 percent increase in operating profit to the company (assuming that there was no commensurate decrease in price). Conducting the same

6. Michael V. Marn & Robert L. Rosiello, *Managing Price, Gaining Profit*, HARV. BUS. REV., Sept.–Oct. 1992.

analysis, but this time having a 1 percent improvement in price (assuming no loss of volume), they determined that operating profit would increase by 11.1 percent.

When one of the same authors, Michael Marn, looked at the impact on the Global 1200 (looking over a five-year trailing period) when doing the same "experiment" more recently, an increase in price of 1 percent would have driven an improvement in the level of operating profit by 8.7 percent, by far the largest improvement when compared with the other profit levers of reducing fixed cost, improving volume, and producing variable cost (see figure 4.4 below).

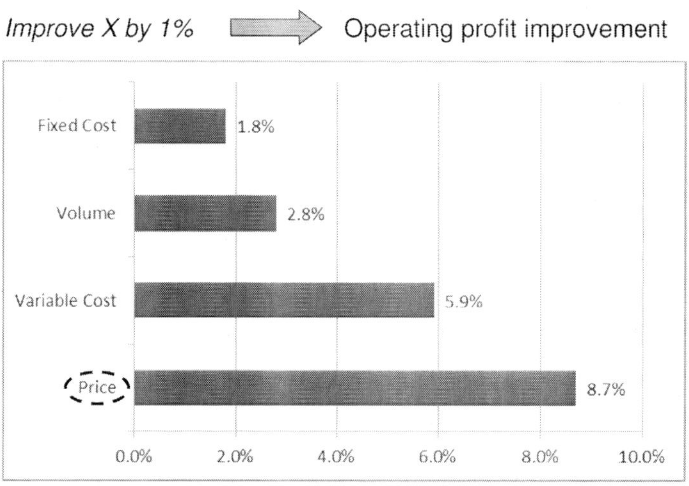

Figure 4.4
Comparison of Profit Levers[7]

In a similar type of study, Robert Dolan and Hermann Simon estimated that 1 percent price realization improvement for Coca-Cola (at the time of the study, 1996) would have boosted net income by 6.4 percent, Nestlé by 17.5 percent, and Ford by 26 percent.[8]

7. Diagram based on Exhibit 1.2, 'Comparison of Profit Levers' included in Walter L. Baker, Michael V. Marn and Craig C. Zawada, *The Price Advantage* (New Jersey: Wiley, 2010), 5.

8. Robert J. Dolan & Hermann Simon, Power Pricing: How Managing Price Transforms the Bottom Line 4 (The Free Press 1996).

All in all powerful stuff, and therefore certainly worth the effort of getting right, with even *small improvements* in the final price received from your client dramatically impacting your overall operating profit.

THIS fundamentally is what this book is about, providing you with a number of suggested approaches, tips, call them what you will, to help you get better at making many of these small improvements in price whilst delivering exceptional customer service and value to your clients.

A Closer Look at Value Pricing

The perceived value of any product or service can be summarized in the very simple equation below.

PERCEIVED VALUE = Perceived Benefit/Perceived Sacrifice.

However, the ability to build or generate value is less simple, and has at its foundation five key principles, these being commonly referred to as the Five Cs of Value.

- Create value for customers.
- Comprehend value to customers.
- Communicate value to customers.
- Convince customers that they must pay for value.
- Capture value with strategic pricing based on value, not cost.

Let's look at each in a bit more detail:

- Create value for customers.
  - It is good practice to continually monitor and evaluate the value expectations of our clients, as these can change. If we can encourage our clients to focus more on the potential value considered rather than the price when making a buying decision, pricing becomes less of a key decision factor (as any good salesman knows!).
- Comprehend value to customers.

- We need to understand what value means, as it's a term that is used regularly. Value is essentially the economic impact (defined in monetary terms) that any product or service has on the customer's business, relative to the price of the best competitive offering. Therefore, value is primarily understood in relation to the other alternatives.
- From an economic point of view, there are three types of "economic value" drivers that we should be aware of. There are those that save clients both time and money (cost drivers); there are those that allow clients to generate more revenue (revenue drivers); and finally, there are those based on feeling clients gets for brand—for example, when someone buys a Rolex watch (called "psychological value" drivers). Of the three, the one which has the least impact on our environment is the final one, although a select number of "Magic Circle" and "White Shoe" firms may be able to operate in this space for certain areas of legal expertise.
- Understanding what value *means* is particularly important in negotiation when looking to define your opening offer (that is, your initial bid to the client), your target price (that is, the one you would be happy to accept), and what you think is the client's "next best alternative" (that is, what they would do if not accepting your proposal). We'll spend a bit more time on this concept when we have a look at how to approach negotiation as part of how we can best Get the Price.

- Communicate value to customers.
  - One of the areas law firms in general have been less good at is how we effectively communicate the value we deliver to our clients. As an illustration, only recently have we seen significant improvements in how law firm proposals are being presented to our clients, with these now focusing much more on client needs and potential value rather than providing a detailed list of how good the law firm is, followed by lots of CVs for the proposed team.
  - We should seek, where we can, to clearly differentiate our value. This is important not only from a marketing perspective but also from a pricing perspective. Sources of differentiation are varied

but may be through factors such as your use of technology to add greater value for the client or your adoption of legal project management principles. Whatever these may be, it is important to the value proposition of any product or service that we provide some sort of tangible or measurable quality by which to evaluate the value being promised. This is where many of us in the field of law miss the mark. By offering tangible and measurable propositions, it's more likely your client will engage you in discussion, which in turn increases the likelihood of you making the sale. It has also been identified that those proposals that have clear value proposition can also frequently command higher prices for the respective product or service. If merely coming up with a generic proposition, which many law firms are guilty of, that is not going to happen.
    - The points of differentiation that are most effective in a proposal are those that seek to address the specific client business problem and that provide a positive bottom-line impact. This requires us to *actually speak to our clients and understand our client's requirements from the outset*, rather than merely pitching with a generic proposal full of our own untested assumptions. Here I am reminded of something I once heard in conversation: "There is no such thing as a price-sensitive client, only clients who've grown indifferent to your differentiation." Useful food for thought for us all, perhaps?
- Convince customers that they must pay for value.
    - If we are unable to convince our clients that they must pay for value, they are likely to view cost as the only differentiator for that particular product and service, and will therefore be content to let the law firms compete purely by offering the lowest price.
    - Whereas for some products or services this may be seen as inevitable, as they are viewed as being more commoditized (a word no lawyer likes, but one that is an economic reality), this may not necessarily be the case when we remember that the experience of, the client relationship with, and service from any lawyer is unique.
    - It is also useful here to know what type of characteristics your clients exhibit, as this allows you to more appropriately engage with each type.

- In *The Strategy and Tactics of Pricing*, the authors identified four key types of clients,[9] the key characteristics of which are summarized below and shown in figure 4.5.

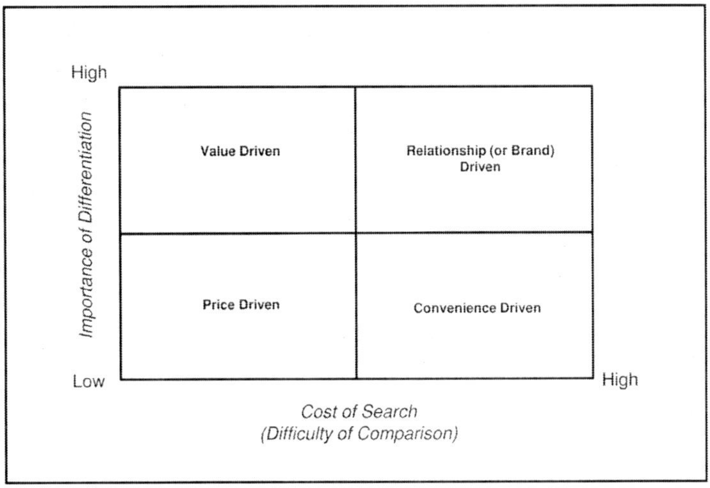

Figure 4.5
Identifying Different Buyer Types
Source: Diagram based on Exhibit 5.3, "Buyer Types," Nagle, *supra* note 1, at 103.

- Value-driven buyers: These clients know what value looks like to them and are likely to have strong analytical approaches in place to determine the actual level of value to them. With this type of client, it's important to first understand what they are looking for, and then be able to determine and quantify your "value add" to them. (There is also a subset of this group called "power buyers," but is less relevant to our industry unless you have one client who is 20 percent or more of your annual revenues, and therefore not covered here.)
- Brand (or relationship) buyers: This group wants a good product or service, but don't want the rigmarole of having to do any in-depth analysis. In many respects, this type of client is

9. Nagle et al., *supra* note 1, at 103–11.

one of the easier ones to deal with—as long as you continue to meet these clients' expectations.

  - Price buyers: As the name suggests, this group is very much focused on obtaining the lowest possible price for the specific product or service, and are the very opposite of brand (or relationship) buyers. If coming across this type of buyer as part of a broader client relationship, it is important that any agreement reached with this specific client is clearly "ring-fenced" so that the agreement you come to in this context does not "cannibalize" or set a dangerous precedent for any of the other agreements you may wish to have with others.
  - Convenience buyers: This is what I'm guilty of when I go shopping with my wife. It is where I don't spend time comparing prices, I just buy where it is most convenient, and then need to recognize that this may mean I pay more than I would normally have for that convenience (hence my wife's objections). The parallel scenario here would be where your client continues to use an incumbent law firm for certain matters rather than these being put out to wider tender, thus potentially paying more for the matter to be done.

- Capture value with strategic pricing based on value, not cost.
  - This one is the hardest to do, especially for a law firm. This is primarily due to the fact that most firms tend to judge the success of any pricing value strategy based on traditional financial metrics, such as return on investment, return on sales, and increased sales volume.
  - In this area our measures should be more comprehensive, and include things such as customer satisfaction, customer loyalty, and other value-added metrics. We'll return to the topic of metrics and measurement in one of our later chapters (Chapter 20), but suffice it to say here that this will be one of the hardest challenges for many firms, given the required shift away from traditional financially driven metrics.

When taking a step back when looking at the Five Cs of Value, I would suggest that the first four are probably "doable" in our industry and act as a good guide as to how we should be setting prices in our firms. The fifth we will hopefully get to over time.

The Management of Pricing

No introduction to pricing would be complete without a brief look at the different types of price management approaches that exist.

There are three distinct levels of price management commonly used.[10] These move from a specific transaction-driven view to one that looks more at the product and market to, finally (and at the most macro level), the industry and the underlying pricing strategy.

- Transactional management:
    - This is where the focus is on managing the exact price charged for each specific transaction.
    - As we will examine in Chapter 7, there are a number of recommended approaches to doing this that are much more comprehensive than just looking at the original quoted price for the product. During this chapter we'll explore in more detail the concept of pocket price, which is a truer reflection on the impact on profit than invoice price.
- Products/market strategy:
    - At this level, we are primarily focused on a customer's perception of our product or service. It is here that our focus is primarily on appropriate price positioning relative to the competition and therefore setting the correct target price for each product or service.
- Industry strategy:
    - It is at this level where we begin to factor in and analyze the effects of future supply-and-demand conditions on price levels in our respective market. If here, you are in a position to anticipate market trends rather than merely reacting to them.

10. Baker et al, *The Price Advantage*, 15–22.

I would guess that many of us are at the first level, but only superficially (this level is ironically the most detailed if being done well), with a few perhaps at the second.

There are traditional barriers or constraints inherent in most law firms that stop us sometimes even from being able to get to any stage of effective price management.

Pricing is one of a few functions in which many people actually *do* it but no one actually *owns* it. Even within a traditional law firm context, those who have a role—or sometimes more accurately believe they have a role—in pricing may include marketing, finance, the COO or CFO (or equivalents), the matter partner, a practice area lead, the executive committee (or other senior body), or managing partner. With so many potential contributors, it is perhaps little wonder that pricing decisions normally suffer from a lack of effective management.

If seeking to rectify this, there are four core areas recommended by the Professional Pricing Society for firms to focus on when looking to improve their pricing decision-making processes and underlying organization:

- Having a clear structure and assigned responsibility for pricing. This would include the capture of information about trends and industry, competitors, the implantation of pricing decisions, and also the monitoring and auditing.
- Having clear pricing policies and procedures, both looking to manage the long-term price decisions but also those in the immediate term.
- Adopting appropriate platforms and tools, where organizational functions are aligned and coordinated using standardized platforms to measure pricing performance.
- Aligning incentives that match (and reinforce) the overall pricing strategy. (For example, these should be based on the level of contribution margin generated, rather than volume or gross-revenue targets.)

Whatever is adopted, this needs to clearly align with your respective firm's structure, culture, process, systems, and overall strategy for your efforts in this area to be successful. Therefore, one of the implied key decisions in any firm is how centralized or decentralized to make pricing management. In a law firm context, this can then be defined as pricing management being driven at a matter, product, practice area, specific jurisdictional or national level, or even regionally or globally for some.

The Law Industry "Report Card": Could Do Better

How are we generally, as law firms, doing against these four areas of "good" price decision making? If this were a report card, we (as an industry) would probably scrape a C—and only if our teacher was being generous.

Many law firms have already begun to address the first criteria mentioned. There is also some movement, though still in its infancy, in both the second and third areas. However, it is perhaps the final area, that of having more aligned incentives, where there is much more work to be done and where some fundamental challenges remain based on our adherence to the traditional law firm metrics of utilization and realization (and in some firms, the concept of "origination credit").

If there was one statement that our teacher would have written on our report card, it would probably be:

> Law needs to recognize that the price should reflect the perception of value possessed by its clients. Law really could, and should, do much better.

Don't forget *(a summary of the key points):*

- Current law firm pricing approaches—cost-plus, customer-driven, and competitive pricing—can severely limit a law firm's ability to drive and sustain profitable growth.
- Good pricing discipline encourages us to be more strategic in our approach—by being value based, proactive, and (appropriately) profit driven.
- Understanding the importance of "value" in our pricing equation is vital.
- Remember the impact of our 1-3-4 Rule™—even small improvements in price can have a significant beneficial impact on your profit.
- Have someone manage or coordinate your pricing decision-making process—many people historically do pricing in law firms, but no one typically "owns" the role.

Chapter 5

Getting Started: Beginning with the End in Mind

In our last chapter we talked about some of the fundamental principles of pricing within a law firm. In this chapter, we're going to cover in a bit more detail what you can do to get started when looking to price a specific matter (our main focus) and how to approach the pricing of a client relationship agreement.

There are also a couple of challenges addressed, later in the chapter, that are more easily addressed than others. Each of them can have a significant impact on both Set the Price and the ultimate perception of value to our clients.

Scoping the Opportunity

What normally happens at the very beginning of this process? The phone may ring, you get an e-mail alert saying "you have one new message," or sometimes an existing client may take you to one side and say, "We may have something you can help us with, would you be interested?"

What is certainly true is that after any of the above occurs, you then need to put your thinking cap on. No longer is it merely a case of dusting down the previous quotation you gave to a client and hope that this does the trick. First, there is no guarantee that the matter will be identical, but also, the days of the client blithely accepting your initial number are long gone.

Let's assume, for the purposes of illustration, that this is a new matter. How do you go about pricing it in today's more challenging market?

Fortunately, a number of the traditional principles still hold true. Scoping is still *the* critical part in determining any fee arrangement. Whether this can be easily defined or not will be based on your professional experience, potentially supplemented by that of your colleagues.

But you're still looking to identify what the key matter stages are (more of which when we get to our Manage to Price section), estimate the duration of the matter (including any possible options that may extend or compress matter duration), and determine the matter's level of complexity or novelty.

If typically working on litigation matters, you'll also need to consider the appropriate jurisdiction (given differences in time to trial) and know which firm is representing the other side (and if you can, the basis on which they are being paid, as this can drive behavior). You then look to see who will be involved, for how long, and potentially from where, if a multinational firm. Only as of this point will you feel more comfortable in trying to determine the potential price.

However, there is one little hiccup here. Nowhere in the scenario outlined above have we recognized the fundamental flaw in traditional law firm pricing. *Costing the matter is **not** the same as pricing the matter.*

I have heard stories of a number of firms that have spent significant efforts in reviewing past performance of their matters to help them more fully understand the underlying cost of conducting them. What this does do is give these firms a better understanding of the potential levels of risk and effort involved in trying to cost a matter (this being higher for more commoditized areas of work).

But there are some important caveats to consider. For example, there's the risk of being either too optimistic or pessimistic about how long the matter may take, thus impacting cost. There is the risk around the level of complexity or novelty of the matter. And there are those risks that we just have no idea exist (until it's too late).

Certainly the efforts of those firms are commendable, and this may allow the respective firms to *cost* with a higher degree of accuracy, but what it will not do is allow the firm to *price* with a higher degree of accuracy, as these are not the same.

Nor is it merely just adding some level of markup onto costs (cost-plus pricing). As outlined in one of the key pricing textbooks, *The Strategy and Tactics of Pricing*, "Cost-plus pricing is . . . in theory, a simple guide to profitability; in practice, it is a blueprint for mediocre financial performance. The problem with cost-plus pricing is fundamental: in most industries it is impossible to determine products' unit cost before determining price. Why? Because unit costs change with volume."[1]

Nowhere is this truer than in professional services where someone's utilization or level of "busyness" is a key metric, even if they are busy doing unprofitable things.

Determining the Options

And yet it is hard. Having identified the "input costs," it can be difficult to then mentally separate these so they do not adversely impact the eventual "matter cost."

One suggested approach here is to model a number of scenarios based on your understanding of input costs. After all, if you think it will take 100 hours to successfully complete the matter, it is still probably going to take 100 hours to do the matter. Then do the same at 110 hours, and 120 hours. This allows you to see the potential impact on cost through changing only one or two bits of information. If nothing else, this helps you approach the *pricing* of this matter with your "eyes wide open" (a phrase we will return to on a number of occasions during this book).

Given the increased scrutiny pricing is receiving in our industry, the proverbial "finger in the air" estimate is no longer good enough for our clients *nor* for our own firm's management.

To help improve the accuracy and development of potential options, many firms have either developed their own pricing and matter estimating tools

1. Thomas T. Nagle, John E. Hogan & Joseph Zale, THE STRATEGY AND TACTICS OF PRICING: A GUIDE TO GROWING MORE PROFITABLY 2–3 (Prentice Hall 5th ed. 2010).

(something that both my previous and current firm have done), or have purchased one of the many available software applications that do the same.

If you have not built or bought your own, a relatively straightforward, simple spreadsheet with a number of key pieces of data can help you quickly do the same—at least initially. This at least means that you are developing cost and pricing estimates on a more *consistent* basis.

Examples of functionality you may want to include could be how to enter (or retrieve) your firm's standard (or "rack") rate and respective costs per experience level or timekeeper (this should be according to the approach you use in your firm, recognizing that these differ across our industry). You would also want to include some basic calculations that allow you to easily enter and review common fee options—for example, those with a straight discount on rates, on a fixed-fee basis, or on a contingent, risk-sharing basis.

Any analysis you do should ideally be *dynamic*—that is, where the analysis allows you to quickly model and assess different pricing options, albeit based on some key assumptions. This gives you a starting point in determining how to best price your matter.

Finally, any results should allow you to assess the options selected against your firm's key client relationship and financial criteria. You should also seek to model a range of different pricing options initially to estimate the likely impact on profitability, as, if nothing else, in any business, the key is to at least recover more in revenue than you spend (if wanting to stay afloat).

We have already talked about the impact of the 1-3-4 Rule™ in the previous chapter, in particular the impact poorly thought-through discounting can have on overall firm, practice group, and matter profitability. Remember, not all revenue is "good" revenue. Again, this type of analysis allows you to see possible outcomes and then make a reasoned and informed decision on where to begin to Set the Price. But we can't stop there, however a good starting point it may be.

Factors such as the impact of competition, the role of price in our client's decision-making process, the ultimate value being created for the client, and your own firm-wide pricing objectives (assuming you have these, and frighteningly not all firms do), all play a role in helping you in setting the *right* price.

You need to consider what's right for your specific client, the specific situation, and your firm (for example, is this work you actually *want*?). It is also good to check what you have offered similar clients for similar types of work, as you should seek to maintain *appropriate consistency of pricing* across your client relationships.

Again, if you typically support litigation matters, you'll also need to consider your potential client's attitude toward when to settle the case (as this will drive cost and potential profitability of the matter). Litigation lawyers who tend to work on a value fee basis (more on that in the next chapter) will typically seek to choose in midpoint between early settlement and trial based on their experience. (This was referred to in a great article by Jordan Furlong as "the pricing of risk in the legal process" and is well worth a read.[2])

If trying to develop options at a *relationship level*, it is also important to review any existing client financial reports that may be available (such as those that show historic profitability by matter, practice area, and jurisdiction, if required), any existing fee arrangements that may be in place (as these will typically be a starting point for any future negotiation), and other good relationship agreement examples that may exist within your firm. And this is all *before* you determine the appropriate type of *fee structure* to adopt.

We'll discuss more about the pros and cons of various fee approaches in the next chapter, so suffice it to say that once you have identified likely costs and factored in the multiple variables above, you then need to work out the *most appropriate* fee approach for your client. This should be a fee approach that clearly aligns with your client's business objectives, one that clearly demonstrates your value to your client, and is one where you are able to perform the work at an appropriate level of profit.

2. Jordan Furlong, *Rise of Pricing Risk in the Legal Process*, LAWYERS WEEKLY (June 24, 2011), http://www.lawyersweekly.ca/index.php?section=article&articleid=1444.

Competition and Resisting the "Race to the Bottom"

A quick word about competition: As we know, the competitive landscape often is setting a clear benchmark or value on what specific types of work can command in the market, and therefore the price. However, it is important to see this in the context of the following—this only matters when clients have multiple options on who can meet their specific needs, and *only then* when price is the primary driver of its decision.

In summary, *if a client is not buying on price, then you should not be selling on price either*. It may pay to do some quick "competition homework" in advance, or else you might be setting a price at an inappropriate level.

There may be instances when you do want to price at, or below, the level of the appropriate competition. This is normally done as a "loss leader." This may be done to either build a relationship with a new client or keep your team busy in times of lower utilization (and should be viewed as the exception rather than the norm).

Adopting this kind of approach can be dangerous, though. In reality, only in very rare circumstances do the small jobs done as loss leaders develop into significant client relationships. Therefore *use your loss leaders carefully*, otherwise you may find that you have many small unprofitable clients, rather than the fewer, bigger ones that you had initially anticipated developing. Once you set an expectation in your client's mind of what you can deliver at a low price, it is extremely difficult to change that perception.

This reminds me of a conversation I had with a senior partner, Richard Godden, whilst I was at Linklaters during the start of the global financial crisis. During a break in our meeting, Richard took a pen and quickly sketched something on a flipchart, which is reproduced (very roughly and from memory) on the next page in figure 5.1.

The value of the diagram was in its simplicity, and yet the point is extremely powerful. You need to remember your market position and the value that you add. Therefore, when reacting to competitive pressures, it is key to ensure that you don't diminish your market position *or* perception of value (as once done, it is very difficult to recover).

Let's take another, this time hypothetical, example to illustrate the point further. We have two associates, Fred and Bob, that we are going to use on

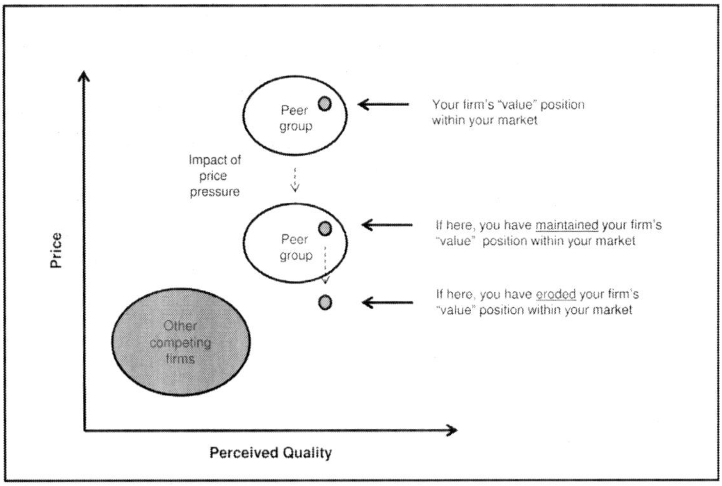

Figure 5.1
Maintaining Your Value Position

the client. They each have an hourly charge-out rate of *$100*, have the same underlying cost structure, get paid the same salary, and have the same skills.

The client wants to use them for one hour each (for the purposes of this illustration we won't talk about different pricing approaches). The client wants a 50 percent discount on each—that is, they only want to pay a total of $100. What do you do?

Well, you have three options. The first is to refuse, but let's assume that you don't. We now have two options left.

- You agree to the client's request, and both Fred and Bob now have an hourly charge at the rate of *$50* each. This is the approach that most of us would probably take.
- *Another* approach is that we agree to the client request, but we charge Fred at *$100* per hour (his normal charge-out rate), but we agree to provide Bob's services *at no charge*.

In both examples the client's final bill, assuming it was only two hours' worth of work, is still $100. The realization on your matter is also still the same, at 50 percent (and the level of profitability is similar too, given the same cost structure).

But there's one key difference, between (1) and (2) above. In the first example, you have now set the expectation in your client's mind that they can get the appropriate level of expertise at *$50* rather than the *$100* they used to pay. However, in the second example, although Bob's services were at no charge, the client expectation of what we would normally pay for someone of this level of expertise remains at *$100*. Now, from your perspective, which is better long term?

Gaining Approval

The last step in this process is around gaining *approval*. "But wait!" I hear you cry. "I'm a partner in the firm, surely I don't need to get approval!" Admittedly, this is not an unusual reaction, but one that is becoming fortunately less common. I say fortunately, but what do I mean?

Let me take a quick step back for a moment and give some supporting context. There are a number of key stages or levels of "pricing maturity" that pricing consultants use to evaluate their clients' pricing capabilities, each varying slightly depending upon the provider in question. These levels range from those that have no infrastructure or effective coordination, to those deemed to be "world class" (the preserve of very few, certainly less than 1 percent of companies).[3]

With my "pricing practitioner hat" on, an optimistic assessment of where we are in general in the legal industry is that we are at Level 2, and even then, at a push. This is the level where we recognize that something is wrong and needs to be fixed, and where we have begun to put some *fundamental* building blocks internal processes in place in an effort to improve.

One of the first requirements of being classed as having "Level 2 maturity" is having some clear pricing processes in place. It is here where you are trying to *gain some control* over what's going on within your organization.

3. The pricing maturity framework concept mentioned is driven from the World Class Pricing Process Maturity process developed by Pricing Solutions, How to Achieve Pricing Excellence, as part of the Professional Pricing Society certification curriculum.

Probably about 40 percent of companies (not just those in the legal sector) are at this level.

(As an aside, progression through the other levels is then driven by the extent to which pricing and value analysis is done, the use of optimization tools, and, finally, the overall maturity and effectiveness of the pricing process.)

Now back to our law firm.

A number of firms are now beginning to move away from being "firefighters" (that is, at Level 1) to play more of a "traffic cop" role in the world of pricing (Level 2). It is here that they are trying to gain a better understanding of *price leakage* through the inconsistent application of their existing discounting policy and through more comprehensive review of the total cost to service a client relationship and, if possible, a matter. (We will talk about this more in the final chapter of this section.)

It is also driven by firms paying much closer attention to *parity* across their existing client relationships, recognizing that clients (like lawyers) typically move within similar professional circles. No law firm wants to be in the embarrassing situation where it is discovered that its best client is receiving a significantly less favorable commercial deal than one of the law firm's smaller clients, all because two clients happened to sit next to each other on a flight. *These* are the reasons that gaining approval is important.

Traditionally in firms, the role of pricing has been left to the discretion of the individual partner, or sometimes department head if there have been initial efforts in place to put in a pricing policy.

But pricing is most frequently an orphan within a law firm's list of roles and responsibilities, with no clear central point of ownership (although this is potentially changing with the rise of pricing directors and similar roles, as is discussed in Chapter 23). Sometimes pricing is owned by the partner, sometimes by the member of the finance team, and even occasionally (though rarely) by those in the marketing and business development function. What is clear is that there needs to be greater *coordination* of pricing efforts in many firms.

A good starting place is through the introduction of rudimentary pricing policies. The pricing policies themselves do not *need* to be very prescriptive. Each needs to give appropriate guidance to what is and is not acceptable within the firm and sets very clear guidelines as to where formal approval is required (and is consistent with your firm's overall culture). At this stage, many are trying to just get their "organizational arms" around the process. Being prescriptive can come next.

I know of a number of firms where only the managing partner can sign off, and of many others where there are clearly defined escalation and approval paths in place. Some firms have also implemented pricing committees, with these becoming involved for complex matters, significant relationships, or innovative pricing approaches. These are becoming increasingly widespread, with both law firms I've worked for having these bodies in place. The common characteristic for all, however, is that there is a senior person (or group of individuals) ultimately responsible for approving the pricing decision. Therefore, my suggestion to you is not to over complicate the approval process, but make sure that you *do* have one.

One final word on approvals: What you have had approved by your appropriate firm body is *not* necessarily what you immediately propose to your client. We'll touch on this important point again when discussing negotiation, but it is really important to make sure you give yourself some *negotiation room* as part of your client discussions without having to go back to seek further approvals (although this technique itself can be powerful in a negotiating context, which we'll also cover later).

We have had a look at some of the key do's and don'ts when looking to Set the Price in this brief chapter.

How we go about this step has a significant impact on how we then seek to Get the Price, and then successfully Manage to Price. We really do need to *begin with the end in mind*.

When determining the price, we need to have a good grasp of what it costs to deliver a service or product, but more importantly we also need to make sure that it is something needed. As Thomas Edison commented, "the secret of staying afloat in business is to create something people will pay for."[4] And people will pay if they understand the value that the product or service will bring.

---

4. Ronald J. Baker, PRICING ON PURPOSE: CREATING AND CAPTURING VALUE 143 (Wiley 2006).

But before talking about how we can more effectively *communicate* our price, let's take a closer look at some of the potential pricing and fee arrangement types that exist, and where these work well and less well. We have put it off as much as we can, but now we are about to enter the realm of the AFA, the alternative fee agreement.

Don't forget *(a summary of the key points):*

- Costing the matter is not the same as pricing the matter.
- Make sure you go into any pricing decision with your eyes wide open, and remember that not all revenue is good revenue.
- If your client isn't buying on price, you shouldn't be selling on price either.
- Beware of "loss leader" pricing, and manage it carefully if you do decide to use it. It often doesn't lead to anywhere—except maybe unprofitable matters.
- When reacting to market pressures, be careful to retain your current market position and the market perception of value as a minimum.
- Having a clear approval process in place is critical—this helps minimize price leakage, ensure appropriate parity among your client base, and maintain the overall integrity of your pricing approach.
- We need to always begin with the end in mind when pricing, as decisions made here subsequently drive our negotiation and matter management approaches.

Chapter 6

Demystifying AFAs: What They Really Are and How They Really Work

No book on the topic of legal pricing would be complete without a summary (at the very least) of the typical pricing approaches adopted by law firms and clients.

A confession:

Unlike some commentators in this field, I am not going to predict the ultimate demise of the billable hour, as I strongly believe that there are occasions when pricing on this basis makes sense (for example, when seeking to clearly define and scope a very complex, multi-jurisdictional matter).

What I am going to predict is that it will become the least used and most scrutinized form of pricing. Hourly based fees will become the exception, not the rule.

So what are our options? Where do these work best and what are some of the benefits to, and related costs of, these approaches?

Not all options are equally appropriate for a matter, and those that are poorly defined and managed from the outset can lead to confusion and ultimately resentment from both parties. It is therefore important before selecting the desired approach to understand its potential strengths and limitations.

The majority of this chapter looks at those arrangements that are most typically employed. Although not exclusive in coverage, this should hopefully both be a useful guide to those most frequently used and point to common variants of each.

But before diving into the different options in more detail, I would like to cover a couple of key points up front—around terminology, adoption, and identifying which approaches could work.

Speaking the Same Language: A Question of Terminology

The key first step is ensuring that we (whether client or law firm) are speaking the same language.

The term itself, alternative fee arrangements (AFA), is a strange one. By its very definition, it is being determined by what it is not—namely, anything that is not based on an hourly rate. This has led to some law firms viewing anything not done against their standard rate as being alternative. To further illustrate the point, the General Counsel Roundtable also uses a relatively broad set of fee approaches in its definition, including volume-based discounts and blended rates, the inclusion of which would have AFA purists up in arms.

It can also imply something else, though—something new, untried, untested, or unproven. It may be hard to adequately counter the last statement about AFAs being unproven (as the wider jury is still out on this point for both law firms and their clients), but for the remaining attributes, the evidence is much clearer. AFAs have been around for a long time, not just in the legal profession but in other professional services firms (accountancy and management consultancy, to name but two). They clearly do have a part to play.

Therefore, a term we prefer to use at Baker & McKenzie is "appropriate fee arrangements" (and we even get to keep the same acronym). Why this subtle shift in naming? Simple. Whatever the agreed fee arrangement is, it needs to clearly align with the economic interests of both client and lawyer; it should be structured to encourage completion of a clearly specified (and identifiable) client objective; and, finally, it should encourage and incentivize the lawyer to identify ways to become more efficient. It is therefore one that clearly reflects the appropriate value of the transaction.

In sum, an appropriate fee arrangement. The word "alternative" just does not cut it.

The appropriate type of fee arrangement will vary depending upon the actual matter in question, and also, frequently, the phase (or segment) of the matter.

It's important to clearly understand, as a law firm, your client's expectations and frame of reference. I can recall vividly a conversation with a general counsel of a European-headquartered client who was keen to adopt an AFA-type arrangement. What he was actually looking for was a volume discount (the conversation itself went along the lines of "the more I spend with you, the bigger the discount I would like"), but as mentioned above, terminology was confusing. In this particular instance, his frame of reference was that he was looking for something that was different from the standard hourly rate. When I have had similar conversations with other clients—for example, large investment banks—they were looking for something very different: an AFA that clearly had an element of shared risk and incentive to be more efficient.

There has also been much debate within the legal press about whether past experience informs the general counsel's view. One school of thought has been that, as general counsel of major organizations are typically 50 years old or older, and have therefore "grown up" with the hourly rate approach, they are reluctant (or at least hesitant) to change, as AFAs are unfamiliar to how they had practiced law when in private practice. Whilst there may be some credence to this view, in my own opinion all this means is that it is even more important to have an open and honest discussion with a client as to what would be the best fee approach.

Finally, an interesting observation I have made since relocating to the United States a few years ago has been how AFAs are viewed—much of the discussion (and adoption) in the United States has typically been around their adoption on litigation-based matters, whereas in some other geographies (for example, the United Kingdom and Australia), adoption has tended to focus on a wider range of matter types (although nearly always "transactional" in nature).

As I am writing this chapter, I am recalling a number of partners in both law firms where I have worked who proactively sought to discuss and explore possible pricing and fee approaches with their clients. Although not all options being discussed may have been appropriate (at least in the client's eyes) for the specific matter in question, what it did do was *encourage a discussion around what was*. We should not be afraid to have that proactive discussion with clients. They, rightly, are looking for us to share our experiences of adopting these with others. Once put into our clients' own framework of business and matter objectives, and their previous experiences, an appropriate solution will be easily found.

"Lies, Damn Lies and Statistics"

So how widely adopted are AFAs? In sum, probably not as much as some think and more than others.

As will be discussed more in the next section (Get the Value), adoption of AFAs is less widespread than initially predicted. Even today, the bulk of legal fees paid are time based, whether this be an hourly rate, an agreed discount to the hourly rate, or similar. Surveys have consistently stated ongoing usage of hourly rates at around 80 percent, and some recent surveys have even suggested that this number is increasing, rather than decreasing—despite the ongoing commentary on this topic within the legal press.

That said, although there is perhaps not the wholesale adoption some predicted, they are being used, albeit at a slower rate than expected. In the Altman Weil 2012 Law Firms in Transition survey, 47 percent of the firms surveyed reported that usage had increased since the previous year. Other surveys, such as the 2012 ALM Legal Intelligence survey and the *American Lawyer*'s 2012 Law Firm Leaders survey, have also pointed to both greater law firm adoption of AFAs and more client requests, at 62 percent and 68 percent, respectively.[1]

In addition, this is where terminology becomes key. Indeed, the fact that a recent ALM survey on the topic was entitled "Speaking Different Languages" further highlights this potential issue. Given the different interpretations of what is meant by an AFA, interpreting actual usage is made much harder than it needs to be.

1. American Lawyer, 2012 Law Firm Leaders Survey (2012).

As Jim Hassett comments:

> [T]he fact that . . . conflicting definitions of AFAs are in wide use adds considerable confusion to an area already confusing enough. If a firm claims that 50% of its work is performed on an alternative fee basis it could mean that they are moving away from the billable hour (under the narrow definition), or it could mean that they are engaging in some creative hourly rate discounting (under the broad definition).[2]

Although I have a preference for the narrower definition, I can certainly appreciate both viewpoints. For those who would like to find out more on this topic, Jim provides an extremely useful overview of recent trends and developments in his book *Legal Project Management, Pricing, and Alternative Fee Arrangements*.[3]

Finding an Appropriate Model

One of the hardest yet most fundamental things to do when running any business is to determine the appropriate pricing approach.

Although the same is true in the legal world, through applying a number of core principles, firms can not only seek to manage the level of their "investment" with a client (and mitigate any potential impact on profitability) but also strengthen their relationship with existing clients, and win new (and hopefully profitable!) business from others.

We talked earlier about what good pricing looks like and some of the key guiding principles, but we did not talk about the most appropriate pricing approach at that time.

So, when looking to price a matter, what are some of the key considerations you should be mindful of?

---

2. Jim Hassett, LEGAL PROJECT MANAGEMENT, PRICING, AND ALTERNATIVE FEE ARRANGEMENTS: WHAT FIRMS ARE DOING 165 (2013).

3. *Id.* at chs. 8, 9.

These should include

- an assessment of the type of work required, by which I mean whether it is viewed as being strategic/bet-the-company-type work (normally less than 5 percent of the work within the legal market), expertise (about 60 percent of the market), or more routine or commoditized (about 30–35 percent of the market);
- your (and the client's) ability to clearly define the scope of work;
- your ability to determine the appropriate staffing model (or leverage); and
- your ability to quantify the potential impact of your firm's contribution (however defined), in terms of value to the client and also in terms of the overall result.

Whilst this list does certainly not intend to be exhaustive, it does highlight some of the key themes that you may wish to consider when determining a *potential* fee approach. In addition, you may also want to consider your own experience in doing this type of work, your previous experience in adopting different fee approaches, etc.

A few years ago, while working at Linklaters, I took a few moments out of my day to see how I could most effectively summarize the gamut of pricing options that existed. Figure 6.1 was my attempt to do so, and one that I'm hopeful still stands the test of time.

As part of that exercise, I identified three key characteristics of the pricing approaches that existed. There were those that mitigated the level of risk to the law firm (and also, it should be noted, to the client, depending on the nature of the transaction); there were those that were more cost focused; and, finally, there were those that were more focused on, and aligned to, the generation of value (appropriately defined for each specific client scenario).

However, there are a couple of additional considerations that are important to acknowledge. The first, although perhaps obvious, is that no one size fits all. Not only does each matter possess different attributes, but it may also be viewed differently in terms of its overall importance and value delivered within the client's organization. Even during the matter, employing a number of fee approaches may be more suitable—each reflecting the

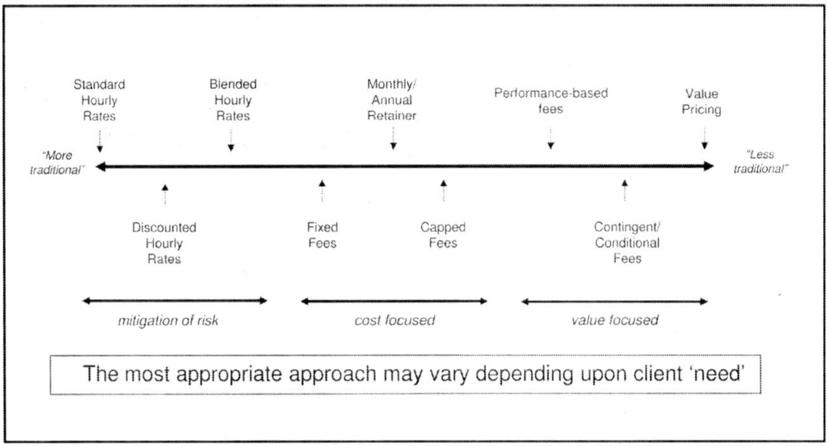

Figure 6.1
More Than the Billable Hour

individual matter phases' or segments' complexity and value. The second, discussed earlier, is the client's own frame of reference.

Looking at Our Options in More Detail

Now that we have quickly addressed the overall context, let's now have a more detailed look at some of the options themselves, starting with those fee approaches that appear at the left-hand side of figure 6.1. (For those that are most familiar, I have provided slightly less information in the interests of space.)

Risk-Mitigating Approaches

The approaches outlined here are those primarily based on time (that is, the input cost). The advantage of these approaches is limiting associated risk to the law firm if matters progress longer, or if the matter requires more resources than initially anticipated.

These approaches are primarily

- hourly rates
- discounted hourly rates
- blended (or banded) hourly rates

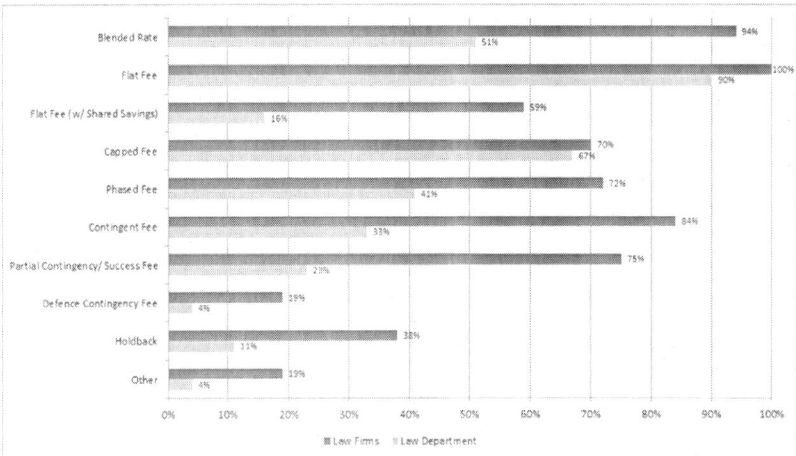

Figure 6.2
Commonly Adopted Alternative Fee Approaches
(The following chart was based on responses provided as part of the ALM survey on Alternative Fee Arrangements. The question asked to participants was, "Of the alternative fee arrangements employed in 2012, which of the following does/did your law firm or law department use (Check all that apply)." ALM Legal Intelligence, *Alternative Fee Arrangements at Legal Departments and Law Firms* 21 (2013).

As each of these approaches are time based, it is also easier for firms to more accurately capture what their input costs actually are (although I continue to be amazed sometimes how infrequently lawyers record their time promptly).

However, as increasingly documented in the legal press, there are a number of constraints and disadvantages to these types of approaches. To name just a few, there is a lack of cost certainty, a lack of transparency, no incentive to become more efficient, and no clear alignment to the client's actual business objective.

Hourly Rates

The Basic Outline

Whether we admit it or not, this is where we all start from. The humble hourly rate, where the price is determined by the time spent multiplied by the appropriate hourly rates for the timekeepers who are working on the matter.

Although perhaps increasingly rare in today's competitive environment, some firms still charge their standard hourly rate (for the defined levels of experience for their respective jurisdiction, and that may also vary by practice area).

Law Firm Considerations

The advantage to the law firm is that they have no risk, it's familiar, it provides a predictable degree of cash flow, and it is also easy to change the underlying standard rate to reflect any increase in cost. But there is no recognition in this model of the *potential complexity or urgency* of the matter in question and the approach by its very nature seeks to penalize efficient working practices. Also, from a purely logical perspective, the amount that one timekeeper can charge is finite—as there are only so many hours in a day.

Client Considerations

For the clients, all the risks sit with them. There is no alignment or reflection of value in the charging mechanism, there is a high degree of uncertainty around the final bill (unless there has been some of the recommended project management disciplines, discussed later, put in place), and they may pay for work that they feel is not required (an extreme example here being the training up of less experienced lawyers). However, some do like it, as it is what they know, and can act as an easier comparison of rates between firms (note this is not the same as comparative value between firms). Finally, it can provide some degree of transparency as to the time being spent.

Discounted Hourly Rates

The Basic Outline

This is the most common variant of the above, where a discount is provided against the agreed standard rate, and is the dominant form of fee approach in today's legal market.

For example, if the agreed client discount is 10 percent and the specific lawyer's rate is $500, the client's agreed rate this timekeeper would be $450 (that is, the fee being reduced by $50 or 10 percent of the standard value). This discount may be specific to named individuals, jurisdictions, specific matters, or time period.

Law Firm and Client Considerations

The pros and cons discussed above in the previous section are equally as applicable here.

Blended or Banded Hourly Rates

The Basic Outline

However you cut it, these are still fully 100 percent hourly based arrangements. These rates can be set in a number of different ways; for example, these may be defined at a jurisdictional level, experience level (most common), or even practice-area level.

It may be one single number (for example, $400 per hour regardless of who actually does the work) or be a single number per experience level (for example, $250 per associate) or jurisdiction (for example, $325 for all work in Mexico). The possibilities here are probably endless.

The Jury May Still Be Out

I can recall a global proposal issued by a major French investment bank a few years ago, in which they had requested as one of the potential options a globally blended rate to be applied at the relationship level, not just for a specific matter. At the time, the firm I was working with declined to submit a single number. This was driven by the valid conclusion that there were too many variables involved in determining what that number should be based on, with the potentially changing profiles of matters to be supported and changes to jurisdictions requiring support, not to mention the level and experience of the lawyers who would actually provide any support. (One other factor here was that it was a multiyear engagement, which created even more potential uncertainty).

Another potential danger here, if clients are asking for this, is that any proposed blend provided by the law firm is likely to be conservative for the very reasons outlined in my example above, and therefore the client is not getting a true representation of what the actual rate should look like. Ultimately, the bank in question decided not to pursue this single-rate approach.

In my experience, blended rates *do* have a role, though. This approach is well suited for work that is rate sensitive, routine, or repeat litigation. Examples here would include employment litigation where there is a single plaintiff. They tend to be less effective where the work is more advisory in nature—for example, intellectual property work, regulatory or privacy work, and antitrust work.

Law Firm Considerations

The key challenge for both law firm and client is around the appropriate setting of expectations, especially around how much partner (versus less senior) time that will be dedicated to the matter.

It can also become quickly unprofitable for the law firm if the initial estimate of the timekeeper mix is inaccurate—for example, where a matter requires more senior partner input than originally anticipated.

Client Considerations

Many of the challenges that relate to the hourly rate approach also apply here, from a client's perspective. But there is one other major consideration—whether work is being performed at a more junior level is appropriate. This situation can often be driven by the law firm's desire to maintain costs within the agreed blended rate.

However, there are also a couple of benefits. First, it is easier to understand and easier to administer than a more traditional hourly rate approach. Second, the level of blended rates may actually result in the spend for a specific matter being reduced when compared with the more traditional approach.

Cost-Driven Approaches

The approaches outlined within this grouping are those based on the premise of providing *better cost control to our clients*, and managing better budgets for ourselves.

These are primarily

- fixed (or flat) fees
- retainer-based arrangements
- capped fees

Let's explore each a bit more.

Fixed or Flat Fees

Of all the non-hourly-based fee approaches being used, by far and away the most popular is the fixed (or flat) fee. In the 2011 ACC Chief Legal Officer survey, over 8 percent of all legal spend adopted a fixed (or flat) fee model,[4] with this number rising subsequently.

The Basic Outline

In its most simple form, a fixed fee is one that is jointly agreed to by law firm and client for an agreed-upon set of well-defined services. This is either for a single engagement, or phase within a single engagement (for example, fixed fees are frequently adopted for the initial due diligence phase of mergers and acquisitions matters or for specific phases in litigation).

Usage of fixed-fee arrangements drive very different law firm behavior when compared with hourly rate–based approaches. It encourages law firms to deploy smaller teams, ensure greater efficiency of effort, and really question how to resource the work most effectively.

However, as with the hourly rate–based approach, fixed-fee matters are completely indifferent to the eventual outcome. All this approach provides in its most basic form is *budgetary certainty.*

Law Firm Considerations

For fixed-fee matters in particular, *efficient staffing and execution* of the matter is key, due to the adverse impact on law firm profitability of being inefficient. Whilst this typically means using the lowest-cost resource, there are occasions where the opposite is true—especially if a partner is able to resolve a specific point of law in minutes based on previous experience rather than the more typical scenario of a relatively junior associate plowing through mountains of legal opinions (and can also support value-pricing efforts too).

4. ASS'N OF CORPORATE COUNSEL, ACC 2011 CHIEF LEGAL OFFICERS SURVEY (2011), *available at* http://www.acc.com/legalresources/resource.cfm?show=1294806 (note: you need to be a member to download the survey).

It can also encourage more overall proactive management—for example, when assessing potential matter options in a litigation case.

The law firm in this instance bears the "downside risk" if work required exceeds the level of the agreed fixed fee. However, a note of caution: using this type of approach can be risky with newer clients until there has been an opportunity to establish a better understanding of expectations and respective style.

Client Considerations

The key benefits for a client in this approach is that they gain *greater predictability of legal cost*, eliminating the risk of these costs increasing through potential changes in law firm effort required to complete the matter (or phase). There is also potentially a strong incentive for the client to increase the number of similar matters under the management of the law firm to help drive even greater economy of scale and mitigate the impact of budgeting inaccuracy through widening or diversifying the portfolio.

Variations on a Theme

Holdback: One variant to the basic fixed-fee model is to adopt fixed fees with some proportion of payment being "held back" based on either law firm performance or, more commonly, matter outcome. Given the amount of fees potentially "at risk" to the law firm, this can counteract any temptation to staff a fixed-fee matter with inexperienced team members, as there is a real financial consequence of underperformance (however defined by the client). From clients' perspective, they are able to objectively assess and set compensation based on the value of the service provided, either via a jointly agreed-to set of criteria determined by both parties in advance of the matter, or independently.

Flat fee by phase (or segment): This is where a fee is agreed for a discrete phase (or segment) of work rather than the matter as a whole. Using a litigation-based example, this could be for initial investigations or pleadings, with a similar arrangement then agreed on for written discovery, depositions, and so on, through to trial. I have also seen this very successfully adopted when there are perceived to be many moving parts to a matter, such as in mergers and acquisitions or corporate reorganizations.

However, this approach provides no incentive to complete a matter more promptly. Although this may not be an issue on some matters, in the majority of litigation cases it will be. Indeed, most clients typically request this fee approach when seeking to gain a potential benefit through paying a lower overall price for an earlier resolution of the matter.

Fixed-fee menu: Fixed fee menus are increasing in popularity. This is where there is a defined list of services and associated costs, or for specific segments (or stages) of a matter. Although well established in areas such as real estate, family law, and corporate secretarial matters, these are also becoming more common in other areas, such as loan agreements.

Portfolio fixed fees: Where there is a large volume of similar matters that need to be addressed, adopting a portfolio fixed fee may be appropriate. In this scenario, the law firm and client would agree on a single fixed fee to cover *all work in scope*. This is often adopted for commercial contracts or relatively simple employment-based matters (for example, immigration and visa requests). The key advantage to the client here is that they achieve an element of *cost certainty*. For the law firm, there is the opportunity to increase overall profitability through the more efficient delivery of matters over time.

There is also a variant to this approach that I have seen adopted. This is where the law firm agrees to conduct a series of matters with a fixed price on a sliding scale—that is, the first five matters are done for $100, the next five for $90, etc. This approach encourages the law firm to identify and implement the more efficient handling of the matters in question, although it does presume to some degree that these matters are very similar in nature, and are therefore ones in which process efficiencies may be easily identified. For the client, there is a clear cost benefit from doing this through the declining level of fixed fee (assuming that the original level of fixed fee is felt to be fair).

In Summary

Fixed fees are appropriate for the vast majority of legal matters (hence its continuing popularity). At the very minimum, it provides greater cost certainty. However, through adoption of some of the variations outlined above, it is possible to directly encourage a greater shared risk of outcome through the law firm having some degree of "skin in the game."

Patrick Lamb also provides an excellent observation in this regard (the comment initially referring primarily to litigation-based matters). The greater alignment of incentives tied to payment can also have another benefit. It can also provide clients with a "much more thorough and accurate assessment of the quality of the case at the outset since firms will be reluctant to make investments in poor cases."[5]

Retainer-Based Fees

The Basic Outline

This can often feel like a supersized fixed-fee arrangement. A retainer-based arrangement is one in which the client agrees to pay the law firm a fee at intervals (monthly, quarterly, annually, etc.) for a clearly defined set of services.

I know of a number of law firms that have found this fee approach to be successful for them and their clients, these firms often having a number of very long-standing retainer arrangements in place, ranging from practice-area-specific arrangements (for example, trademark portfolio management or employment matters) to ones that span multiple practice areas. One very well-known example of the latter is the relationship between Tyco, a U.S. industrial conglomerate, and Eversheds (a United Kingdom–based firm), which was originally established as of 2007 and renewed for a fourth time in April 2013, covering Tyco's legal needs across Europe, the Middle East, and Africa.[6]

The scope of the retainer agreement can be as wide or narrow as appropriate, covering matters within a specific area of law, to ones that are focused on a specific matter (for example, during litigation for as long as the case remains active).

For the law firm there is an additional benefit: it can also act as a valuable marketing tool for the law firm, as it potentially removes any barriers

---

5. Patrick Lamb, Alternative Fee Arrangements: Value Fees and the Changing Legal Market 19 (Ark Group 2010).

6. Yun Kriegler, *Tyco Renews Fixed-Fee Contract with Eversheds*, THE LAWYER (Apr. 26, 2013), *available at* http://www.thelawyer.com/news/latest-news/tyco-renews-fixed-fee-contract-with-eversheds/3004271.article.

to the client picking up the phone and seeking instruction on other matters outside of the agreed retainer scope.

Law Firm Considerations

This type of arrangement has a number of advantages for a law firm. It encourages greater efficiency, a clear upside if using resources wisely, and it supports better cash flow (as these types of arrangement typically bill on a monthly or quarterly basis).

Like fixed- and capped-fee arrangements (looked at next), strong project management is key to ensure the most efficient use of time. These disciplines are also essential to ensure that you are only conducting those activities in the *agreed* retainer scope as part of the retainer.

Finally, you need to ensure that there is the ability to "correct" the level of retainer based on client desire to increase or decrease the scope of services covered (based on actual or anticipated usage) and the actual profile and volume of work done under the existing retainer. Having a number of agreed checkpoints with the client is therefore recommended throughout the retainer agreement's lifetime.

If considering adopting a retainer with one of your existing clients, it is recommended to review the related matter history for the 12 to 24 months previous to try to get a feel for the typical volume and profile of work proposed to be covered in scope.

The beauty of retainer-based agreements is that they are well suited for a wide range of specific work areas (for example, trademark management, employment-related matters, commercial contracts, defined advisory advice) and can be as broad or narrow in geographic coverage as appropriate.

Client Considerations

This approach primarily gives the client certainty of legal spend for the specific matters included in scope, and also provides greater budgeting and cash-flow certainty driven by the agreed payment periods.

Law firms using retainers should also make sure the client is fully informed on the profile and volume of work being conducted, as clients may perceive they are getting less value for money under the retainer agreement if the level of work that particular month is relatively low.

In Summary

Retainers are becoming increasingly more popular as a fee approach for both law firms and clients alike. The key to its success will be the ability of law firms to continue to demonstrate that they are able to deliver "more with less" at appropriate levels of quality. Good expectation management and reporting is key to the success of these types of arrangements.

Capped Fees

The Basic Outline

In this scenario, fees are charged at the agreed hourly rate until fees reach a maximum limit for the agreed matter. If law firms need to perform additional work on the matter to successfully complete it, it's on their own dime. It's the hourly rate "with consequences."

Law Firm Considerations

This is perhaps the least preferable of all the pricing approaches listed from a law firm's perspective. There is no opportunity for an upside, as you get paid for the work conducted if under (or at) the level of the agreed cap even if doing so with great efficiency, but there is a potential for significant downside if you misjudged the level of the cap.

However, it does implicitly promote better efficiency in that you are more aware of the budget available for the matter.

Client Considerations

This provides the client with some degree of certainty around the final cost of the bill, as there is a defined upper limit. There is a potential danger, though. As the matter gets closer to the cap, more junior lawyers may be asked to support the matter by the law firm in an attempt to stay within the overall agreed budget.

Variations on a Theme

"Risk collar" based fees: This approach is based upon charging an agreed hourly rate around an estimated budget for a matter (the cap), with risk sharing if fees are above or below the cap.

As part of this fee approach, there is an agreed "dead zone" or "no-man's-land" established, where there is no adjustment to fees if in this range. If work is completed under the originally agreed budget, the law firm shares a percentage of any savings generated. Alternatively, if work is completed over budget, the client would receive an additional discount on fees over and above the agreed dead zone (which may result in a further reduction in fees over and above the original discount or even no additional charge).

As a simple illustration, if the agreed dead zone is $90–$110 and all fees below $90 are split 50-50 and above $110 are split 25-75 in the client's favor, the following scenarios could occur:

- If fees amounted to $80, the law firm would receive $80 + 50 percent of the difference between this amount and the lower cap ($90). They would therefore receive an additional $5 on their expended rates—that is, $85 in total.
- If fees amounted to anything from $95 to $105, they would receive the amount expended.
- If fees amounted to $130, they would receive the higher cap ($110) plus 25 percent of the difference between this amount and the remainder (25 percent of $20 = $5)—that is, $115 in total.

As Patrick Lamb comments, "this model creates incentives to do less work but without the corresponding incentive to obtain results." From a client's perspective, therefore, it is useful to also tie an element of payment to matter outcome as a way of further encouraging the legal team.[7]

In Summary

These forms of arrangement shift some of the commercial risk to the law firm. It is, in many respects, a halfway house. It is certainly better for a client than the standard hourly rate in that it does transfer some element of financial risk to the law firm, and encourages better cost management, but

7. LAMB, *supra* note 5, at 22.

it does not create the kind of incentive as a contingent-based fee (either full or partial) does.

Value-Aligned Approaches

The final set of approaches outlined is more value aligned to our client's business objectives. These include approaches where there is an element of risk or reward based on either the actual outcome and/or law firm performance. These are the approaches that are currently least adopted by law firm and client alike, but where there is the greatest opportunity for both.

Fee types applicable here in summary are

- performance-based fees,
- contingent (or conditional) fees, and
- value-priced fees.

Performance-Based Fees

The Basic Outline

This is very similar in approach to the "holdback" mechanism we discussed when looking at fixed fees. This is where some proportion of payment is being held back based on law firm performance.

As with the holdback example, depending upon the amount of fees potentially at risk to the law firm, this counteracts any temptation to inappropriately staff a matter, as there is a real financial consequence of underperformance (however defined by the client). This is normally around 10 percent to 15 percent of the total fee for the matter, and can be more. It can also be applied both to hourly fee or fixed-fee arrangements.

From the client's perspective, they are able to objectively assess and set compensation based on the perceived value of the service provided, either via a jointly agreed set of criteria determined by both parties in advance of the matter or independently.

Law Firm Considerations

This is a very good way to align the fee more closely to actual performance on a matter, and also allows the client to have some degree of influence over the final bill to be paid.

I tend to find that the greater value of this approach is that it is also extremely valuable in that it encourages immediate client feedback on performance (and therefore allows you to address any potential areas for improvement quickly). If seeking to adopt this approach, do so with your more regular clients (rather than new ones) to ensure a more informed assessment of your performance.

Client Considerations

This approach gives the client some control of the final fee and encourages them to give immediate matter performance feedback (which will hopefully help on future matters). Depending upon the agreed criteria used to determine the level of performance, this may result in additional administration, therefore a *few simple metrics* are recommended as part of any evaluation criteria. (For example: Did the law firm add value? How well did the lawyers understand the client business objectives? How well did they work with the client team? Etc.)

In Summary

As mentioned, this is a great way for a law firm to encourage more frequent client feedback, and also share some degree of commercial risk with the client.

Contingent or Conditional Fees

The Basic Outline

In a contingency-based fee agreement (also sometimes referred to as conditional fees, especially in the United Kingdom), a law firm will have the level of its fee payable determined in its entirety on a successful outcome (however defined). This is most commonly adopted by plaintiff lawyers (think personal injury claims as one example here), but is now moving into the defense arena too (see also reverse contingency on the next page).

For these types of agreements, it is critical that the manner in which the potential success fee is agreed on before the matter commences. Whilst this is sometimes left to the client's own discretion, it is more often better to agree on the payment against an agreed set of criteria (ideally these should be few in number and very easily and objectively measurable). This helps avoid any difficult discussions at the matter's conclusion, and also clearly aligns expectations from the outset.

This approach can be used on its own, or in combination with other fee approaches, such as discounted hourly rates or fixed fees (see also partially contingent fees on the next page). Indeed, it sometimes makes good sense to adopt this in conjunction with another fee approach, as this ensures (from a law firm perspective) that there is some degree of interim cash flow throughout the lifetime of the matter, which may make the law firm more amendable to putting a significant proportion of its fee at risk.

Law Firm Considerations

This approach is very popular if acting as the plaintiff but is rarely used in transactional work. I would certainly never recommend it if being done on a fully contingent basis, although I have seen this very successfully used within both law firms I have worked for under a partially contingent fee arrangement for major mergers and acquisitions and securities matters in which an agreed percentage of fees are put at risk.

An important caveat: Not all jurisdictions allow contingent-based fees to be used, especially outside of the United States (for example, these are not allowed under local bar rules in Belgium and Germany), so do check your appropriate bar rules before proposing.

Client Considerations

If adopting a fully contingent fee, the client benefits from not having any initial expense when pursuing the case, as this is borne by the law firm (in some respects, the law firm acting as the client's "banker"—a concept that some law firms are more comfortable with than others!). The flip side for the law firm is that they can potentially gain an even bigger "upside" through seeking to improve the client's ultimate award.

Variations on a Theme

Partially contingent fees: In some respects this is a hybrid fee approach. A law firm will typically receive a proportion of its normal hourly fee, payable as the matter proceeds. They will also receive a final lump sum (or success fee) at the conclusion of the matter, depending upon the final outcome. Again, agreement on what constitutes success is key.

Reverse contingency: This fee type is becoming more commonly used in defense litigation matters where the level of contingent fee is based on a percentage of the amount saved for the client in the matter. The fee amount is determined as a percentage of the difference between the estimated level of potential exposure and the corresponding amount (if any) paid by the client, either via damages, as part of a settlement, or any litigation costs that have been avoided. At the outset of the matter it is key that both parties agree what constitutes fair value; for example, what if the client loses the case and is also liable for the other party's costs of full litigation?

This approach can be used on its own or in combination with other fee approaches, such as discounted hourly rates or fixed fees. As with contingent fees, it sometimes makes good sense to adopt in conjunction with another fee approach, as this ensures (from a law firm perspective) that there is some degree of interim cash flow throughout the lifetime of the matter, which may make the law firm more amenable to putting a significant proportion of its fee at risk.

Like the standard contingency-fee arrangement, this approach shifts some of the potential downside risk to the law firm, more closely aligning law firm and client incentives. It can also help strengthen the partnership between both parties, as there is a greater understanding of clients' level of overall exposure and potential legal costs and therefore impact on their business.

For a law firm, there is a stronger financial incentive to obtain the *most favorable* result possible. It can also drive better and more-targeted staffing and working approaches due to the potential economic upside for doing so cost-effectively.

This approach is best adopted when there are large, complex matters in which the client needs the best possible result (however defined) but wants to manage the overall costs of litigation. Typical areas may include intellectual property litigation or antitrust defense matters. It requires a strong relationship between law firm and client (as indeed most AFA approaches do). Finally, this should only really be used where there is an opportunity to directly quantify the impact of a successful outcome on the client's profit-and-loss statement. Not only does this make it easier to determine any contingency payment but can also be used to more easily "sell" internally to both parties.

In Summary

Contingency or conditional fees are increasing in popularity, with law firms and clients alike due to the potential upside in fees for the law firm and potential reduction and better management of cost and cash flow from the client's perspective. This in part can be attributed to the number of variants that can be applied, briefly summarized above. However, as with many forms of AFA, it is really critical that both parties *identify what is meant by "value" at the outset*, or as close to, of the matter. With so much riding on this definition, it is frightening how little effort is frequently devoted to this step, and yet the consequences of not doing so often lead to client and law firm dissatisfaction and a client-counsel relationship in need of urgent repair.

Value-Driven Pricing

The Basic Outline

This is potentially the hardest to get right, and in some respects could be seen as the holy grail of legal pricing. It is where the level of the fee is determined by the estimated value the legal work has contributed toward the overall client business objective. (We will explore the concept of value more fully in the next section.)

I have seen this used most successfully (although not exclusively) on major transactional matters (for example, merger and acquisition deals and Initial Public Offerings (IPOs)). The key here is having an agreed assessment of what constitutes value and how the value will therefore be measured (and payment assessed). Do this at the start of any significant matter rather than at the end or midway through, as it ensures a much clearer alignment between law firm and client.

Law Firm Considerations

In this scenario, the law firm can further strengthen its client relationship with the upside of recovering higher fees. It clearly helps drive greater client satisfaction through the *common pursuit of value*. The law firm may also potentially receive a fee larger than it would have if adopting one of the more traditional pricing models outlined earlier.

However, a firm's comfort in proposing this type of fee approach often comes down to the confidence and experience of the individual matter partner in being able to determine where value can be delivered to the client and the firm's ability to deliver to this. In this option, whether the legal work required takes two weeks, two months, or two years, the fee paid by the client would be the same. This approach is completely time *in*dependent.

Client Considerations

For a client, it is an easy sell, with the amount of fees payable directly tied to the value contributed by the legal work conducted. However, similar to the law firm, a client's in-house legal team may not be comfortable in being able to determine what value means in the specific matter context—or even worse, not have their assessment acknowledged by others within the organization. (This leads into a broader question on the perceived value of in-house legal teams within some organizations, as they strive to become more akin to "trusted advisors" to the business.)

Variations on a Theme

Although I have seen these typically adopted on single, large matters, there is no reason why this approach could not be used for a portfolio of smaller, similar matters.

There are also two other approaches that are worthy of mention here, one well known, the other perhaps less so: those of percentage-based fees and the concept of the Value Adjustment Line.

Percentage-based fees: In my view, this has always been a bit of a hybrid—in part fixed fee, in part value-based fee—and, as such, doesn't really satisfy either criteria particularly well. The fee itself is based on the estimated size of the transaction, which will be determined as an agreed percentage of the total transaction. This assumes that larger transactions require more legal support and that the support required is more critical. However, in the legal context, big does not necessarily mean complex or difficult. Therefore, solely driving a fee from this basis, whilst advantageous to the law firm conducting the work, is not one that would encourage (or sustain) a long-term client relationship. Although these issues can be addressed (through the adoption of a sliding-fee scale based on transaction size), they can result in greater scrutiny (not in itself unwelcome) and divert management attention (which would be unwelcome, and potentially have greater consequences).

From a law firm perspective, the benefit is that remuneration is based on transaction size, not hours expended, with this being able to be determined with some degree of accuracy at the transaction's outset. But this approach raises a number of potential issues. For example, what happens if a transaction were to stop midway through, prior to completion? How would fees then be determined? What if the work required is more complex and takes longer than both parties estimated at the outset? None of these issues are insurmountable, but early recognition *and* discussion of them is key.

Although I have seen this used in a number of practice areas (and indeed investment banks have operated on this model for years), I have come across this most regularly on mergers and acquisitions and real estate–related matters.

As a client, there are a couple of key benefits: The fee is known at the beginning of the transaction, and therefore requires less management attention to billing. This allows more attention to be focused on what really matters—the progress, and contribution, of the legal work.

However, there is also a flip side. Some clients may worry that the work ultimately done is actually less complex, or completed more quickly, than originally thought. Being blunt, you pay for what you get—if the fee is truly linked to the value of the transaction, this issue becomes a nonissue (and indeed the converse is true for the law firm, who may find the work more complex and time-consuming than initially estimated yet receive no upside for additional effort).

The Value Adjustment Line: This second approach is something that is not as widely covered in the AFA literature or portfolio of options. It is a concept developed initially by Ralph Palumbo (of the Summit Law Group) and further successfully adopted (and advocated) by the Valorem Law Group (and I am sure subsequently a few others).

Why it is worth including here is because it is an excellent example of how even adoption of hourly based fees (though not only these) can be adapted to *more closely align* to the concept of shared risk and value. Although potentially harder to implement in larger law firms, it is something that all should be aware of and seek to adopt if possible.

In its simplest form, billing is as per the traditional hourly rate model, but then there is a key twist. The client is then able to adjust that value of the bill upward or downward to more accurately reflect the value (however defined) that they feel was delivered.

Although certainly a risky approach, it has a number of excellent benefits:

- immediate feedback on performance (as reflected in the bill)
- quicker payment
- lower accounts receivable (as there is no debate about the amount to be paid—at least from the client's perspective)
- (perhaps most importantly) a clear demonstration by law firms adopting this of the belief in their ability to deliver value effectively to their clients

In Summary

Each of the varieties mentioned above are useful arrows in your AFA quiver, but "use wisely" is perhaps the most pertinent advice here.

. . . And Not Forgetting

For completeness, it's also useful to briefly summarize one final fee arrangement type, which incorporates the hourly rate. Although I am strongly of the view that this is not an AFA in the truest sense of the word, it at least includes elements that provide greater benefit to the client than the pure hourly rate–based model.

Volume Discounts

The Basic Outline

This is where an increasing level of discount is granted when an agreed threshold fee income volume is exceeded.

It is very important to *be specific* about any volume-based discount structure that will be applied.

For example: Is it based on work billed at the standard rate or the agreed client rate? Do the following thresholds incorporate all work done for the client only for specific matters or business units? And is this discount threshold based on the work that has been billed (but yet to be collected) or work for which income has been received by the law firm?

Law Firm Considerations

For law firms, this can provide an incentive to their clients to provide more work if set at an appropriate level. (Tip: For any volume-based discount structure to work, the thresholds included need to be ones that are *potentially achievable* but also provide a stretch, or aspirational, goal for the relationship. Otherwise, you are merely providing an additional discount for no real return.)

Client Considerations

Although the key advantage here is that the hourly rate cost will decline based on the appropriate final discount to be applied, this can create a different problem in that those using the service later on benefit from lower costs, compared with those who were using the law firm during the earlier stages.

In Summary

This can be very effective if used appropriately, but be clear on its structure from the outset.

So what does it all mean?

Non-hourly-based billing approaches are here to stay. The billable hour will, however, continue to have a place (albeit diminishing) at the table, driven by client preference and nature of complex matters. For all others, though, the move toward appropriate fee agreements is inevitable.

This means that we need to begin to separate or decouple cost from price. It also means that we need to proactively engage with our clients to understand how we can better align our fee approaches to their own business objectives. We need to keep it simple, otherwise it just won't work. And finally, we need to become much, much better at capturing (and analyzing) matter performance for those matters not being done on the hourly rate (which may include broadening the type of metrics we include). We are going to look at this very topic, that of matter analysis, next.

Don't forget *(a summary of the key points):*

- Hourly based fee approaches are very likely to become the exception and not the rule for law firm pricing—but they still have a role to play.
- Be sure to understand what your clients mean when they ask for an AFA—this term can mean different things to different people. Check up front.
- We should move away from calling these arrangements as "alternative" (they have been around a while) to "appropriate"—a term more reflective of the value of the transaction for the client, and that aligns the economic and efficiency interests of client and law firm alike.
- Have a proactive discussion around possible pricing approaches with your client—and remember, that no one size fits all (even *during* a matter).
- Trust and a commonly shared understanding of what constitutes value are the two essential ingredients in making AFAs work successfully for law firm and client.
- Be clear on the basis of the fee approach adopted from the outset of the matter.

Chapter 7

The Power of Pragmatic Analysis

One area where there is still insufficient focus is the analysis of pricing performance. With the increasing use of *appropriate* fee arrangements (AFAs) by law firms, the need for pragmatic pricing analysis is key.

If this were a book more generally on pricing, supporting pricing theory, and the analytical approaches available, we would be introducing approaches like

- *Van Westendorp*, a technique for determining consumer price preferences by asking respondents direct questions about the expected price of a product in the context of different scenarios of usage),
- *Gabor Granger*, which uses direct questions about the likelihood of purchase at certain price levels, exposing psychological thresholds,

and finally, if then also factoring in the overall value proposition in addition to setting an appropriate price level,

- *Conjoint analysis* in its many guises (such as Adaptive Conjoint Analysis or Discrete Choice Modeling), all of which are excellent ways to look at understanding how choices (or trade-offs) are made and consequently the importance of product attributes and price.

Thankfully, for our purposes at least, it isn't.

Any analysis conducted has to be simple to do, recognizing first what we are looking for the analysis to tell us; second, recognizing what tools we have available (which, in law firms, are primarily spreadsheets or simple databases); third (and most importantly), *making it appropriate and relevant* for those in law firms.

Although we are seeing the rapid increase of those in law firms with pricing experience and who are familiar with the approaches outlined earlier and the methods of conducting such analysis (for example, myself, John Strange at Baker Botts, Toby Brown at Akin Gump, Vince Cordo at Reed Smith, and Chris Emerson at Bryan Cave, to name a few), the adoption of one or two of the more basic techniques will suffice for many—at least for now.

Albert Einstein and "Insanity"

Past performance is not an indicator or guarantee of future performance. How many times have you seen this phrase on the bottom of your financial investment statements? While it is true that the past is no guarantee to the future, it does provide a strong directional sense of likely outcome.

After all, no less than Albert Einstein himself observed that "insanity" was "doing the same thing over and over again and expecting different results." Yet when law firms price their legal services, this is what tends to happen time and time again. We use the same data, same approach, and often the same people as last time expecting a better overall result and then have a profound sense of disappointment when we fail to achieve this.

And yet, given the volume and complexity of what we typically do within our firms, this can sometimes act as a smoke screen making it nearly impossible to be able to understand what is actually happening on our matters from a pricing and profitability perspective.

The Essential Building Blocks

There are a number of essential building blocks required to help law firms conduct better analysis.

The prime one is the ability to segment, or look at, matters more at the activity or task level. Some of you may already be familiar with this type of approach if using task codes for some of your clients (task codes are a way of capturing task-based detail, normally used with e-billing systems, and is an area we will return to in more depth when discussing legal project management approaches).

One approach taken by many firms here is also to encourage the pricing of matters at this more granular level. If pricing by specific task (or at least group of similar tasks), this provides you with a solid baseline from which to conduct any subsequent analysis.

This also reduces the likelihood of being asked questions such as "We priced the matter at $10,000 last time, but we didn't do too well. What can we change?" and yet with no ability to determine where the matter took more time than the original estimate, as it was priced only at the matter level, rather than by phase or task. Those who typically support pricing within law firms (whether this be a specific department or function, or those in finance) are, by and large, talented people, but not even they are able to—without appropriate data—determine where the matter actual performance varied from the original estimate, and therefore help inform future pricing efforts.

Pricing at this more granular level can easily be done either through using third-party software applications (for example, Thomson Reuters Engage suite of products) or by "homegrown" tools. But each does involve a change of approach or mind-set from those developing the price estimates initially. Whether the current reluctance to do so is driven from apathy, fear of accountability (that is, the unwillingness either internally or externally to be held to the initial estimate), or the fact that this is seen as difficult to do, few firms to date price at this level consistently across all their key practice groups.

For any pricing analysis to be useful, it needs to have some level of detail. Pricing by phase or task helps get there quicker.

We shouldn't forget other sources of data, though. This may range from any volume discount or relationship discounts that may be applied to the impact of relationship "value adds" (for example, free time via "hotlines" or variable payment terms) and so on. The aim of this analysis is to be as comprehensive and insightful to our specific needs as possible, but doing this in a more pragmatic manner (recognizing the potential resource and skill constraints that may exist).

Two Indispensable Tools

There are two tools that in my mind are indispensable for those who are seriously looking at conducting pricing analysis from a law firm perspective, both of which are easy to do. These are dispersion analysis and waterfall analysis. Neither of these types of techniques is new, but they are new to many law firms.[1]

Each supports the concept of being better at managing matters and can help us stop leaving money on the table. This analysis should be able to be prepared (relatively) quickly by your pricing team (if in place) or finance department once they understand what you are looking for.

Before going on to describe each approach in more detail below, a quick observation: If you are a partner or fee earner in a law firm, the following analysis may sound complex. It isn't. However, if you are not too keen to get your hands dirty looking into this, I would highly recommend that you request someone in your finance, pricing, or practice management team to do so on your behalf. The results *will* be worth it.

Dispersion Analysis

First, don't be put off by the name. Although sounding like it has come from the depths of some university or college class on advanced statistical analysis, it—in this context—is much more simple, yet still very valuable and enlightening.

Take the following situation: How many times have you spoken with a fellow partner or fee earner in your firm about a matter in which profitability (or realization) has been less than desired? When I have had this type of discussion in the past, the typical response has been, "Ahh, yes, that is a one-off because of [insert reason here]." But is it?

One of the unfortunate aspects of being so engaged on a specific matter is that, sometimes, by being so much in the detail, you are unable to take a more holistic view of what is happening—either at a client, practice area,

---

1. Michael V. Marn & Robert L. Rosiello, *Managing Price, Gaining Profit*, HARV. BUS. REV., Sept.–Oct. 1992. This article provides a good overview of both the Pocket Price Waterfall and Pocket Price Band concepts.

or even individual partner level. It really is a case of sometimes not being able to see the forest for the trees.

What dispersion analysis allows you to do is get a very quick snapshot of client, matter, or responsible-fee-earner performance across a range of different parameters. It allows you to quickly see whether the pricing challenges identified really are a one-off or are part of a broader, hitherto unseen pattern. And then this allows you to focus on those areas that will really make a tangible difference.

Getting Started: Conducting Dispersion Analysis

When getting started, I would recommend that you do two "views" of the data. The first should be focused on the level of effective discount you are giving on specific matters, and the second focused on the level of profit being generated for the same sample. Each should then be filtered by your own specific criteria—for example, by client, office, and practice area—but identical to allow both results to be meaningful. (Note: If feeling really adventurous, you can even use the waterfall analysis described below to determine the level of effective discount being provided. Regardless of how detailed you seek to make this, dispersion analysis is still a very valuable tool in your firm's analytical toolbox.)

A simple way to get started is as follows:

Step 1: Capture your base data. Prepare (or have prepared by your finance team) a standard client report or practice-area report in your typical spreadsheet application (for example, Excel).

This should include key data fields such as matter name, client name, lead partner, fees generated, costs incurred, etc. The more data you include, the more cuts (or views) of data you can make. Table 7.1 provides an example of what this could look like.

Table 7.1: Sample Data for Use in Dispersion Analysis

Typical Fields Included	Rationale for Inclusion
Client name	This allows you to filter on/view by a specific client or group or related/similar clients
Practice area (and/or sub-practice area)	This allows you to filter on/view by specific practice area of matter type
Responsible partner	This allows you to filter on/view by responsible matter partner
Matter name (and any other unique reference)	This provides a unique identifier for the record. You may also wish to include any specific matter or PO related number
Matter fees (at your firm's standard or "rack" rate)	This allows you to determine the actual discount from your firm's standard rates for all attorneys involved
Matter fees billed	This allows you to determine the discount from your firm's standard rates vs. what you have *billed*
Matter fees collected	This allows you to determine the actual discount from your firm's standard rates versus what you actually *collected*
Matter discount	This field is typically calculated separately. This can be done both for fees billed and fees collected. I refer to the total discount (of both combined) as the "effective discount"
Matter profit margin	This field is typically calculated separately, and is used when preparing a profit margin dispersion analysis

Step 2: "Pivot" your base data. Take the data generated during Step 1 and put into a PivotTable or similar (if in doubt how to do this when using Microsoft Excel, look at the help function—it really is surprisingly useful!).

What I have found to work well in the past is to use fields such as client, office, and practice area as "page" entries, as shown in figure 7.1 on the next page, with other data fields for total costs. After you have done this a few times, you will quickly be able to determine your preferred view. (Remember you may want to do *two* versions of this PivotTable, one to review the discount offered and the second on the level of profit generated.)

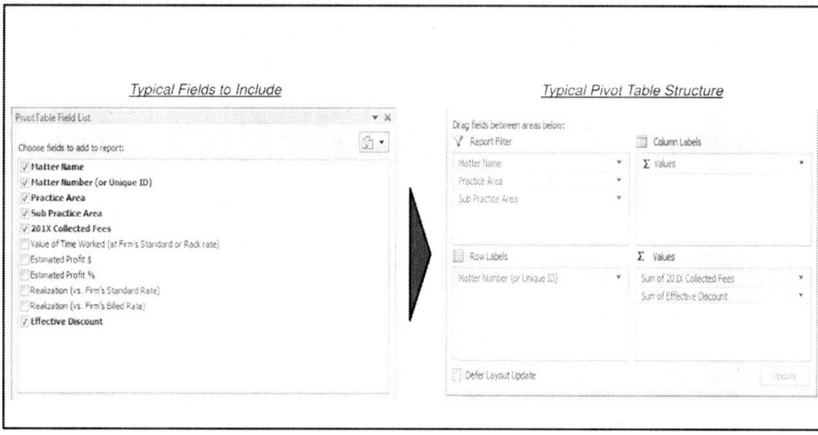

Figure 7.1
A Sample Pivot Table for Use in Dispersion Analysis

Step 3: Making the data compelling. One major advantage of conducting dispersion analysis is that it provides a very strong, visually compelling chart that can easily be used in discussion with key decision makers within your firm as seen in Figure 7.2.

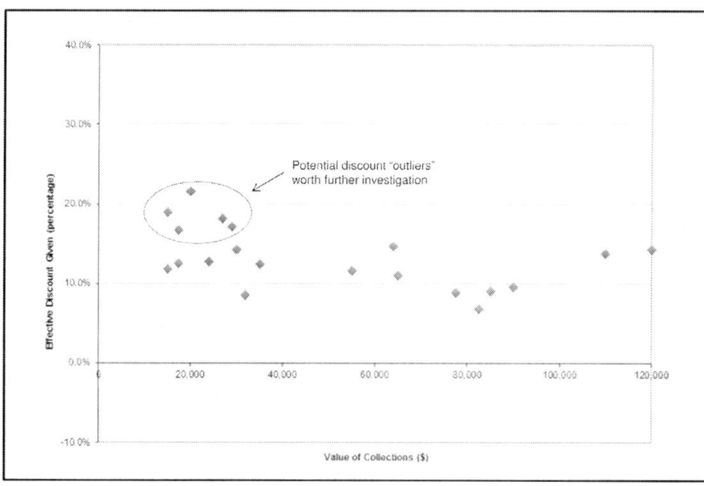

Figure 7.2
A Sample Dispersion Chart

The best method for doing this is to use the "scatter chart" option available in most spreadsheet graphical tools (although I have done this using Excel, similar functionality is available within applications such as Numbers if using a computer based on the Apple software suite). An example of this is shown in figure 7.2. Another variation of the dispersion chart is called the pocket price band. An example of what this looks like is shown in figure 7.3.

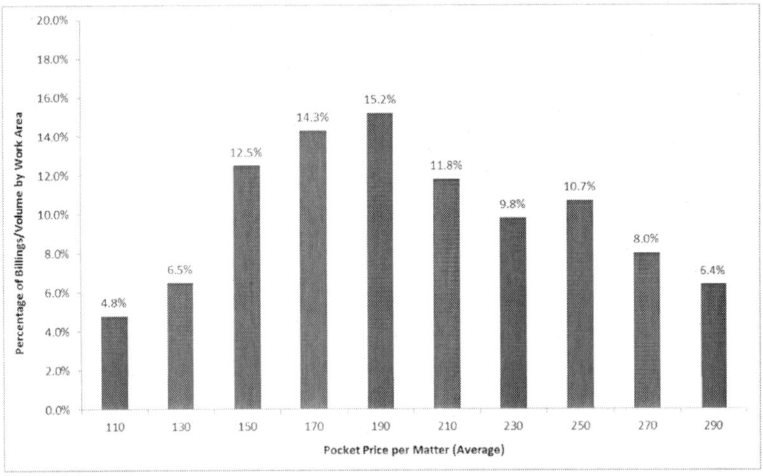

Figure 7.3
A Sample Pocket Price Band Graph

Similar to the dispersion chart, understanding the variations in the pocket price bands helps you get better at managing *transaction-based* pricing opportunities (as discussed briefly in Chapter 4).

The basic width and shape of these bands can help tell a valuable story, as not only are people normally surprised at the width of the bands identified, but also which clients are at the extremes of the bands (with clients often perceived as profitable being at the lower end of the band, and vice versa).

It also allows you to see where your existing pricing and discounting policies (if these are in place) are being adhered to, how much of your work is being "sold" at deep discounts, and so on. One additional area you may find helpful to do this is by practice area, client, or even individual fee earner to further determine the effective contribution per hour worked.

I have a personal preference for the dispersion chart as I think it allows you to highlight key variances quicker and supports a more interactive discussion, but obviously choose whichever approach you prefer, and that you think will be most successful and easily adopted within your firm.

Making Data into Information

Initially you receive some data, which through good analysis we need to turn into information. And yes, I acknowledge that there is always the issue "garbage in, garbage out," but let's be honest, we all need to get started somewhere, and this allows you to more systematically sift through your garbage and get better over time.

This allows you to quickly determine what "good" looks like for your own firm. Each firm will be different based on its respective expectations of margin, realization, nature of matters supported, and so forth.

Okay, it is a reactive approach, but it helps *inform* future pricing decisions, encouraging those directly responsible for the client, practice area, or matter to see what good looks like, should seek to replicate, and become more proactive for future matters.

Also remember the 1-3-4 Rule™ discussed earlier when reviewing this information—the potential contribution of being able to reduce the discount by just 1 percent will typically add 3 percent to your existing level of profit margin. Conducting dispersion analysis allows you to see some "quick hits" to focus on, and help you do just that—as does this next recommended approach, waterfall analysis.

Waterfall Analysis

Another useful tool to consider when conducting pricing analysis is known as waterfall analysis, or the pocket price waterfall.

This allows you to identify the true cost of delivering your services to a client. Typically, many firms focus on either the list price (that is, the rack rate or standard rate) or the invoice price (that is, the billed rate) and therefore forget to consider the full range of elements that impact the final transaction cost.

The way law firms traditionally view price is therefore incomplete. Management information provided is often limited in its view and provides one or more of the standard rate, the discounted rate (that is, the billed rate), and the received rate (that is, the collected rate). However, that is only *part* of the picture. What the pocket price waterfall allows us to determine is the impact of those typical off invoice items that we traditionally forget.

Some of the more common elements include

- the impact of volume discounts over the duration of a matter (or client relationship),
- any early payment discounts that the client may receive,
- any rebates the client may receive, and
- the cost of money to your firm if the client typically pays invoices beyond the agreed payment terms.

For example, how often have you reviewed the profitability of one of your client relationships at the end of a year only to realize that you have not included the impact of providing a secondment, training, or other value-added service that you had offered as part of your proposal? Each of these can have a significant impact on your overall client profitability if not managed closely.

In addition, don't forget the impact of travel and disbursement expenses that cannot be charged back to the client (for example, through your agreement to accept its outside counsel guidelines), as these, too, are a cost and have an impact and yet are often forgotten when assessing overall client profitability.

As one commentator noted: "[P]ricing becomes much more interesting when you adopt the pocket price waterfall view. All of a sudden, it is more than just setting list prices and standard discounts."[2]

It also identifies more avenues for you to explore when looking for that additional 1 percent price improvement.

2. Walter L. Baker, Michael V. Marn & Craig C. Zawada, The Price Advantage 29 (Wiley 2010).

If proof were needed, have a look at the illustrative diagram figure 7.4 to see how our standard rate can be impacted to the provision of these other, often forgotten, elements.

Of course there will be a number of very legitimate business reasons why you may wish to invest in the client, but what this approach allows you to do is to *recognize the impact* of these and then allow you to *manage* them accordingly. It allows you to go into any discussion with your eyes, if not completely wide open, at least seeing some daylight, and helps mitigate any potentially nasty surprises down the road.

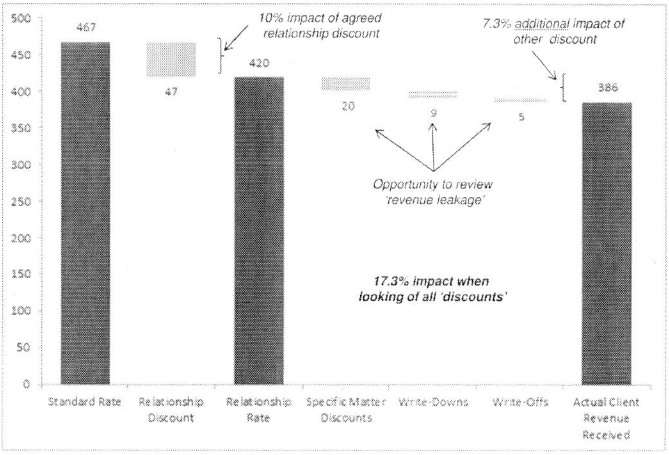

Figure 7.4
Identifying Revenue "Leakage" Through Waterfall Analysis

As we observed earlier in this section, even a small change in pricing performance can generate a significant benefit. Therefore, if we take the time to look at each specific element identified as part of the pocket price waterfall, we can quickly begin to see how we can deliver even greater contribution—with our pricing hat on, it really does not matter whether we are looking at something that is classified as being an "on invoice" item or an "off invoice" item. Ultimately the impact on profitability is still the same, yet how many of us really look at those other elements?

Getting Started: Conducting Waterfall Analysis

Step 1: You may feel restricted in your ability to do this given the technical infrastructure you may have in your firm to support financial reporting. However, with some slight amendment in how you currently collect your existing financial data, you are likely to be able to get a more comprehensive, and therefore a more useful, view of the profitability of each of your clients and of the products and services that you provide them.

It is also worth bearing in mind that you may also have to capture this information from a number of different sources. Some of it is not typically held within your financial systems, especially when considering the impact of secondee relationships.

Step 2: Capturing the information. The easiest way to do this stage is to have a very simple spreadsheet with the key types of data you are capturing across the top of the page and in the values represented underneath. An example of this is shown in figure 7.5.

Step 3: Presenting the data. As with the dispersion chart, this is most effective when presented visually, as it allows you to quickly identify the true gap between your list price and what then becomes the pocket price. It quickly allows you to see where the greatest opportunity is and, therefore, where you will want to focus the majority of your effort to help improve profitability. Figure 7.4 showed an example of how this may look in practice.

There are a number of resources available on the Internet to help you determine how to easily graph this information (some of these are listed[3]), or you may have resources within your own firm that can easily do this for you (for example, within your finance team). Although relatively simple to do, if I were to explain it here, the chapter will become significantly bigger!

3. Some sources include *Waterfall Charts Using Excel*, CHANDOO.ORG (Aug. 10, 2009), http://chandoo.org/wp/2009/08/10/excel-waterfall-charts/, and *How to Create Waterfall Chart in Excel in 2 Minutes*, DATABISON, http://www.databison.com/how-to-create-waterfall-chart-in-excel-in-2-minutes/ (last visited Jan. 3, 2014). For those who prefer a short video tutorial, try either Contextures, Inc., *Create an Excel Waterfall Chart*, YOUTUBE (Oct. 19, 2010), http://www.youtube.com/watch?v=LT4KxLtlQNA, or Excells Fun, *Excel Magic Trick #246: Waterfall Profit Chart*, YOUTUBE (Feb. 4, 2009), http://www.youtube.com/watch?v=FhA54KniEZ0.

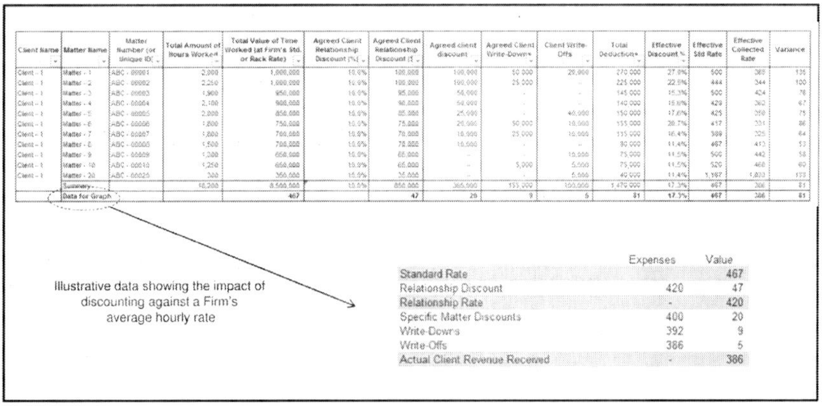

Client Name	Matter Name	Matter Number (or Unique ID)	Total Amount of Hours Worked	Total Value of Time Worked (at Firm's Std. or Rack Rate)	Agreed Client Relationship Discount (%)	Agreed Client Relationship Discount ($)	Agreed client discount	Agreed Client Write-Downs	Client Write-Offs	Total Deductions	Effective Discount %	Effective Std Rate	Effective Collected Rate	Variance
Client - 1	Matter - 1	ABC - 00001	2,000	1,000,000	10.0%	100,000	100,000	50,000	20,000	270,000	27.0%	500	365	135
Client - 1	Matter - 2	ABC - 00002	2,250	1,000,000	10.0%	100,000	100,000	25,000	-	225,000	22.5%	444	344	100
Client - 1	Matter - 3	ABC - 00003	1,900	950,000	10.0%	95,000	50,000	-	-	145,000	15.3%	500	424	76
Client - 1	Matter - 4	ABC - 00004	2,100	900,000	10.0%	90,000	50,000	-	-	140,000	15.6%	429	362	67
Client - 1	Matter - 5	ABC - 00005	2,000	850,000	10.0%	85,000	25,000	-	40,000	150,000	17.6%	425	350	75
Client - 1	Matter - 6	ABC - 00006	1,800	750,000	10.0%	75,000	20,000	50,000	10,000	155,000	20.7%	417	331	86
Client - 1	Matter - 7	ABC - 00007	1,800	700,000	10.0%	70,000	10,000	25,000	10,000	115,000	16.4%	389	325	64
Client - 1	Matter - 8	ABC - 00008	1,500	700,000	10.0%	70,000	10,000	-	-	80,000	11.4%	467	413	53
Client - 1	Matter - 9	ABC - 00009	1,300	650,000	10.0%	65,000	-	-	10,000	75,000	11.5%	500	442	58
Client - 1	Matter - 10	ABC - 00010	1,250	650,000	10.0%	65,000	-	5,000	5,000	75,000	11.5%	520	460	60
Client - 1	Matter - 20	ABC - 00020	300	350,000	10.0%	35,000	-	-	5,000	40,000	11.4%	1,167	1,033	133
	Summary		18,200	8,500,000	10.0%	850,000	365,000	155,000	100,000	1,470,000	17.3%	467	386	81
	Data for Graph			467		47	25	9	5	81	17.3%	467	386	81

	Expenses	Value
Standard Rate		467
Relationship Discount	420	47
Relationship Rate	-	420
Specific Matter Discounts	400	20
Write-Downs	392	9
Write-Offs	386	5
Actual Client Revenue Received	-	386

Figure 7.5
Supporting Data for Conducting Waterfall Analysis

You can also extend this concept of the pocket price waterfall to become a pocket *margin* waterfall.[4]

Whereas the pocket price waterfall works well when selling more standardized products or services, you may find that the margin waterfall is better for the vast majority of your matters. This is best suited for where products or services are more typically tailored to specific client situations. The approach provides additional valuable insight, and is perhaps more representative of the work that many of us do within our firms.

The basis is still the same as before, although "pocket margin" is defined as being the pocket price of a transaction (or relationship) minus any of the direct costs identified (for example, negotiated discounts) and any account-specific "cost to serve" items. This can act as a good indicator or measure of a transaction or relationship's overall attractiveness.

After all, how often have we gone ahead and agreed to a deal with a client (or indeed, in our personal lives) and then realized after the fact that it maybe wasn't such a good deal after all (the purchase of time-shares or similar comes to mind). Doing this analysis helps reduce these occurrences.

4. BAKER ET AL., *supra* note 2, at 39–44.

Why All This Is Worth the Effort

The benefits of using price waterfalls are numerous. However, the four main benefits are

- higher profits, through the ability to be able to pinpoint revenue leakages and where you can optimize pricing at a matter level;
- improved control, as this allows you to become much more data driven in how you approach measuring the effectiveness of your existing pricing processes;
- better planning, through being able to review pricing at a number of distinct pricing components (for example, the impact of volume discounting or late payment); and
- value-based negotiation, providing you with valuable information to support your client negotiation. It will also allow you to be more consistent in applying any discounting or pricing approach. Ultimately, this will help you maintain both the integrity of your pricing across your client base and appropriate profitability.

A Quick Word About Competitive Intelligence

Our focus so far has been on our internal information—that is, the information we have captured ourselves when working on matters with our clients. However, it is also important to recognize the value of external information.

There are a number of ethical considerations that we need to consider when using external competitive intelligence, such as the means of capture, storage, and dissemination of this information. However, there are a number of products now available in the marketplace that make the capture of this information much easier (and that also conform to the ethical guidelines in place).

These products range from those that seek to capture publicly available information, often allowing you to get information on specific firms, and even specific individuals (for example, Valeo Partners), to those that aggregate information from e-billing or time-entry systems (for example, Peer

Monitor, SkyAnalytics, and Tymetrix), where information is more aggregated and around a "basket" of selected firms.

It is important to recognize that not only are many of these resources available to us as law firms but also marketed, targeted, and used by our clients. Therefore, our clients may be in a much stronger position to be able to determine what they see as being the right price for a product or service that we provide than we typically are. (Remember the concept of competitive pricing discussed earlier.)

There are a number of well-known examples of law firm clients using these tools to identify potential alternative law firm providers for key services and also as a mechanism for lowering the cost from the existing law firm for the services already delivered. Although not all clients are currently in this position, there is clearly an emerging trend.

However, in my opinion, there are some current limitations to the value of these tools. Unsurprisingly, given the evolution of these products, they tend to be very United States focused (this is, in part, due to e-billing being more prevalent in the United States than in other regions, and also given the "home" of the providers themselves).

They have also tended to focus on litigation-based matters and pricing (given the volume of litigation-based matters being captured via e-billing systems), and therefore the utility of these products may be more limited if you are working for a law firm that has a broader international presence and indeed a broader portfolio of practice areas. In their defense, these providers are acutely aware of these limitations and are actively seeking to address these gaps.

In addition to these, there are also a number of surveys that you can subscribe to (or purchase) that are issued at periodic intervals throughout the year.

You may also capture useful competitive intelligence in discussion with your client or from lateral hires (again, we need to be mindful of the ethical use of this data). In more traditional sales-based organizations, the most useful source of information is the company's sales force. They have the most contact with the end customer and can gain insights from those customers on the competition. In the legal world, the sales force is our partners, and yet how many partners view themselves in that way and therefore take the opportunity to ask questions that will help capture this type of information in a meaningful fashion?

Be Comprehensive in Your Outlook

In my experience, although each of these sources of market intelligence on its own is useful and can provide a directional sense of what is happening within the marketplace, one source is not enough.

The real value is when you begin to take a much more comprehensive view of the pricing information that you have both within your firm and available externally, as you can then begin to develop a much more useful picture to help inform and guide your pricing decisions.

Potentially, one of the hardest things to do is have a central repository for this information, and find a way to make this more easily available to those who need it at "point of need." Given the sensitivity of some of this information, it may not be appropriate to make it available to all via an intranet or similar. Therefore, it's important to consider what the best approach is within your own organization to best hold and communicate this information. What is useful, however, is to have one individual within your organization responsible for the capture, collation, communication, and management of this information within your firm.

One note of caution, however: The cost of gathering competitive intelligence can be high both in terms of money (for example, through subscribing to some of the resources outlined above) and also in time. Therefore, before embarking on this path, it is best to have a clear view of *what* you're trying to capture and more importantly *why* you're trying to capture this information.

Dr. W. Edwards Deming, one of the forefathers of the total quality management movement and of the plan-do-check-act philosophy, is said to have commented: "What gets measured gets attention. What gets attention gets done." (This quote, and derivations of, has also been attributed to a wide range of other management thinkers, such as Peter Drucker and Lord Kelvin).

Through taking some time to conduct more structured pricing analysis, you are more able to identify where to focus your firm's efforts. Although more firms today are doing some form of pricing analysis, this tends to be at too high a level to be really meaningful.

Effective pricing involves a number of small things being done extremely well. The approaches outlined in this chapter, if applied, will enable you to do just that.

But this statement also holds true for what we have discussed in the whole of this section. The small things matter and do make an impact. As we will see through the remainder of this book, this principle also applies to how we Get the Price and then Manage to Price.

Often, much of our work done during this Set the Price stage, where we have carefully conducted analysis and developed appropriate pricing options, becomes unstuck as we go through the process of agreeing on a deal with our client and then working on the matter itself.

Nowhere is this more apparent than in the next step of our framework, Get the Price. This is due to our inability to effectively articulate and demonstrate our value to our clients, and then compounded by poor negotiation. We will now turn our attention to these areas and, more importantly, what we can do to get the "small things" right.

Don't forget *(a summary of the key points):*

- Law firms have a wonderful opportunity to improve and better understand their pricing performance through some simple analysis.
- The two indispensable tools are dispersion analysis and waterfall analysis, techniques commonly adopted elsewhere but only now becoming more widely used within the legal community.
- Don't overcomplicate what you are trying to accomplish—make it relevant and appropriate.
- Be comprehensive in your analysis and your outlook (especially if conducting competitive intelligence), but have a clear plan.
- The way that law firms traditionally view price is incomplete—remember to look at "off invoice" items too (such as volume discounts or rebates).

Step Two: Get the Price

Chapter 8

There and Back Again: A Question of Value

One of the most overlooked elements when pitching to a potential client is sadly (and perhaps slightly ironically) the value proposition itself.

Too often a law firm proposal merely states how good the respective law firm is in the subject matter in question, how many offices, clients, and awards they have, and then, finally, the cost. Often, there is very little about the actual matter in question or the client itself, and—if there is—this can often be found toward the end of the proposal. Without going into lots of detail about what is wrong with the above scenario, it is clear that this will not be compelling to any prospective client.

However, defining the value proposition can be difficult.

In 2008 the Association of Corporate Counsel (ACC) launched the ACC Value Challenge. Its stated intent was to "reconnect the value and cost of legal services." This seemed to both catch and further define the mood of increasing dissatisfaction in the hourly rate (which has been well documented elsewhere).[1]

Looking back, in some respects the ACC was extremely wise when launching the initiative by choosing not to define what was meant by the term "value" in this context. It merely suggested that its respective members

1. Further information on the ACC Value Challenge may be found at http://www.acc.com/valuechallenge/resources./

discussed with their retained outside counsel what this term could mean for them and then how best to realize (and reconnect) the value to cost. This acknowledged, tacitly at least, that the term "value" would mean different things to different people.

However, whilst recognizing that one definition would be too generic in nature, the lack of one has inadvertently created confusion both for corporate counsel and law firms alike and has, in part, contributed to the adoption of appropriate fee arrangements (AFAs) being less widespread than initially predicted.

Not only are law firms trying to determine what value they can add for clients (more on which later), but frequently clients' in-house legal teams themselves are struggling to define the value *they* provide to their own organization.

Remaining Vague About Value

Looking at this theme in a bit more detail, I would like to take a slight step back and borrow heavily from a useful study done a few years ago by Nabarro, a United Kingdom–based law firm, aptly titled "General Counsel: Vague About Value?"[2] The key reason for doing so is that I think this provides a helpful framework for us to consider when trying to determine the value that we, as lawyers, can provide to our clients.

What stood out from this survey were a number of key points, and although not necessarily directly applicable in all client situations (or indeed, jurisdictions), certainly provide some key *directional* observations that I think are relevant to all.

As part of the study (and also the previous one conducted), Nabarro introduced the concept of the value pyramid for the in-house legal function. This effectively divided tasks conducted by an in-house legal function into one of four levels. Tasks within the first level involved those that had

2. NABARRO, GENERAL COUNSEL: VAGUE ABOUT VALUE (2011), *available at* http://www.nabarro.com/downloads/General_Counsel_2011-2.pdf.

the potential to deliver the greatest value to the business (such as strategic planning and introducing commercial opportunities), and those in level four were seen as the "essential but 'bread and butter'" type of activities (such as "getting the job done" and working with stakeholders). Figure 8.1 outlines this in more detail.

The survey unsurprisingly found that general counsel (in particular) were keen to move the perception of their function toward those activities near the pyramid's pinnacle (shifting from a 3 percent figure for those tasks at the top level to 29 percent by 2015).

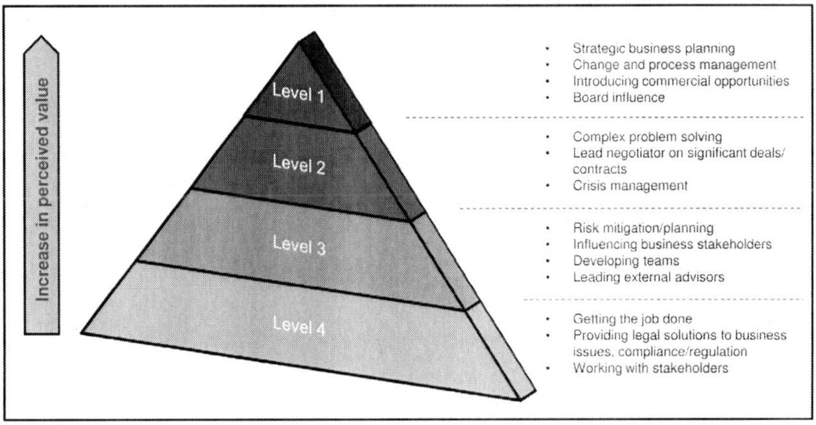

Figure 8.1
The Value Pyramid
Adapted from: NABARRO, *supra* note 1, at 2.

The key survey findings (for our purposes, with italicized emphasis added by me) were as follows:

- Just over half of the general counsel surveyed said that the in-house legal team was recognized as adding value to the business, with some going on to state that the team was "*not felt to add substantial value, or that recognition was partial or superficial.*"
- Eighty percent of general counsel agreed that *improving cost-effectiveness* was either important or very important.

- Fewer than half saw external lawyers (that is, us!) as partners in delivering *financial value*, with over three-quarters *not quantifying the value-added services* received by law firms.[3]

All in all, not a very rosy picture for either the general counsel or external law firm, with there being a sense of "much activity" going on but little recognition of the relative contribution of each.

Rather than waiting for our clients to therefore determine how we can deliver value to them, we should become much *more proactive* and *make it easier* for them to both recognize what value we are delivering to them and also *communicate this value* within their own organizations. Those that grasp this early will be much more successful in both the conversion rate of their pitches and also in the strengthening of their client relationships.

Given the importance of demonstrating cost-effectiveness stated within the survey, the reality of how this is measured in many organizations is very primitive, with an overreliance on the absolute value of external legal spend rather than what this means within the overall business context. It is here that we (the law firms) have a further opportunity to clearly articulate the value we can add—for example, in terms of supporting revenue generation (for example, supporting mergers and acquisitions or commercial-contract-related matters) or mitigating potential costs (for example, avoiding costly litigation via alternative dispute resolution approaches, or similar).

As to further quantifying the impact of external law firms on business, the main reason given for not measuring the contribution of the value-added services was primarily due to the difficulty of actually measuring these. Again, this is something that we should be able to address within our overall value proposition with a little application.

Finally, many general counsel surveyed felt that the law firms they used did "not really understand the importance of value, quality and cost in delivering their services, or the need to invest in the relationship."[4] Where they (the law firms) did, often the value being delivered was not then being

3. *Id.* at 5.
4. *Id.* at 18.

generally appreciated across the client's business. Again, a solution should be able to be found if we try.

In its conclusion, the study pointed to a number of key areas where I believe we, as law firms, can add significant value—*if* we take the time to think about it:

- General counsel needed to *demonstrate greater value* if they were going to "climb the value pyramid."
- There was more scope for general counsel (or in-house legal teams, more generally) to *show economic value* through cost-effectiveness and innovation (including the innovative use of technology).
- General counsel should *engage with their external lawyers more readily when discussing financial value*, and also when seeking to quantify the value of the value-added services.
- General counsel should consider an appropriate system of *performance measurement* (both in-house and external).[5]

Whether you agree with the survey's conclusion or not, what this clearly points to is that our clients often need help in being able to both *quantify and articulate* the value that in-house and external legal teams provide.

Therefore, any value proposition that we propose should seek to *directly* address these key points, in the context of the matter at hand—this then being further reinforced by our chosen pricing and delivery approach.

Where AFAs Come In

We know, as a general rule, that a client does not want to buy a lawyer's time. It is the expertise that comes with that time that is important. Expertise that (hopefully) will help the client achieve its business objectives, however defined.

It was this realization that has initially helped drive the move toward clients requesting AFAs (for it was they who were more proactive in asking

5. *Id.* at 29.

for these types of arrangements), this move representing a conscious effort to drive better cost control through how a fee approach was structured rather than having a greater focus and rigor around the adherence to certain billing processes.

However, success has been mixed. I personally know of some clients that are not fans of AFAs, and seek to continue adopting agreements based upon the billable hour. That is their decision, made for appropriate business reasons and in light of their respective previous experience.

For the vast majority, though, they are looking for something more. As part of the Acritas 2012 Sharplegal market survey (and re-quoted in the *American Lawyer*), one in-house lawyer of a billion-dollar retail giant echoed what many others have felt. He believed that the relationship with his external legal counsel is "going to have be more value-driven than rate-driven."[6]

So for these individuals, what constitutes value?

The first thing to acknowledge is that law firm clients realize value from their respective law firms (and lawyers) in a number of *different* ways. It may range from the more tangible areas, such as cost control and the total absolute cost of a matter, to the specific legal expertise being provided (and the associated knowledge transfer to the client). It can include the certainty of outcome, both financial and legal (indeed, for some clients, cost predictability and management of cash flow may be as important as the actual amount). It can also encompass the speed of resolution or completion of the matter (something that can be extremely important, for example, in litigation or merger and acquisition matters).

Through adoption of AFAs, there is also another potential key benefit, although one often overlooked—the *saving of time and effort expended* by in-house counsel in managing matters and reviewing law firm invoices line by line (or managing a third-party provider to do so). Adopting AFAs can free up those lawyers to focus on what is more important to their own organization rather than drowning them in administrative, non-value-adding tasks. Working alongside external counsel can further add value to the

6. Quoted in Everybody's Talking at Me, Aric Press, THE AMERICAN LAWYER (27 FEBRUARY 2013), *available at* http://www.americanlawyer.com/PubArticleTAL.jsp?id=1202589232002.

in-house team through the transfer of specific matter knowledge or provision of bespoke training sessions on emerging legal trends.

Add into this mix the significant (most likely unarticulated) value already being delivered by the in-house legal team in the execution of legal work, including institutional knowledge; day-to-day working relationship with the corporate teams; and understanding of specific stakeholder interests and incentives.

Clients now should also rightly expect broader thinking from their legal providers, not only of how to best manage the matter but also anticipating (and managing) any potential risks or issues throughout a matter through effective matter management. Adoption of AFAs helps further drive this better matter management discipline within law firms (although I believe it is equally vital in hourly based arrangements too).

The challenge to all of this is in capturing and articulating these key elements of value in a compelling and meaningful fashion, and aligning these to the appropriate business *and* matter-specific objectives. That is where law firm and client need to work together, to make the in-house legal team's role, overall contribution, and value easier, more visible, and recognized.

The reason that many still adopt hourly based billing structures is because it provides a "veneer of precision" in the absence of anything else. Now is the time for law firm and client to jointly develop the "anything else."

Using AFAs Sensibly to Drive Greater Value

If value is therefore key, how can both law firm and client develop and implement appropriate fee arrangements that meet (or ideally, surpass) expectations?

A fundamental requirement is *trust* between both parties. While a number of law firms and their clients have attempted to implement AFAs in new relationships, only very few have been successful. Why? Those that failed typically had not had time to develop a sense of trust in the relationship, leading to misaligned objectives, expectations, and finally results.

Where trust exists between law firm and client, there is a fundamental shift in the relationship, encouraging greater partnering behavior between both parties. This in turn helps support an enhanced degree of communication (frequent and as often as appropriate are good guiding principles) between both. It means that the right discussions are held when budgets are being developed, when fee approaches are being defined and assessed, and when determining what is the right "quality" for the matter (striking the right balance between quality and efficiency). Put bluntly, it means that both parties are pulling in the same direction and against a shared view of success and value.

Before blindly embarking on an AFA, therefore, both law firm and client should consider the following three key points as a minimum:

- How will the proposed commercial arrangement support the (client's) business in achieving its goals?
- What are the elements of potential value that are most important to the client (and does the proposed commercial relationship support this)?
- How will both parties best measure and track how value is delivered? (This will help in both being able to clearly articulate the value delivered internally, and also be used as a basis for future, similar arrangements).

Typically (though not exclusively) these arrangements are based on three common approaches: fixed fees, contingency-based fees, or a modified version of hourly fees (including some element of risk sharing or incentive to drive further efficiencies, such as performance-based or holdback fee structures), many of which we discussed in Chapter 6.

Take time up front to structure these arrangements appropriately. This helps increase the likelihood that the results achieved will at least be in the ballpark of initial expectations around the value to be delivered.

Taking It to the Next Level: The Kano Model

If wanting to explore the concept of value further, you may wish to look at the concept of the Kano model.[7] I am indebted to my ex-colleague, Ori

7. For information about the Kano model, go to http://www.kanomodel.com. In addition, a useful summary may also be found here: *Kano Model Analysis*, MINDTOOLS.COM, http://www.mindtools.com/pages/article/newCT_97.htm.

Weiner, who mentioned this to me in passing while we were talking about ways to better align price and value (more about Ori later).

For those unfamiliar with the model (as I was), it is a theory of product development and customer satisfaction developed by professor Noriaka Kano (hence the name) in the 1980s.

The model's purpose is to help you better understand what value your customers place on the features of your product or service. It helps reduce the risk of providing a product or service that overemphasizes features that have little importance or (conversely) miss the must-have requirement.

To help do this, Kano determined that a product or service could have three different types of attributes or properties:

- a **threshold** (or basic) attribute (that is, those things a customer would expect to see)
- a **performance** attribute (that is, something not necessary but that is known about and would increase the customer's enjoyment of the product or service)
- an **excitement** attribute (that is, those things the customer didn't even know they wanted, but are very, very happy when they find they have them).

In reality, there is also a fourth attribute: **not relevant**. These are the features of a product or service that a customer doesn't care about.

These attributes have also been typically referred to as being delighters/exciters, satisfiers, dissatisfiers, and so forth, depending upon the source material. Fundamentally, these are all the same.

Threshold (or basic) attributes are those that directly impact the level of customer satisfaction by their absence or inclusion. If these basic attributes are not present, the customer is immediately dissatisfied. Even if they are present (but there are no other attributes present), the customer may also be unsatisfied overall, as can be seen in figure 8.2 on the next page.

As you can probably work out, it is the *performance* attribute where most products or services compete (think back to a recent proposal or pitch and see what I mean). Importantly for our purposes, it is this attribute that *primarily drives the price that a customer is willing to pay*. This may be related to someone's specific skill or knowledge, or a specific feature of the product.

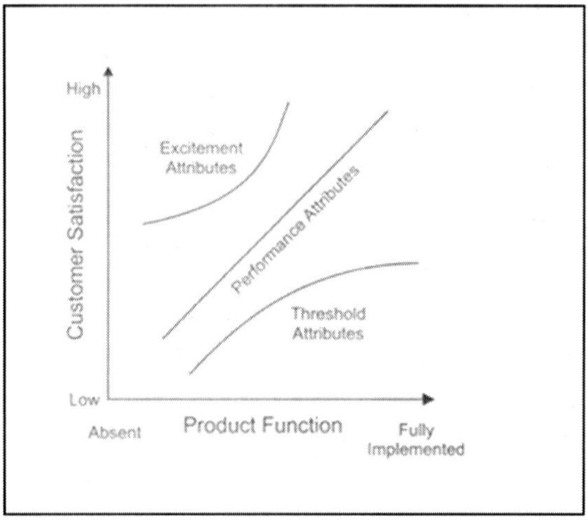

Figure 8.2
The Kano Model

Finally, we have excitement attributes. These are the things that people don't really expect to get but that really delight them when present. Some commentators have gone as far to note that "even if few performance attributes are present . . . the presence of an excitement attribute will lead to high customer satisfaction."[8]

What does this look like in practice? Let's take a simple example from outside the legal world first—a car.

- Threshold/basic attributes could potentially include the steering wheel, having an appropriate number of seats, the car exhaust, wing mirrors, etc.
- Performance attributes could potentially include engine capacity, model and make of car, etc.

8. For information about the Kano Model, go to http://www.kanomodel.com.

- Excitement attributes could potentially include heated seats, cup holders, the in-car entertainment system, etc.
- Not relevant attributes could potentially include tire size, tire brand, etc.

Now let's translate this concept to our world.

- Threshold/basic attributes could potentially include the overall price, experience of conducting similar matters, etc.
- Performance attributes could potentially include the seniority and experience of the proposed team, use of law firm/client "collaboration" sites, etc.
- Excitement attributes could potentially include the presence of the "star" partner who is the acknowledged go-to person for these types of matters.
- Not relevant attributes could potentially include where the team are located.

Why does this matter? If we can take the time to work out what will really engage our clients, which features (or attributes) we must have and which are nice (and mutually advantageous) to include, and which add *real value* to the client, we can become much more targeted in how we deliver our legal services and also the cost of doing so.

None of this is easy, I admit, and is certainly not something you would wish to do for all the clients you work with or services you provide. However, using the 80-20 rule, there is merit in doing this for your larger, more significant clients, or for those products and services you provide on a frequent basis.

Work out what really matters to you and your client by going through the following key steps:

- Identify all the features or attributes of your product or service (especially those you *could* include to please your client).
- Categorize each of these attributes or features as being one of basic, performance, excitement, and not relevant.
- Make sure you include all the threshold (or basic) attributes (discarding those that are not relevant).

- For those you identified as excitement attributes, which of those can you add? Which ones will *most* improve the potential level of your client's satisfaction (and will hopefully lead onto future matters)?
- Think through those attributes that you may need to trade (either performance attributes for excitement ones or vice versa).
- Most importantly, *add only those that still allow you to price at a level you think your client is prepared to pay* (and at one you are confident you can deliver at an appropriate level of profit margin).

From my own experiences, one example springs quickly to mind.

When looking to respond to a potential client's global panel request, I and the rest of the client proposal team were considering a range of possible value-added services. These ranged from the more traditional areas, such as providing a number of training sessions, access to certain precedents, through to others perhaps less familiar, such as an agreed number of secondments, client hotline, and others in a similar vein.

One thing became quickly apparent as we began to run the numbers. When adding up all the elements of our potential proposal (which also included an agreed level of discount to hourly rates), it became clear that it was becoming potentially "unprofitable" to respond—certainly in the fashion first anticipated.

In hindsight, what we then did was exactly as the process outlines above. We looked at each potential feature, worked out what was essential and nice to have, and then worked out what we could then offer to the client that met its requirements. We then looked to see what we could offer that would bring the excitement factor to the client. (By the way, we won the pitch.)

Finally, one word of caution: It is also important to recognize that, with the passage of time, what was once an excitement attribute can become one that is seen as basic or essential, as more and more customers begin to expect this feature as a standard (think of smartphones and cameras). As an example, a decade ago, any major international law firm having a capability in Islamic financing was probably viewed as an excitement factor by some more progressive clients looking for expertise in this area. Today it may merely be viewed as a performance or even basic attribute, depending upon the client's business model.

Our clients' expectations change over time. We need to remember to also change ours too.

Learning from the Romans

The Ancient Romans had a word for it. *Pretium.*[9]

Some readers will know that this is the Latin term for price. However, fewer may know that it is also the term for value. Put simply, our Roman friends used the *same word* to reflect price and value. They understood the *fundamental connection* between price and value in any economic transaction. Indeed, as any good pricing practitioner would tell you, price only makes sense when seen in the context of the potential value delivered by the purchase (whether that value is quantifiable or not).

When properly structured and implemented, appropriate fee arrangements can enhance the long-term partnership between companies and their outside counsel in the creating, and sustaining, of value for their organization.

Adopting approaches that are commercially pragmatic and simple, being flexible in which approach to adopt during each stage of a matter, and encouraging the ongoing sharing of information will all help contribute to delivering compelling results. Those law firms that realign or shift their goals to be consistent with their clients' will be those that succeed.

However, nothing can replace the *dialogue* between law firm and client. For lawyers, this means we need to listen and respond appropriately. For clients, this means a need to be much more specific about what is important to them and how this will help drive value, both at matter-specific and business level (as ultimately the question of value is the client's to make). And for both, it means speaking a common language based on trust, openness, and honesty.

There and back again. It still is a question of value.

---

9. Hermann Simon, *The Magic Word: Pretium*, PRICING ADVISOR, Sept. 2012, at 8, *available at* http://media.pricingsociety.com/publications/Pricing_Advisor_Newsletter_Sep12.pdf?elq=15d0cb09625e4a3d9949bfe86d89c4cd&elqCampaignId=56.

Don't forget *(a summary of the key points):*

- Law firms need to become better at defining the value they provide clients—from the proposal stage onward—and then measuring it (for both us and our clients).
- Clients realize value in different ways—we need to engage with them to determine how we can best support their business objectives.
- Taking time to determine what elements of our service add *real* value (and those that, conversely, do not add any value) will allow us to become more targeted in our value proposition, delivery of services, and price.
- The ancient Romans clearly linked price and value in the Latin word *pretium*. They understood the fundamental connection between price and value in any economic transaction. We need to do the same.

Chapter 9

The Two Ps: Part 1

Pitching to Win

You have done the hard work. You have priced the matter, you have identified the value add to your prospective client, and then . . . BAM!

You discover that you need to *formally* pitch to get the work, and if that was not enough, the process is being run by the client's procurement team (a nebulous term that seems to cover a wide array of activities, none of which lawyers are particularly keen on—or, at least, so it seems).

What makes a successful pitch, and how can we best work with procurement? Over the next two chapters we will explore each of these in a bit more detail.

I have perhaps some unusual experience in this area.

As a management consultant I was often asked to help drive business development activities with current (or potential) clients (and then deliver the resultant project).

But perhaps even more relevant is that I was, for the vast majority of my management-consulting career, primarily a procurement consultant. In that role, I designed procurement programs on behalf of clients (including legal services), I conducted negotiations and e-auctions on behalf of clients (including legal services), and now that I am "poacher turned gamekeeper," I continue to participate in procurement discussions—but this time from a law firm perspective.

What follows are some of the key pieces of advice people much wiser than I am were kind enough to impart, which hopefully means that you don't need to make some of the mistakes I have along the way and can repeat some of the successes. The advice is not exhaustive, and indeed a list of suggested reading is contained elsewhere, but it will hopefully give you a few key pointers of do's and don'ts on your way to successfully winning more work and suddenly having lots of "procurement buddies" at your client (if you like that sort of thing).

First, I would like to cover some useful do's and don'ts on pitching.

Pitching to Win

Pitch. Defined by the Oxford English Dictionary as "[noun] a form of words used when trying to persuade someone to buy or accept something; [verb] to make a bid to obtain a contract or other business."[1] But we know the real meaning: beauty parade, beauty pageant, or similar (depending upon where you are from).

And if we don't win the pitch, we have a number of readily available reasons why we didn't. These typically range from those relating to the firm ("we are too small/big for them"; "they wanted [insert name of a key individual here] at our competition") to price ("we were too expensive") to random musings ("the client doesn't have a clue what they want"). All are said to make us feel better.

But how can we avoid going through this often frustrating exercise? By pitching to win.

When preparing to write this section, I spoke with one of my colleagues, James, at Baker & McKenzie about what makes a successful pitch. (As are a number of major professional-service organizations, we are fortunate to have a number of highly skilled individuals who focus on driving forward the more complex pitches, and in providing coaching to the client pitch teams). James broke it down into the following six key steps, which pretty much align with other recommended best practice in this area.

1. *Pitch*, MERRIAM-WEBSTER, INC., http://www.merriam-webster.com/dictionary/pitch.

1. Be organized.
2. Know your audience.
3. Solve the problem at hand and price appropriately.
4. Preparation and practice make perfect.
5. Give the great presentation.
6. Gather feedback.

Let's look at each a bit more.

Be Organized

Planning is key—pitches typically have a very swift turnaround time. If matter specific, this can be a matter of hours (worst case) to a few days. If a relationship panel, this can sometimes be as much as two to three weeks (although the level of details requested is commensurately bigger). Regardless, there is typically very little "fat" in the timing.

Having a clear plan from the outset allows you to be more effective and allows you to focus on the key themes and messages—not trying to herd the "pitch team" into a room. Most importantly, it gives you time to *think* about the client's problem.

As part of any pre-pitch planning, there are probably four key steps to consider. The first is probably the hardest to do.

Meet with (or At Least Talk to) Client if Possible

This is very useful as a way to change any misconceptions you may have had about the pitch itself (whether this be process or subject matter), and it allows you to meet the key decision makers (and also introduce any key members of your potential team). It also allows you to identify very early in the process what problem the client is seeking to address, what they think they need to do (which may not be actually what is needed) and also the key selection criteria.

There are some suggested techniques outlined in our next chapter ("Dealing with Procurement") when trying to secure that all-important meeting.

But that is not enough—to develop a compelling pitch, it is important to do some background research.

Do Some Background Research

What is your (potential) client looking to do? Have they been in the news recently (there is nothing more embarrassing that attending a client meeting being unaware that they have either been acquired or have acquired someone else—especially if splashed across the front pages of the financial or industry press). What work have you done that is similar that could act as a compelling credential? What pricing approaches did you adopt, and how profitable were they? The more recent the examples you can find, the better.

Assess the Opportunity

Too much time in law firms is spent responding to every request for a quote. Sometimes we need to say no. This may be because we are very busy and would struggle to support the matter appropriately (a nice problem to have), or that it doesn't sit in our "sweet spot." The key is, however, not responding to everything. The amount of effort firms devote to pitching for opportunities that they are never going to win is huge.

One approach used very successfully by other professional services firms (specifically those in consulting and accounting) is the prequalification of any pitches *before* the pitch team actively starts working on the request. In one of my previous consulting firms, there would be questions asked if margin was not at the expected level or where business development effort exceeded 10 percent of total potential revenues (this of course assumes that business development effort itself was being tracked). Whilst such an approach may not work for all, having someone from your firm's management team or practice group "kick the tires" may help you decide where your pitching efforts may be best focused.

The other important consideration here is *can* you work for the potential client. Do you have the right skills? Have you checked whether you have a potential conflict? Do you have the right relationship?

This last point is often overlooked. There was a study done a few years ago that sought to determine the likelihood of pitching success based on whether the respondent had a lot of exposure to the client, some exposure, or no exposure. Unsurprisingly, those firms that had no exposure to the client were unsuccessful *100 percent* of the time in securing work. So, ask yourself, are you there to make up the numbers or do you have a realistic chance of success? If you responded 'yes' to the former or have any hesitation *at all* answering the latter, stop now and wait for the next potential opportunity.

The Pitching Team

Finally, make sure you have a good team around you from the outset. Play to your own organization's strengths. Who are the key partners you should include when developing the content and approach? Who from marketing and business development should be involved? Are there specialists you should speak with (for example—and in line with this whole book's premise—those involved in pricing and/or legal project management)? Are you forgetting any associates that you may wish to have involved as part of the client team? Is there an opportunity to get them actively involved from the start? The overall goal should be to put your best foot forward.

Know Your Audience

It is vital to understand what makes your client tick. How have they performed in their respective market(s)? What are their key initiatives, challenges, and opportunities?

Much of this information can be gathered very quickly in today's world, if willing to do a few searches online and spend time reading a client's annual report (it is amazing how few do!).

As part of this, we are looking at not only how best to address the client's broader *business* context but also the *pitch* context. Finally, don't forget the *personal* context too—at the back of every decision maker's mind, they need to make sure they hire someone who is going to (at best) make them look good, but (as a minimum) will not make them look bad.

For example, some key questions you should be thinking about:

- How many law firms are they speaking with?
- What are they looking for from their advisors?
- What are their main business concerns and are there any potential changes looming?
- What does the client like (or dislike) about working with you or other incumbent law firms?

- What are they looking for in terms of pricing? (You might as well address the proverbial elephant in the room quickly!)
- What would success look like for *them*? Now? In a year's time?

Although some of these you can easily answer through doing online searches or reviewing the original request, a number of them—especially those that are personal—can only be done in discussion with the client themselves. Again, it comes back to the comment made earlier—if you have no (or limited) direct contact to find out more and test your understanding of the problem at hand, what real chance of success do you have?

Solving the Problem at Hand and Pricing Appropriately

This is all about building the proposal itself, and is where the majority of the effort lies. If putting a number against this, from the initial query to the final presentation, this is probably where 60 percent to 70 percent of your (and the broader pitch team's) time should be spent.

It is about having that initial kickoff meeting with the broader pitch team, structuring the document, and finalizing the commercial proposition.

The Initial Kickoff Meeting

The pitching clock ticks down very quickly. When having the initial kickoff meeting with the pitch team, make sure that everyone is aware of the key milestones during the pitching process—who is responsible for completing which area, who reviews and when (remember to include someone to review the *whole* document to make sure it all makes sense), who is responsible for producing the final document (and ensuring it gets to the client *on time*). Each is an obvious question, but in the heat of battle mistakes are unavoidably made—unless you keep a tight watch over them.

So clearly set expectations and accountability from the outset, even if there are only two or three of you working on the proposal. And meet every day, even if only for five minutes to discuss progress (and address any issues arising).

Structuring the Document

It is here that we need to interpret what the client wants; these may be explicit needs, or implicit. I am sure like many of you, I have been in a situation where I have understood the client to want one thing, only to discover they wanted something else!

Another key consideration here is also how experienced the client is in the area of law in question; they may not be fully aware of some of the potential opportunities or pitfalls that may lie ahead. This is something law firms working in some of the emerging economies are experiencing. After all, you don't know what you don't know, and you only know it if exposed to it.

It is also important to identify the benefit to the client in each area mentioned where possible (remember our discussion on value earlier). If it doesn't help the client and add value, why are we doing it? All too often proposals focus on features primarily, not benefits.

A poor example in this regard would be a statement such as, "We have over 20 partners in our firm who can help you." A much better example would be, "We have a number of skilled and experienced partners who will help you quickly and cost-effectively navigate the issues at hand."

Finally, remember to *focus on your client*. You are preparing for them, after all, aren't you?

When (much) less experienced, I was guilty of the cardinal sin of proposal writing (I hope I have improved since). The vast majority of my early proposals (before being checked by those much better than I) were very focused on the firm I was working for at the time. The early part of the proposal would focus on who the firm was, where we had offices, who the team was, recent awards, and so on. Notice anything?

Yep, you noticed it too—not one mention of the client yet, and we may be 50 percent or more through the proposal. How do you think that would be received? Not well, and yet many proposals submitted to our industry's respective clients still make this fundamental mistake.

How much better (and novel) would it be to structure the document around the client's key concerns and issues? Within the first few paragraphs (or slides, as more and more proposals are being presented in PowerPoint or similar), summarize your understanding of the client's issue, how you are well placed to help the client (stating specific examples and benefits), and the commercial proposition (that is, pricing!).

If you need to talk about your firm's offices, other capabilities, team, and accolades, keep it brief.

Pricing Appropriately: Determining the Commercial Proposition

A key theme throughout this book is to understand and *know your value*. Remember that "hours" does not equate to "value" (however defined). Similarly, when pricing, we should *charge for our wisdom, not the hours expended*. The following episode from history illustrates the dilemma faced by many lawyers.

James Whistler famously recognized the challenge during his libel case against John Ruskin, the Victorian art critic. He was challenged by Ruskin's lawyer, Attorney General Sir John Holker, during cross examination on his fee of 200 guineas for painting *Nocturne in Black and Gold—The Falling Rocket*. The painting itself had taken him only two days to complete from start to finish.

The dialogue that day in late November 1878 was as follows:

> Holker: "The labor of two days is that for which you ask two hundred guineas?"
> Whistler: "No, I ask it for the knowledge I have gained in the work of a lifetime."

And that neatly sums up our problem, both in the price that we charge for our services and also in the way in which we seek to communicate them.

All the hard work spent during our initial Set the Price phase will come to nothing unless we can articulate the value we will deliver in a compelling and meaningful fashion.

The Set the Price phase is also positioned first for a reason. Too often when preparing a proposal (regardless of industry) the pricing section is often left to the end. This, in part, is because many people view it as too hard. As a result, typically during the last 60 minutes of time available prior to the submittal of the final proposal, pricing can still be the section or slide remaining resulting in frenetic last-minute proposal team activity to determine and then gain any approval for the final pricing proposed.

This results in two fundamental issues. The first is that the pricing proposal is then, as a result, poorly thought through as "we just need to put a 'reasonable' number in the section" (or at least that is the view). The second is even more worrying. If pricing is left to the end, how is it possible to accurately reflect the value of your proposal to the client if you are unsure of how the proposal will be priced and what the price will be? It is *pretium* gone wrong.

Arguably one of the reasons that pricing is one of the four Ps of the marketing mix (first expressed by E. J. McCarthy in 1960), alongside product, place, and promotion is that, in addition to being the only revenue-generating P in the marketing mix, it is also something that is *inherent in the communication and marketing* of one's product's or service's value to the buyer.

Preparation and Practice Makes Perfect

Despite opening myself up to accusations of stating the obvious, it is vital to practice your proposal presentation (if you are required to present to the client as part of the process).

Where Fools Rush In

What is perhaps less obvious is that this should be done *three* times. "How?" I hear you cry! "We're busy and don't have time to do this. We have other, more pressing matters (pun intended) to attend to." The phrase "busy fools" comes to mind, where people run from one crisis to another.

The reason it is recommended that you and the pitch team rehearse three times is quite simple really. Think back to the initial proposal rehearsal you have on your pitch (once you have been able to corral everyone into the same room, ideally, or at least the same conference call). In reality, the first meeting is more of a sense check on the proposal, not a rehearsal at all. At best, you may agree who is actually going to present each section to the client (for example, the relationship partner may focus on the relationship, the matter/responsible partner may focus on the content, etc.).

The second rehearsal (if you have one), is a bit better. This is where you review any amendments identified during the first meeting, and check what each is going to say (although still not hearing *what* will *actually* be said).

Putting an End to "Ums" and "Ers"

A personal bugbear of mine is how poorly I have seen some otherwise extremely capable people struggle when it comes to presenting. I do not mean to diminish the level of anxiety or trepidation that they feel, although this can be made easier by preparation. It is more the repetition of "ums" and "ers" that frequently puncture the presentation. If you do not present well (or at least with a modicum of confidence), what impression do you think this gives the client? If I could be king for a day, one of my edicts would be that going on a presentation-skills course should be mandatory for any senior lawyer—especially if involved in pitching.

It is in the third rehearsal (if you get that far!) where the "sparkle" or "magic" is produced. It is when all the individuals present act as one team (not individuals who only have their own section to worry about and then "switch off"—it happens—often in full view of the prospective client!). Handovers are seamless between presenters, content is crisp and the pricing and value messages are clear.

At each stage, practice the pricing part of your presentation. This is where you are most likely to face the greatest challenge from the client. Be comfortable and confident in your approach and supporting facts and figures. (Some suggested approaches on how you can do this are covered in the next chapter.)

Nowadays, especially with our reliance on slides when presenting, practice and appropriate rehearsal is even more important. I remember (when a management consultant) having prepared a presentation for myself and the lead partner at the time. There are two reasons I remember this vividly: one, it took all night to pull the materials together (it was a very short-notice presentation), and the second, more important reason was the lead partner just decided to talk about the overall approach and benefits. No presentation slides were used. The materials were available (and sitting on the desk in front of all participants), but not used—as they typically are—as a crutch. The structure was the same as the slide materials, but the level of engagement with the client was markedly different. It became a structured discussion and exploration of the issues. Being comfortable with the subject matter was key. (The pitch was won, in case you were wondering).

Imagine attending a (prospective) client's panel presentation with your pitch team with no rehearsal, intending to use the slides as the crutch. (Again, without wishing to state the obvious: *never* just repeat the words on the slide—clients can read—use these words as jumping off points, provide some "color" to your message, not just the monotone words on the slide.) You turn up ready to present and the client then either mentions to you that they just "want to talk" and/or switch off the projector. If you haven't prepared properly as a team, haven't rehearsed your key messages and haven't rehearsed your handovers among the team, it is not going to be very professional and the chances of success will be nominal at best.

It May Seem Unimportant, But . . .

Not only is rehearsal important for any pitch, *adequate preparation is also vital*—there *is* a distinct difference between the two. We will cover how best to prepare for the client negotiation in Chapter 11, but for now we will focus on the proposal or pitch presentation itself.

When preparing, you should have an answer to some basic questions as a minimum.

- Who is attending from the client? Do we know them? Which parts of the client's business are they from? (This is particularly important if from the client's procurement department, a topic we will cover in Chapter 11.)
- What do they like/dislike? What style works best with them? (Do they like numbers, charts? Do they like short presentations?)[2]
- What questions can you expect to be asked? (One tip I was given when starting my consulting career was: Think of the worst possible question you could be asked, and prepare for that—then repeat the process until you have covered all the possible variations).

2. One of the best books I have come across that addresses the topic of different styles and is a great introduction to the topic is by Robert Bolton and Dorothy Grover Bolton: PEOPLE STYLES AT WORK . . . AND BEYOND: MAKING BAD RELATIONSHIPS GOOD AND GOOD RELATIONSHIPS BETTER (2009).

- Where is the meeting going to take place? How long does it take to get there?

This last point is sometimes overlooked, and often underappreciated at best.

Build in Travel Time!

A colleague once told me of the merger discussions between a major German retail and investment bank and a smaller, more "traditional," British investment bank. The British bank's negotiation team flew into Frankfurt for the negotiation meeting on *the day* of the meeting. (For those who are maybe less familiar with time zones in Europe, there is a one-hour time difference between the United Kingdom and Germany, with the United Kingdom being an hour earlier). The meeting was due to start at 9:00 a.m. Regardless of your airline carrier, flights rarely land when they are supposed to. To cut a long story short, the British team was late for the meeting, and this caused significant senior-level heated discussions between both parties. The meeting was rearranged, this time in the United Kingdom. Despite the time difference working in favor of the German banking team, they did the right thing—they arrived the evening before. They turned up rested, prepared . . . and on time. You may think this will never happen to you—it will. At least once.

Make sure you have extra copies of everything you need. Not only your presentation materials but also power cables and so forth. Also be aware of your client's preferences. Some clients may not want physical copies of everything due to their personal preference or company's corporate social responsibility (CSR) policy—find out their preference before the meeting. A number of law firms have extremely valuable guides to areas of law, but these are often over 500 pages thick and sit on a shelf. Doesn't it make more sense to provide a "soft copy"?

And one more thing—do an online search on the client and the meeting participants on the day of the presentation itself. You never know what might turn up and how that might impact your pitch.

Giving the Great Presentation

This is the bit where the rubber hits the road: the pitch or presentation itself.

Although fortunate enough to have seen a number of very strong presentations, there is one that stands out. While working on behalf of an insurance client as a procurement consultant, I was helping manage the panel process for a specific area of consulting expertise (on Six Sigma, which was a very popular topic within "progressive" financial firms at the time). On this particular day in the penthouse boardroom of my client, we had a series of potential-supplier presentations as to why they were best qualified, why their pricing proposal made sense, and so on. It was getting to the end of what had become a very long day. And then, the fifth and final group came through the door (they were from another well-known global consulting firm).

They began to place "slide billboards" around the interior walls of the boardroom. They then started the presentation, and after the initial introductions, the team members proceeded to discuss their respective billboard, and we (the client) all moved to the next one (and so on) until we reached the end, closing with a brief question-and-answer session.

It was clear they had given thought to the presentation style, made sure they involved everyone in the team, and had rehearsed (probably at least three times). They won the pitch, not only because they had the appropriate skills (others did too), but they had successfully engaged and energized the (client) audience. They had made their pitch and the content memorable.

While not suggesting that you adopt this approach directly, the key message is to encourage thought about how to make your presentation and pitch engaging and memorable. From the beginning, through the middle, and right to the end.

This anecdote also illustrates another theme: the possible advantage of going last when pitching, although it is something that is hard to control unless your client specifically asks you to choose a time slot. Not only does it give you slightly more time to prepare but your client's recollection of your presentation will be more recent and fresh. It allows you to address the key concepts of your pitch quicker (as a lot of the preamble will have been covered multiple times by others).

Finally, once the pitch is finished, exit "properly and positively." There was a phrase used during the Blitz in London during the Second World War, which was, "careless talk costs lives." Although not of the same magnitude (or consequence), it means do not discuss how you felt the pitch went until safely away from the client's premises (or wait until the client is safely away from yours, if hosting). Similarly, be careful what you write down in view of the client and leave lying around.

Gathering Feedback

Whether you win or lose the pitch, get feedback. Have a debriefing with the internal pitch team and also with the clients themselves.

Ask typical questions such as how your proposal compared with your competition and which other firms were being considered. Ask what was the key factor as to why the winning firm (it may be you) won. What would have made a difference to the tender outcome? Was there anything your team did in the pitch that stood out (both for good and not-so-good reason!)?

From a pricing perspective, where did you finish up? If more expensive (and having lost the pitch) what was the key percentage variance or difference in approach? If successful, how did your pricing compare? (Remember that you may not have been the cheapest. Indeed, if delivering the appropriate value, you shouldn't necessarily be.)

The phrase "you lost because you were too expensive" is a very easy response to give a law firm as to why it lost a pitch—it is expected, it is not personal, and it is easy. It is often used as the catchall phrase to cover a multitude of sins; for example, the client did not rate your capabilities or did not like the team (or a specific individual in the team). So when being told you were too expensive, probe, ask insightful questions, and use this information when pitching next time (as it is a very valuable source of competitive intelligence).

In closing, always leave a positive impression regardless of outcome. When speaking with the client on an unsuccessful pitch, ask how you can best continue your relationship with them. They will look on you more positively next time. We will cover the area of feedback more fully as part of the Review the Price section, but next, let's focus a bit on the role of the procurement team, a group becoming increasingly influential and visible in the "law firm buying" process.

Don't forget *(a summary of the key points):*

- If needing to pitch, have a clear plan from the outset—this gives you time to think about the client's problem rather than reacting to document preparation.
- If you are unable to gain access to your client during the pitching process (for example, to clarify your understanding, or "test" possible approaches), seriously consider whether you should pitch.
- Do not leave the pricing section until the end. Price and value are inextricably linked, and the theme of "value" needs to be in evidence throughout your proposal. You can't realistically talk of value if you don't know your price.
- Practice, practice, practice. Learn from the experts. You should practice your pitch presentation three times—only by the third time will you sound convincing to yourself, your team, and to your audience.

Chapter 10

The Two Ps: Part 2

Dealing with Procurement

Procurement. A word defined by one dictionary as the act or process of procuring,[1] which doesn't seem to help much. More useful is the following definition: "Procurement is the business management function that ensures identification, sourcing, access and management of the external resources that an organisation needs or may need to fulfill its strategic objectives."[2] Other terms are also often used to mean the same thing (although be aware that the scope of each is slightly different in a purist's mind), such as "purchasing," "sourcing," "supplier management," or simply "buying."

What is undeniable, however, is that those who are involved in whatever variant of the term "procurement" you wish to use are becoming increasingly more involved in the buying of legal services, and now have a valid seat at the table.

Although I have heard many lawyers wistfully wish for the days prior to the global financial crisis and what that meant in terms of demand (lots) and pricing pressure (little), the industry now recognizes that these days are gone for good. But the global financial crisis also had an interesting by-product.

1. *What Is Procurement?*, WebFinance, Inc., http://www.businessdictionary.com/definition/procurement.html.

2. CIPS Australia, the Definitions of "Procurement" and "Supply Chain Management", 4, *available at* http://www.kbresearch.com/cips-files/The%20Definitions%20of%20Procurement%20and%20Supply%20Chain%20Management.pdf.

With the greater attention being given to an organization's balance sheet and external expenditure, the need for organizations to get a better grip on external costs was paramount, with most large companies spending anywhere between 40 percent and 60 percent of their income on external goods or services. Unfortunately for those in the legal profession, that included us.

External legal counsel can often be one of the top three or four cost items for an organization (information technology is frequently up there too). Whilst this will vary from company to company, it is often near the top, and with that brings focus.

One commentator noted that in 2008 (pre–financial meltdown), professional services (defined here as being legal services, management and IT consulting, accounting, and financial advisory providers) "are together estimated to have been worth $1.2 trillion, larger than Mexico's GDP and about the same size as India's."[3] Of that amount, about $580 billion was estimated to be the value of the legal-services market, according to Datamonitor (a research firm), of which about half was in the Americas (North, Central, and South) and about a third in Europe.[4]

For many companies seeking to navigate through the choppy waters of late 2008 and 2009, a key area to potentially reduce external expenditure was therefore legal services. Enter procurement stage right.

Although initially there was certainly a mismatch of skills and expectations in a number of companies as to what procurement would be able to deliver (and also a certain degree of reticence from those in legal to allow procurement to enter their world), this has now become less prevalent.

Yes, it was true that, initially, many procurement resources were more familiar with buying office supplies, or other "easily definable" services. Yes, it was true that this meant there was a keen focus on cost (often to the detriment of everything else). And yes, it was true that there were bumps along the road with legal teams often of the view that procurement did not understand the complexity of the work they did, nor the importance of relationships when using external legal services, and would pronounce these

3. Fiona Czerniawska & Peter Smith, Buying Professional Services 7 (2010).
4. *Id.* at 8.

facts loudly from the rooftops. (The same arguments were also voiced by others who traditionally used other professional services, such as accountancy or management consultancy.)

From procurement's perspective in the early days, there was also frustration. There was limited *objective* information available to help support any buying decision, the services required were (and often still are in some areas) relatively hard to define, and the individuals involved in making these decisions were frequently very senior within respective organizations, making procurement's job even harder.

The skills required in this type of situation were very clearly different from buying pens and pencils. As David Cheyne, at the time the senior partner of my previous law firm, Linklaters, observed "(W)hat we're not sure about is whether the average purchasing manager understands the different services firms provide and what differentiates one law firm from another. Some have come from buying bulk services or products where you can specify your requirements precisely and negotiate a discount without compromising quality. The concept of value for money in a professional services context is more complex: you can end up paying over the odds for routine work and getting poorer quality advice on important transactions."[5]

Jack Welch once notoriously said that "engineers who can't add, operators who can't run their equipment, and accountants who can't do numbers become purchasing professionals."[6] What General Electric's legendary boss was reflecting is, however, a common perception of the function, regardless of how it is stated: namely, that the purchasing/procurement function is little more than a necessary evil in business.

Thankfully, today these once valid concerns are less to the fore. Procurement has "grown up" when it comes to helping companies procure their legal services, and now have a valid seat (for the most part) at the table.

So now that they are there, how can we best work with them—for both our and our client's best interests?

5. *Id.* at 44.

6. Quoted in Steffen Fuchs, Gillian Pais, and Jeff Shulman, Building superior capabilities for strategic sourcing, McKinsey Insights, May 2013, *available at* http://www.mckinsey.com/insights/operations/building_superior_capabilities_for_strategic_sourcing.

Understanding How Procurement Sees the World

Procurement professionals will seek to place you as a supplier of services—or, more specifically, the services you provide—into one of four different "boxes" or segments, as they seek to manage the area of external spend. These are strategic items, leverage items, bottleneck items, and routine (i.e., noncritical) items.

This approach was first developed by Peter Kraljic, and appeared in the *Harvard Business Review* in September 1983.[7] It is called the Kraljic portfolio purchasing model, and is shown on the next page in figure 10.1.

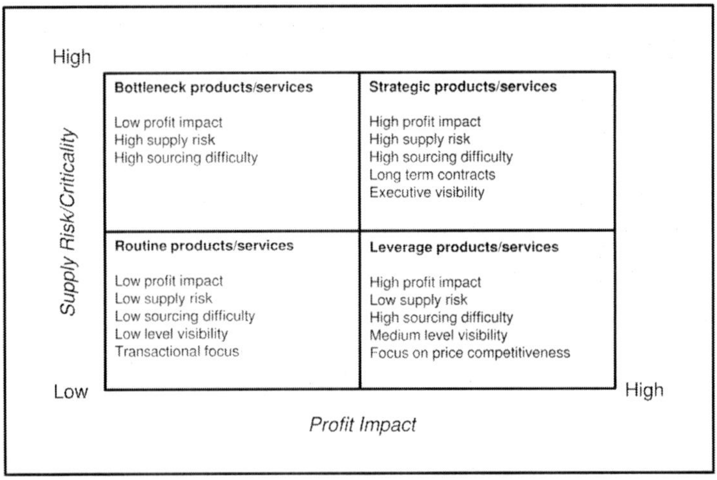

Figure 10.1
The Kraljic Portfolio Purchasing Model (or How Procurement Sees the World)
Source: *Using the Kraljic Portfolio Purchasing Model*, REDACTIVE MEDIA GROUP (June 2, 2010), http://www.supplymanagement.com/resources/how-to/guide-to-supplier-appraisal/using-the-kraljic-portfolio-purchasing-model/.

The main intent of the model was to help those performing purchasing-related activities determine how best to maximize the "security of supply"

7. Peter Kraljic, *Purchasing Must Become Supply Management*, HARV. BUS. REV., Sept.–Oct. 1983, *available at* http://www.nevi.nl/sites/default/files/kennisdocument/LEV-PORT-art-013-bl.pdf. The diagram is from http://www.supplymanagement.com/resources/how-to/guide-to-supplier-appraisal/using-the-kraljic-portfolio-purchasing-model/.

whilst also reducing costs. It also encouraged those in purchasing or procurement to begin to think more strategically rather than transactionally, a key theme of Kraljic's original *Harvard Business Review* article.

Those items that are seen as strategic are those that have a high impact on the client's potential profit, and also a high risk of supply (i.e., there are not many companies who can provide these services). It is here that most law firms would like to see themselves, but very few actually attain. It is where there is a long-term relationship between both parties (either ongoing or proposed).

Next in terms of profit contribution come those classified as leverage items. These have a high profit impact but a low supply risk, meaning that there is a wide variety of possible firms that can supply this expertise or service. This is where there is typically a lot of switching between suppliers (think about the intent behind some of the client RFPs or panel requests you have participated in). In the nonlegal world, this is where you would typically see a high volume of orders being placed as one way of driving down product (or service) cost.

Bottleneck items are those that have a low impact on profit but have a high level of supply risk. Despite their relatively low individual impact on overall profit, the absence of these products or services can have a major impact. In the nonlegal world, this is where you see companies intentionally over-ordering as a means of securing supply.

The final segment is for noncritical items. These have both a low impact on profit and also have a low level of supply risk. It is here where there is typically very little differentiation between products and services provided.

As seen in figure 10.1, the level of executive attention also varies, as does the level of internal approval required to authorize purchases.

Very few law firms reach the strategic level of classification in the eyes of their clients, with the possible exception of the "White Shoe" and "Magic Circle" firms in the United States and United Kingdom, respectively, and the odd major national firm elsewhere. It is also important to recognize that law firms offer a variety of services, some of which may sit here (for example, major mergers and acquisitions activity) and others elsewhere (such as "vanilla loans," or low-level employment issues). Therefore, the approach taken by a client's procurement team may vary depending upon the nature of the service being requested.

What is generally true, however, is that the level of focus dedicated to you as supplier of services increases as your overall contribution to the client organization becomes more critical. Therefore if you are a firm that is acknowledged to be contributing significantly to your client's bottom line (as discussed earlier in this section), you should reasonably expect to have a number of general relationship-focused meetings during the year.

Understanding the Procurement Mind-set

Armed with a basic understanding of how procurement may view us as a supplier of services, it is also worthwhile to take a few moments to outline the typical characteristics of procurement professionals, as this can help us more effectively tailor both our pitches and day-to-day engagement with them.

In many respects, their approach to their role is driven by their preferences. As a general rule, people in procurement roles are methodical and ordered, numerate and analytical, detailed and thorough, and comprehensive in their view of their category (or specific task).

Having been an ex–procurement professional, these themes ring true. Those in procurement are looking for the tangible outcomes from the successful tender, they are looking for proof and the ability to measure (in part so they can quantify their own contribution), they are seeking evidence that you can do what you say you can do, they want to be able to quickly quantify the overall organizational return on investment, and finally, they want "demonstrable value." In sum, they want you to make it easy for them to come to a decision (or at the very least, a recommendation).

Understanding the Procurement Process

Overall, the procurement tender process is pretty standard across all clients and industries. Timings between each stage may vary depending upon the complexity of the tender itself, but the key steps are relatively consistent (although they should be tailored as appropriate). The process itself is shown in figure 10.2.

For significant opportunities, such as regional or global panel appointments, the key message here is that we (as law firm respondents) receive the tender document and then (at best) probably have 10 days to turn this around, at the same time making sure we have put together a compelling proposal.

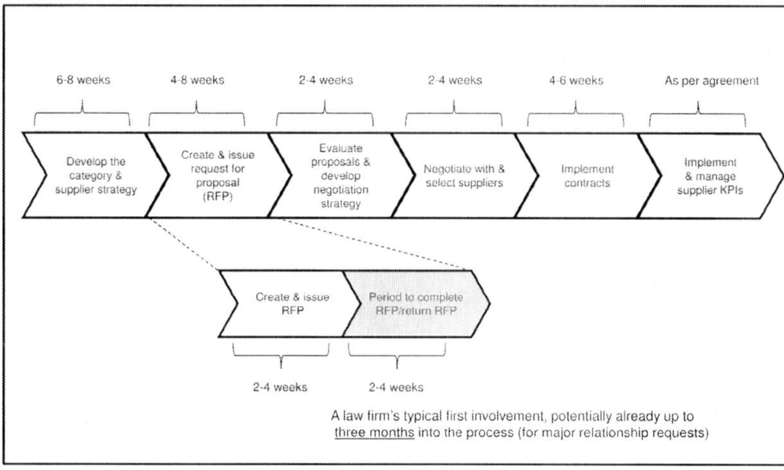

Figure 10.2
A Typical Procurement Tender Process

However, the client and their procurement team have probably spent upward of six to eight weeks prior to this time looking at possible requirements, evaluating the state of the market, gathering feedback on existing law firm performance (sometimes even asking for data from the law firms themselves, such as the previous year's billings and key business areas supported), and even potentially determining what they are prepared to pay for the services being requested.

A similar, although truncated, process is adopted for other matters where procurement is involved.

Once you understand the process, no large tender should come as a surprise. If it does, it clearly indicates that you don't have the relationship you perhaps thought you did with the client. Even if you are not informed in advance of every forthcoming significant tender opportunity, knowing the key stages of the process (particularly for panel-based arrangements) can help you anticipate the process and associated timings. You can then start to "position" and sense-check your proposed value proposition with your client away from the white heat of tender preparation.

Having a Formal Procurement Process: The General Counsel's View

A United Kingdom–based survey on the topic of procurement within law firms from a general counsel's perspective (conducted in 2012), highlighted a number of pros and cons of conducting a formal procurement-driven process.[8]

On the plus side, the benefits of doing so were being able to point to better value for money, greater transparency, and "audit-ability" of the process (an area of increasing importance to many firms). Each of these three themes was identified as being of key importance by 40 percent or more of respondents. Other themes identified also included this being a good way of generating greater confidence in the eventual decision, allowing the process to be seen to be more rigorous, and providing greater bargaining power.

The challenges identified were in some respects more revealing. The key reason for not doing so was the length of time taken, with over 75 percent of respondents identifying this as a reason not to conduct a formal process. Indeed, at time of writing, there have been three major organizations that have either revised the timing of their legal panel process or dramatically amended the tender request itself—each in recognition of this very point.

However, others included the lack of flexibility in applying the selection criteria, the lack of tailoring the process to a specific legal situation, the lack of consideration of "softer" measures, and that it was "unnecessary," with the belief that the same conclusion would have been reached through personal knowledge.

Involvement of nonlegal professionals in the process was only identified last (with 16 percent of the respondents' votes)—those of us who are more

8. Acritas, Procurement Web Survey (2012).

optimistic may see this as signaling a shift in the perception (and contribution) of engaging with procurement over the last few years.

There Is More Than Just Cost

There is no denying that cost is one of the key decision criteria when assessing which law firm to use. But we would do well to remember that it is not the only one, as Melania Wenstrup outlined in her article "Putting Your Best Foot Forward: Bidding to Procurement."[9]

There are probably six other key factors, or drivers, being looked at.

The first, and a recurring theme in this section (and indeed book), is *value for money*. It is easy to say, but it is key that we articulate succinctly what this means for our client, as discussed earlier on.

The second is *service quality*. The level of service quality will vary dramatically from one law firm to the next. Therefore, the more we can do to make the comparison easier, the better. If nothing else, you want to ensure the client is comparing at least "pieces of fruit," if not "apples to apples," and make it clear what makes you better than your competition (at least in your own eyes).

The ability to successfully manage, or at least *mitigate*, *risk* can also play a part. The way in which your legal advice can help mitigate risk to the organization, whether in the manner in which contracts are drafted and managed, or to more significant litigation claims, the ability to help "make the problem go away" for many can sway a decision (as an analogy, think of how firms sometimes employ management consultancy firms to make, or at least implement, difficult cost-cutting decisions).

The *use of technology* is also another factor that is increasingly being considered. If you use technology (whether this be your own tools or those that are from a third-party provider), highlight what this is and, more importantly, give specific examples as to how this can help the client—for

9. Melania Wenstrup, *Putting Your Best Foot Forward: Bidding to Procurement*, *in* BUYING LEGAL: PROCUREMENT INSIGHTS AND PRACTICE 61–66 (Dr. Silvia Hodges ed., 2012).

example, the advantages of a client portal where the client can instruct matters, review progress, and share information pertaining to the matter.

Then come what Melania terms *hard drivers*, which I think is a great term. These are the things, as an ex-boss of mine used to say, are the "golden nuggets" and are the items that procurement can "bank" as part of the process. These are elements such as those that make a sustained contribution to profit, drive growth, and mitigate risk. Examples of hard drivers include any pre-agreed discount to hourly rates, savings made from fixed-fee arrangements, and free time (such as for when transitioning from any incumbent provider to you). As we mentioned earlier, whatever is listed here ideally should be easily measured and quantifiable.

Finally come the *soft drivers*. It is important that we don't forget about these, which include your ability to work across different cultures, your approach to diversity (which is becoming increasingly important as a criteria), and also how you currently approach corporate social responsibility (briefly mentioned when we discussed pitching earlier), and how you would do so in partnership with them.

Earlier Engagement Means Earlier Results

The earlier procurement teams are involved, the more comprehensive they are, looking at key factors such as the value and quality of service provided. If they are excluded until very late on, their focus will tend to be exclusively on price, which, although we can mitigate to some degree through applying some of the principles outlined in this section, still makes our job much harder.

Depending upon the type of legal work being sought, and at what stage procurement is involved, the level of savings varies. What is true though is that the earlier procurement is involved, the greater the overall level of savings are.

Let's look at a typical panel process as an example. Before even selecting which suppliers to use, procurement teams will be looking at savings of at least 5 percent, if not more. This is done through a combination of reviewing internal budgets for external legal spend, looking to harmonize which services are purchased, and through doing a market assessment to determine the going rate for specific work types (see Chapter 22 on the role of technology and the rise of "big data" for more information on what our clients are now doing in this area and what we can also be doing). If you then add into this mix the responses received from the issued requests for information and requests for proposal (that is, where we come in), it is perhaps more understandable how this figure of 5-plus percent becomes seen as a benchmark.

Post-supplier-selection savings can then generate up to a further 5 percent once the law firm (or firms) has been selected, through the negotiation of commercial terms and identification of further efficiency improvements. Without really trying too hard, suddenly procurement is sitting on "savings" of 10-plus percent.

A Cautionary Tale

I remember being told of an anecdote of a senior lawyer (let's call him Alan) being asked to quickly visit the client's procurement head to finalize the contract. When doing so, he was met by the procurement head demanding that the law firm immediately agree to reduce his firm's hourly fee by at least 15 percent, otherwise the conversation was over before it had really begun. Sound familiar? What is maybe less familiar is what happens next.

Alan, who had been in the process of taking his papers out of his briefcase, so he could have the discussion, puts them back. He then moves to stand up and says, "I'm so sorry, I totally misunderstood what this conversation was all about. I thought it was about protecting your company from losing a potential (multi million-dollar) claim. I didn't realize it was about saving ($75) an hour. I'm obviously not what you're looking for. I'll be on my way."[10]

Given that the procurement head had been tasked with appointing Alan on favorable terms, he was now very clearly on the back foot. He, like many

10. Recounted in David Kean, How Not to Come Second: The Art of Winning Business Pitches 59 (2006).

inexperienced procurement people, had mistaken price for value. Alan just reminded him of the difference.

Two morals of this story: the first, is you will sometimes come across this type of negotiation (covered in the next section), but two, hold your nerve. They want you, otherwise why have the discussion?

The Secret of Every Good Boy Scout: Be Prepared

You are dealing with procurement. Procurement professionals are trained negotiators and have an eye for detail (or at least should have) as mentioned earlier. You are therefore going to want to be as prepared as possible for any meeting that involves them.

There are a number of key activities you can do to ensure that you put your best foot forward.

- Understand the role of procurement and what the decision-making process is. What role will procurement play? (Are they coordinating review and feedback, are they focused solely on the commercial aspects of the proposal, and what can you do to make their life easier when reviewing your response?)
- Understand how responses will be evaluated. This can help drive where you and your team spend the effort when pitching (for example, is it not better to spend time highlighting how your proposal will help the client achieve their stated objectives, rather than spending time determining whether you have 25 or 26 associates in a specific practice area?). It is also important to recognize what normally happens when a response is received. Key decision makers in the business will receive either the whole document or only the part specific to them. Therefore, your responses need to be able to easily stand alone to ensure that any reviewer gets to see the whole picture. Also be aware that the way in which responses will be evaluated may differ section by section—for example, some being done on a scale of 1 to 5, others being a simple Yes or No criteria.

- Determine, if you can, how the service is viewed (for example, is this seen as a high-value, strategic service or not?). This will help you focus on both the likely pricing of the service, staffing, and key value messages.
- Determine how you can best demonstrate your value and expertise (for example, using some of the techniques outlined earlier). Include a number of case studies, as this can also help encourage the reviewer to give you a higher score.
- Work out what questions you want to ask them directly, and indeed others in the client organization.
- Review the tender early to ensure you fully understand the requirements of the response and specific request. If in doubt, clarify any uncertainty quickly. However, I would also like to add a couple of caveats here:
    - Only ask those questions that will allow you to prepare a compelling proposition and in a way that demands an answer (and it is clear why you are asking the question, and how it will help your overall response).
    - Be careful what questions you ask, as you can sometimes reveal your response and negotiation approach by accident (for example, "Would you be willing to consider a single hourly rate regardless of level/practice area/jurisdiction?" clearly signals that you are considering offering a blended rate or retainer-type fee agreement).
    - Do not ask the obvious (for example, where the information is already available on the client's website, or worse, in the document itself).
- Plan your submission (remember the previous section Pitching to Win).

The final two tips here are covered in the next chapter, but for the sake of completeness are here:

- Plan your negotiation from the start.
- Plan for your meeting with them (including establishing clear roles and responsibilities—for example, who will be the point person for the procurement representative, who will take meeting notes, etc).

Influencing the Procurement Decision

There are a number of ways we can positively influence the procurement (and client) decision to be more favorable toward us.

The procurement survey mentioned earlier highlighted five key findings.[11] These were (in summary) as follows:

- Understand and then specifically address the client's requirements within your proposal—focus on and clearly articulate the benefits you will bring.
- Embrace the process (which is maybe over-optimistic, but the sentiment should be there at least and, as a minimum, you should be open to discussion). As one quote I came across commented, "If my suppliers all look and act the same, then I'll treat them that way. But if you can find a way to stand out, and demonstrate how this unique characteristic benefits my business, I'll certainly listen and may spend more. And if you can educate me on how to measure the performance of suppliers I know little about you're very likely to look good on the report card."[12]
- Be clear on the fees you intend to charge and also any assumptions made—it is useful to make any "apples to apples" comparison easier here to ensure that the client compares "like with like." (One top tip here is to provide a couple of options with the variation to each clearly stated. When wearing my procurement hat for a moment, not all law firms are the same, and therefore their respective understanding of the issues and complexity to be addressed will differ, framed by their experience. You need to ensure that the client can quickly see what they will get as part of your proposal.)
- Be transparent and specific—both in how benefits will be measured and also in your fee estimates. Demonstrate the value you bring using hard facts and figures.

---

11. Acritas, Procurement Web Survey (2012).

12. Timothy C. Corcoran, *Why CEOs Love Procurement*, *in* BUYING LEGAL: PROCUREMENT INSIGHTS AND PRACTICE, *supra* note 8, at 26.

- And finally, conform to the process—submit documents in the right format and respond on time. (It is amazing how often this is not done. Why start off on the "back foot" by submitting late? And what impression does this leave of your organizational skills?)

Ultimately, the key to all the above is to make the buying decision easier.

There are, however, sometimes a few hurdles to overcome when trying to prepare your response, especially when trying to conform to the process. Let's discuss two of the most common ones here.

Getting Access to the Key Decision Makers

I am sure you have seen examples of RFP documents that clearly state (often in bold text) that you may not contact anyone except the identified procurement contact throughout the tender process. Typically the first inclination is to acknowledge this and move on. But on closer inspection, is this restriction appropriate? If you are unable to speak to anyone except procurement during the process, how can you tailor your response to what the client needs (noting that stated needs can often be different to the actual needs).

If you are not already the incumbent provider, how are you supposed to get the appropriate context (and if you are the incumbent, you should have already known about this and been prepared)? And what of those other firms that just ignore the restriction in the first place?

To recap, if you do adhere to the rules, you are probably already at a disadvantage—you have no way of preparing a compelling response—and those who ignore the rules or are the incumbent are already ahead.

Although this may not be easy, you need to find ways to gain access. Remember the comment in the previous chapter about the success rate in pitching of those who had no relationship with the client? If you are not getting access, you need to question whether you should actually pitch and expend the effort if you are only going to be unsuccessful. Ask yourself what else you could be doing with your time. Therefore spending a concerted 10–15 minutes trying to build a case for a meeting or call doesn't seem too bad an investment after all, does it?

Responding to the Proposal Template Provided

Another common frustration is with the proposal templates you are often required to complete. Not only are these sometime ungainly in terms of format and structure but they can restrict your ability to respond as fully as you may like (for example, there is a United Kingdom–based global bank that restricts every answer to 250 words or fewer per question). With the increasing use of electronic platforms to manage this type of process (for example, via software tools such as Ariba), the restrictions only seem to get more frequent.

However, it is important to respect and use the template provided. More likely than not there will be a number of responses being evaluated and the template designed to make comparison between each and allocation of sections for review easier (for example, a recent banking panel pitch I was involved in had over 100 respondents!). What is also important is to answer each part of the question and not to refer to other responses elsewhere in the document (as a reviewer of this specific question may not see the others referred to).

Finally, it may be tempting to include lots of supporting information alongside your formal response. This may include standard brochures on your firm's capabilities or those specific to the area of law in question. The question to ask yourself is, are these actually going to be read and reviewed? Having been on the other end of this process while a procurement consultant, being inundated with volumes of supporting documents from each participating firm was certainly not fun, and the business users *very* rarely even read them.

What is better is to provide a short and succinct e-mail or letter highlighting the key points of your proposal, the strength of your current (or desired) relationship, and an offer to provide additional supporting information if helpful. This is much more likely to be shared with all reviewers, and it also allows you to quickly highlight those key messages you want to filter through from your proposal.

What It Takes to Succeed

I would like to finish this chapter with a quote taken from a recent article that encapsulates this issue, and our challenge, well.

"It appears that those with most to fear from the increasing role of procurement are those which do a poor job at differentiating from the competition, those whose prices are loosely linked, if at all, to the perceived value for the buyer, those who lack sophisticated tools to measure quality, and perhaps those that have relied too long on a single influential point of contact to sustain the relationship."[13]

It is time to face the procurement challenge head-on. Engage with procurement where you can. Enough said.

Don't forget *(a summary of the key points):*

- Procurement, as a function, is becoming an increasingly important player in the traditional law firm–client relationship.
- Take time to think through how procurement views the services you provide and you (as a supplier to their organization), and tailor your messages accordingly.
- Engage with procurement where you can.

13. *Id.* at 23.

Chapter 11

Preparing for Your Negotiation

It never ceases to amaze me how good lawyers are at negotiating on behalf of their clients, but often turn to jelly when being asked to negotiate with a client on behalf of their own firm.

As part of our Get the Price section, the focus on good negotiation skills is key. We've already discussed the rising influence of procurement and competitive tendering in our clients' law-provider assessment process. We've also touched on the topic of value, an understanding of which is vital when effectively communicating why a product or service is charged as it is.

However, this all counts for nothing if you then crumble during the negotiation with your client.

Although many are guided by the words of John F. Kennedy, who said, "Let us never negotiate out of fear. But let us never fear to negotiate,"[1] it is often easier said than done.

This chapter is going to give you some hints and tips about what you can do to strengthen and improve your existing negotiation capability, something you've had for much longer than you probably can remember. You have been negotiating ever since you were old enough to disagree with your parents about whether you should eat your green vegetables or not, or question why you cannot watch your favorite TV program during dinner. We

1. John F. Kennedy, Inauguration Speech (Jan. 20, 1961), *available at* http://www.jfklibrary.org/Asset-Viewer/BqXIEM9F4024ntFl7SVAjA.aspx?gclid=CNfcxqWst7gCFYo7Ogod9TMAdg.

all negotiate every single day with our colleagues, our partners, children, friends, and acquaintances. *Negotiation is an everyday event.*

It is also a skill that can be easily learned, and indeed there are a number of books (some of which are referenced under further reading) that will guide you in more detail through the process. What I'm looking to accomplish during this chapter is merely to stop you from making the silly mistakes that cost you, and also to give you an understanding of the overall negotiation framework.

Even the small steps mentioned here will add significant profit to your bottom line, whilst also ensuring that you have the right commercial framework for your matters, and hopefully a stronger client relationship.

What Is Meant by "Negotiation"

The term "negotiation" can mean different things to different people. For most, it typically means something along the lines of a formal discussion between people who are trying to reach an agreement or compromise. The fundamental requirement here is that there is a "gap" or difference in what both parties claim to want at the outset. It also, by definition, means that there has to be *at least two* or more parties involved, with the greater the number, the potentially greater complexity of the negotiation itself.

Another definition (and one for which I am indebted to John Morton, who taught me much about negotiation) is the following: a negotiation is "a transaction in which both parties have a veto on the outcome."

This, for me, sums it up quite well. In negotiation, we sometimes feel *obligated* to reach agreement, even if it is not in the best interests for either party. In John's alternative definition, he rightly points out that any party can actually say no, although we seldom do when seeking to win more legal work for our firm (whereas in our personal lives the converse is probably true—for example, when looking to buy an expensive item such as a car).

For those who have a more pessimistic view of fee negotiations, and negotiations more generally, the very act of negotiation can also be viewed as one or more of the following:

- a personal attack on the value that you are bringing to the client
- a way for the client to exert more control
- a way for the client to be more obstinate
- a form of rejection
- a block to developing a stronger relationship

However, we need to recognize that in today's environment, negotiation is merely a natural part of the buying process. It's also a chance for us to *demonstrate our commerciality*, something that clients are looking for us to demonstrate on their behalf if we are successful in winning the matter. It also provides a way to *strengthen our relationship* with the client and *increase overall client loyalty*. When put like that, it should not be seen as being so daunting and, *when done well*, is something very beneficial to your overall client relationship.

Some of these perceptions of negotiation may be in part due to the different styles of negotiation that exist. If you think back about your own experiences, you may recognize some of them, from the bluster, hard bargaining, and slightly aggressive style to those that are very conciliatory, calm, and productive. For example, if you've had the opportunity to travel overseas, especially to either the Middle East or Far East, you may come across haggling for your holiday trinket, which is all part and parcel of the buying process in some of these regions.[2]

But for those of us in legal services, it really boils down to two different stances. The first, sometimes known as *positional* negotiation, is where one party "wins" and the other "loses" (assuming there are only two parties in the negotiation). The second is more *collaborative*, where both parties feel

2. Steve Gates, The Negotiation Book: Your Definitive Guide to Successful Negotiating (Wiley 2011), provides a good summary of the different styles involved in negotiation. Chapter 2 discusses the negotiation clock face covering eight key types of negotiation behavior, ranging from those bartering and haggling through to dealing and to partnering.

that they have "won," or at least recognize that they both have something to gain from their agreement.

Positional negotiation is often characterized as one of suspicion, is competitive, is public or formal, and is generally intolerant to the other side's viewpoint and where parties can quickly become emotionally involved. It is also typically, for the reasons just listed, a one-off discussion. Once done, you're seldom tempted to go back. You may also hear of this type of negotiation referred to as *distributive*, where the parties compete over a fixed sum of value. In this instance, the key question is, who *claims the most value*, with the gain of one side being to the detriment of the other?

On the flipside, *collaborative* negotiation is one that is more trusting, is more tolerant, is more cooperative, and is one in which the parties are more emotionally detached (note that this is *not* the same as being disinterested) and is more informal. It's an approach that encourages a longer-term relationship and is one that is recommended for those of us working in the legal sector. This type of negotiation is also sometimes referred to as *integrative*, in which the parties cooperate to achieve maximum benefits by integrating their interests into an agreement. These types of deals are all about *creating value and claiming it.*[3]

What Makes a Good Negotiator?

What makes a good negotiator? In my view, what makes someone successful in this area is a combination of *being resourceful* (due to rapidly changing information as part of negotiation), of *being patient* (as you need to guide the other party to understand your point of view, this requiring more time), and of *being firm* (not only in the face of aggressive negotiators but also when you're seeking something from the other party or, indeed, when you're prepared to walk away). They also tend to see any fee negotiation as a good opportunity to create value through constructive dialogue and engagement with the other party (or parties).

3. Harvard Business Essentials, Negotiation 3 (2003).

It is also important not to confuse *negotiation* with *selling*. These are two distinct processes and skill sets. When engaging in selling, you focus on the value of your offering, and how this helps clients achieve their business objectives. It requires clear explanations, justification, and a well thought-through, rational case. Negotiation, on the other hand, is around the process of planning, questioning, listening to the other parties, and then making a (counter) proposal.

Those who are strong in negotiation also recognize that once you start negotiating, you have to stop selling. If you keep your head in "selling mode" during a negotiation, this implies that you feel the need to validate your proposal or value proposition to your client—which in turn means you are likely to make an unnecessary concession (that is, give away something of potential value that you did not need to). At this stage you need to forget selling (if your client was not interested in what you had to offer, you would not be at this stage anyway) and put yourself into a "negotiation mind-set." Doing so means, first, understanding the key stages of the negotiation "dance."

The Negotiation "Dance"

How do *you* approach a client fee negotiation? Do you take time to think through the process and plan accordingly, or is there the inclination to put the date and time of the meeting or call in the diary and then remember to think about it in a taxicab on the way to your meeting or a few minutes before your call? Perhaps the second scenario sounds extreme, but unfortunately is surprisingly common.

Many things have a beginning, a middle, and an end—a negotiation is no different, although we typically jump immediately to the middle. (This characteristic is part of a typical lawyer's personality trait, referred to as higher urgency—more on which later.)

The beginning is before you actually have that physical meeting: the planning phase.

The middle is then also typically split into three, this also having a beginning, a middle, and an end. However, in this context the beginning is where you are trying to determine the difference between your proposal and what the client is willing to pay (sometimes referred to as "finding the gap"). The middle here is then trying to reduce that gap. And the end? It's when you have reduced that gap and reached agreement.

Finally, what *all* good negotiators do is then review the performance—what went well, less well, and what would they change in future.

Figure 11.1 sums this up.

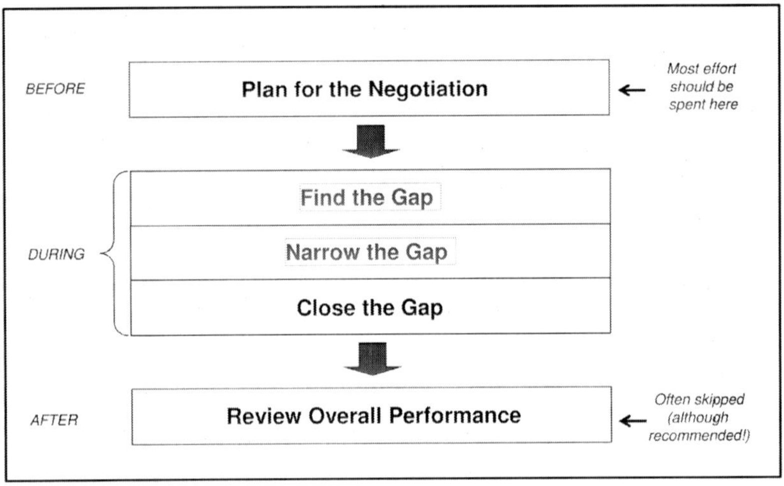

Figure 11.1
The Structure of a Typical Negotiation

Let's now take a closer look at each for the remainder of this chapter and the next.

Rehearsing Your Steps: Planning for Your Negotiation

Those who are seen as excellent negotiators didn't get there by chance, but by effort, application, *and above all planning*. The importance of planning for your negotiation cannot be emphasized enough, but what does it actually entail?

Although not an exhaustive list, it would cover a number of the following, some of which we will cover in more detail:

- having a strong understanding of all the relevant factors that may influence the outcome of the negotiation (for example, this may include any client feedback on previous performance on matters, likely competition, and what is influencing the client's decision)
- determining what potential negotiation items or areas there may be (for both parties) (obvious ones here include cost, but may also include proposed scope, timeline, fee arrangement structure, or even knowledge transfer)
- determining what information you wish to share, and wish to receive
- working out your negotiation "targets," potential concession approach, and walk-away points
- working out other, potentially more creative, strategies that you may wish to introduce during your negotiation

It is important also not just to focus on what your position should be but also *put yourself in your clients' shoes* and see it from their perspective. This is what the client's procurement professional will do (if they have them), so we need to too.

Those mythical "expert" negotiators we hear about but seldom see do this *and more*. They understand from the outset what levels or "negotiating chips" they have, and they know when to play their hand.

Consider the following:

- Preparation generates information.
- Information (in a negotiation context) is power (defined as the ability to influence the climate, style, strategy, and outcome of the negotiation).
- Preparation creates "power."
- *Preparation is 90 percent of negotiation.*

If information is therefore power, how do we start capturing it? Read on.

The Information Exchange

The more we know going into a negotiation the better. In terms of capturing information, there is a simple process that can help.

Getting Information

First, what information would you like to find out from your client? For example, this could include information around what its budget is for this matter (if not already shared), who the key decision makers are, if there is any event at the client that may impact the outcome of the matter, whether they have done this type of matter before, and who else they are speaking with.

Not all the questions asked will necessarily be answered, but we typically have an inner voice that recommends that we stay quiet and do not rock the boat. When asking these questions, you'll be pleasantly surprised at how frequently your client shares this information willingly.

Giving Information

Similarly, there will be some information that you are very keen to share with the client. The intent behind this is to strengthen your own negotiation position through managing *from the start* your client's expectations. Examples here may be your experience in conducting similar matters, reminding them how complex the matter may be (and by implication your ability to successfully deliver), or even how busy your firm is (again, with the implicit message that they need to act quickly to secure your services).

In sum, this is a great opportunity to influence the discussion from the start.

The "Do Not Share" Information

Just as there is information you are keen to impart and receive, there may be information that you do not want to share with your client.

How many times, when asked a direct question by someone, have you immediately and instinctively answered only to think a few minutes later, "Oops, I maybe should not have said that." Potentially worse is when you are asked the same question and appear evasive, either through an over-lengthy pause or some other characteristic that indicates to your client they may have raised an important point.

Although it may sound counterintuitive given that we may not intend to share certain types of information, it is important that we prepare for the eventuality that questions relating to this information are asked by the client, and that we have concise and readily prepared responses to deflect these questions.

I'm sure you can think of a number of things immediately that you would not wish to share in this context, but a typical example to illustrate the point could be your need to keep your immediate team busy (and therefore would be prepared to do the work at a much lower cost).

The "Where Did That Come from?" Information

There will always be a question you did not prepare for. One that comes completely from left field. Answer it as best you can, and move on.

Remember to also take some time to review any available resources you can within your firm or public sources to help you build your information "picture." And if going into the meeting with a colleague, make sure that they are also aware of which information you're looking to get, give, and, importantly, keep.

When I have delivered negotiation training courses, the one phrase I have used on many occasions to summarize what the training is looking to achieve is "*building greater commercial confidence*." Recognizing a lawyer's personality and reliance on rational and analytical thought, *nothing* contributes more to this objective than having a good grasp of this vital step. Be secure in your information.

Determining Your Targets, or When to Say Yes, and When to Say No

The last step prior to the negotiation itself is working out when you're likely to agree to the deal and, as importantly (yet often ignored), when you will gracefully say no.

When having fee discussions with our clients, we very rarely consider declining the opportunity, and yet with the benefit of hindsight (from a *financial* perspective at least), we probably should have on more than one occasion.

Back to Front: When to Say No

When planning your negotiation, think through when the deal, based on your current understanding, does *not* work out for you and where you are better off doing something else.

"Something else," in negotiation parlance, is often referred to as either a best realistic alternative, or BATNA (the acronym standing for the "best alternative to negotiated agreement"). My ex-colleague, Ori Weiner, refers to it simply as the "next best thing," and indeed this is exactly what it should be.[4] If you did not do this piece of work for this client, *what would* be the next best thing? Depending on your own circumstance, this could be doing work for one of your existing clients, engaging in a proactive business development activity, or even taking time out to recharge your batteries so you can come back more refreshed.

This position could be driven by having to provide an excessive discount to win the instruction, or timelines are seen to be too tight to allow you to successfully complete the matter with appropriate quality, or when you perceive that you're being used as a "stalking horse" to try to lower the existing provider's fee. You will know it when it appears.

The point here is that you *have an alternative*, an alternative that you have determined *from the outset*, rather than finding that you have either agreed to a deal that does not work for you (for whatever reason) or awkwardly declining the instruction (and let's face it, you'd be unlikely to do this step) in the heat of the battle. If you remember back to our alternative definition of a negotiation, what you have now done is defined your *veto*. With the multifaceted nature of negotiations today, it's recommended that you work out your veto for each of the *substantive issues* to be discussed (recognizing that some will be more important than others).

4. Ori has written a great book, which goes into many of the concepts outlined here in much greater detail and is an invaluable resource for those in the legal sector (or any professional service firm) wanting to understand more about fee negotiation. ORI WEINER, HIGH IMPACT FEE NEGOTIATION AND MANAGEMENT FOR PROFESSIONALS (2013).

Establishing Your Veto

You now have a clear point at which you can say, "no thank you." This means you now have some very defined limits (note: these may change in the light of new information shared during the negotiation itself and therefore it is good to keep in mind how you may wish to revise this position).

No lesser authority than Harvard has stated that no negotiator is in a "weaker position than one with no alternative to a deal. In this case, the other side can dictate the terms. . . . [Those parties without an alternative option are] . . . a deal *taker,* not a deal *maker.*"[5]

Now that you've established your alternative option to doing work on the matter, and given that you know your starting offer (which is likely to have been included within your proposal), you can now begin to work out the intermediate steps—that is, your negotiation approach.

Working Out the Steps

Now we should think through what our "targets" are. We know our extremes (and we may even have a good idea of our client's extremes too, as, remember, they will also have a veto).

Target setting significantly influences the eventual outcome of a negotiation. Despite its impact, it is the step that people most frequently get wrong.

There are differing views on how to set targets, with some suggesting you merely ask for more than you want (what Roger Dawson refers to as the "maximum plausible position") to others suggesting you add a fixed percentage markup on your price.[6] My personal approach, and the one I was trained in and would strongly recommend here (take a bow, John Morton), is one in which you set an *ambitious* target, one that is not too high but, importantly, not too low either (the latter more frequently done, leaving potential money on the table). In other words, the target should be *ambitious but also realistic.* Where we define this target will set the tone of the forthcoming negotiation.

5. Harvard Business Essentials, *supra* note 3, at 21.

6. Proposed by ROGER DAWSON, Secrets of Power Negotiating (1999), and PATRICK COLLINS, Talking Your Way to What You Want: Negotiate to Win! (2009), respectively.

Karrass and Target Setting

Studies have shown that those who achieve most when negotiating are those who set ambitious but realistic targets.

In one well-known experiment involving 100 professional negotiators from the aerospace industry, conducted by Dr. Chester L. Karrass (one of the original pioneers of negotiation training), it was found that

- those with higher aspirations got better results,
- they *always* "won" against those with lower aspirations (even when those with lower aspirations had greater negotiation skill and more perceived power), and
- those skilled negotiators who had higher aspirations won even when they had less power.

In sum, if you have set targets that are ambitious and realistic, you are more likely to do well.

Setting a "good" target is influenced by a number of different factors. First, by the quality of information you have available to you and any understanding you have of your client's potential veto. Next comes your own level of ambition (and confidence, in part supported by the information you've gathered), and finally your own negotiation skill and expertise.

One way to simply do this is to take a piece of paper, draw a straight line through the middle (left to right or vice versa) and at one end (left) put your veto (that is, the *lowest* number you would be prepared to accept before doing something else). At the other end, put your estimate of your client's veto (or the next best option). If you have been able to estimate your client's likely negotiation steps or increments, put these down on the paper too.

Everything in between the left-hand side of the line and the right-hand side of the line is now potentially where we *may* reach agreement with our client.

From here, we can now begin to work out what our potential negotiation steps or increments may be and, as importantly, what our initial or opening position will be.

Our opening position should be set at a level that allows us, through the process of negotiation, to achieve our target. Similarly, we need to ensure that we do not set this too high that we actually significantly exceed what we believe to be the client's veto, or otherwise it will be a very short conversation.

An example is shown in figure 11.2.

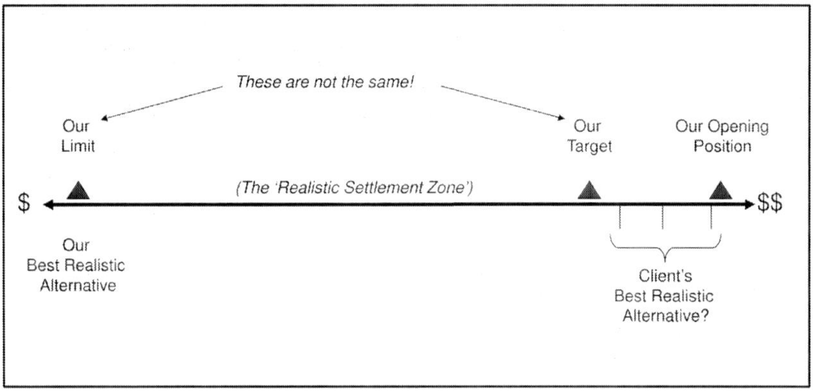

Based on the Harvard Negotiation Project approach (1978)

Figure 11.2
Establishing Your Target

There is one other useful consideration here. If you do not know much about your potential client on the other side, you may wish to consider a slightly *higher* opening position than you would under normal circumstances. This is for two reasons. The first is that you may only have some limited information on hand, and therefore have a risk that any assumptions you have made may be flawed. The second is that if this is a potentially new relationship, you will appear more cooperative if you make a larger concession.

You will not get this step right every time, but with experience, this process becomes easier and easier as you deliver your messages with greater commercial confidence.

So you have done your preparation—now it's time for the negotiation dance itself to begin.

Don't forget *(a summary of the key points):*

- We negotiate every day and have done so since birth. It is also a skill we can learn.
- A good negotiator seeks to create value for all parties (win-win). This is what we should strive to do in our client relationships.

- Preparation is vital and is probably 90 percent of negotiation. It gives you a solid grounding for the forthcoming discussion. Don't rush to the discussion itself or you may regret it.
- Better information (gained through preparation) helps you feel (and act) more confidently throughout the negotiation itself. It gives you greater commercial confidence.
- Think through in advance what information you wish to share, receive, and (as importantly) keep to yourself.
- Take time to think through what your targets are—what do you hope to achieve, what is your opening bid, and when do you "walk away"? Also put yourself in your client's shoes—what are their targets (to the best of your knowledge)?

Chapter 12

Conducting Your Negotiation

This is the time that the preparation (outlined in the previous chapter) pays dividends—the heat of the negotiation battle (or dance).

There are three main activities or stages that we go through at this time. The first is trying to *determine what the actual gap* between your proposal and your client's evaluation of the matter's worth is. The second is where you seek to try and bridge or *narrow the gap*. And the final one is where you seek to close the gap and reach a mutually acceptable *agreement*.

(There is one further stage we outlined in the negotiation process, that of doing a performance review after the negotiation has concluded. We will address this specific stage during one of our later chapters.)

So without further ado, let's have a look at the first stage, determining the gap.

Finding Your Rhythm: Determining the Gap

First Impressions Count

As we all know, first impressions count—no more so than in a negotiation. These opening exchanges can have a significant impact on the overall outcome.

Similar to how your parents, partner, or boss may have told you for social or business meetings, you need to be confident and demonstrate confidence (but not any arrogance) from the outset.

There may be people in this meeting (or the call if not meeting face-to-face) who you are being introduced to for the first time (potentially from the client's procurement team) or you know well.

It is therefore important to *strike the right tone*, and also—especially if dealing with multinational clients—being culturally aware and sensitive, as this, too, may dictate how long the initial introduction lasts for (this being anywhere from two to three minutes in the United States to significantly longer in some Asian countries and range from a perfunctory exchange of business cards and handshakes to more wide-ranging discussion). Before attending the meeting, ask your colleagues what their experiences have been if they have worked with this client or similar.

Even at this very early stage, you need to be projecting an atmosphere of trust among all parties—as these first impressions count and they *do* matter. Projecting confidence is also very helpful in a number of ways. First, if people believe that you are confident, they will be more inclined to believe that you are competent, and finally, with other people treating you as more competent, you will also begin to feel more confident. All in all, a virtuous circle!

Getting Down to Business

Okay. You've done the "meet and greet" (hopefully well), and now it's time to get down to business. This is the time when all your hard work in preparing for the negotiation pays off.

It is here that you now begin to exchange and trade information. Before going into this in more detail, I want to quickly highlight a technique used by many successful negotiators to get this process off on the right footing—the three-button (or opening) statement.

The Negotiator's Secret: The "Three-Button Statement"

One of the most powerful negotiation techniques is the opening statement, one always used by good negotiators. This is also sometimes referred to as the "three-button statement," based on the three key topics addressed at this stage. These are relationship, power, and agreement.

I confess that when I was still earning my negotiation stripes, I was a bit skeptical as to the utility of the three-button statement but quickly became a convert, as it is immensely powerful.

The *order of the statement is very important.*

Relationship comes first—this is a short statement about the overall proposal you have made and your current (or desired) relationship with your client. *Then* power. This is where you implicitly refer that you have some power (that is, something the other party wants—for example, specific expertise in this type of work, previous familiarity with a similar matter for the client, etc.). And finally, agreement. This is where you indicate that you believe that agreement between all parties is possible, and also starts generating some momentum toward reaching a deal.

The timing of when you use this is also important. It is *not* the first thing you will launch into, as you will (hopefully) have some more social, introductory conversations first. However, it is done early, when beginning to share and exchange information (remember the last chapter?).

Why not at the start? Because good negotiators will potentially adjust their statement based on the early exchanges of information (specifically the power button—for example, when you may find out in discussion that our client needs the matter concluded very quickly).

Its overall intention is to help signal or flag to the other side that the relationship is perhaps more balanced (or even slightly weighted in your favor) than they may have originally have thought. It also allows you to signpost potential themes you may wish to return to later during the negotiation itself.

A very basic example is outlined below to give you a flavor of what this can look like.

- "We are very pleased to be able to meet with you again today to discuss our proposal on XYZ matter." (the relationship button)
- "As you may know, we have worked on the last five significant matters of this type for clients very similar to yourself, clearly understand the issues, and have achieved favorable outcomes in all." (the power button)
- "I am sure that, after today's discussion, we will be able to come to an agreement as to how we can best jointly proceed." (the agreement button)

Try now saying the three statements on the previous page in a different order. It just doesn't have the same impact. Remember: *RPA*—relationship then power then agreement.

Don't use the same statement every time, though! It should be short, concise and to the point. You don't need to spend lots of time changing the basic structure, but you *do* need to modify, tweak, and adjust for each specific client instance . . . and then practice it so it sounds confident and credible.

Exchanging Information

What this step does is helps confirm the basis of the negotiation. It gives you an opportunity to check any assumptions you may have made on scope, fee structure, timing, and so forth. It helps you identify any potential risks of constraints that impact the matter. And it also allows you to check and gently probe what is of key importance to your client.

What you don't want to do in this stage is merely engage in asking questions, and telling your (prospective) client your information. This should be a trade of information, and this helps build trust for the negotiation to come and also allows you to better manage the flow of information you wish to give, get, and keep. I would also recommend that at this stage you try to communicate the important information early, but at an appropriate level of detail.

When asking questions, also try making these as open ended as possible. And when asking questions, *listen to the answers*. In our professional life, we have probably attended one or more effective presentation courses, but I think I can safely state that only a small number of us, if any, have attended an effective listening course, and yet this skill is so important when negotiating. Not only is hearing what is said important, but as Peter Drucker observed, "The most important thing in communication is hearing what *isn't* said."[1]

1. Peter Drucker, quote available at http://leadershipdynamics.wordpress.com/2012/03/29/more-leadership-insights-from-peter-drucker.

Indeed, a study conducted by Neil Rackham and John Carlisle, which monitored the behavior of labor and contract negotiators engaged in actual transactions, noted the following,[2] also shown in table 12.1.

Skilled negotiators ask twice the number of questions that average negotiators do. The questions asked were done so with a specific purpose, to elicit real information and then to test their understanding, with the skilled negotiators then summarizing where they felt both parties were in the process. Oh, and they listened to the other party's answers. (These findings have since been reproduced, with similar results, in a number of other professions.)

Table 12.1: The Extent of Information Gathering Behaviors

Activity	Skilled Negotiators	Average Negotiators
Asking questions	21.3%	9.6%
Testing for understanding	9.7%	4.1%
Summarizing	7.5%	4.2%
Total	38.5%	17.9%

Source: Based on table 8.1, G. RICHARD SHELL, BARGAINING FOR ADVANTAGE 145 (Viking 1999).

Ready, Aim, Fire!

Now the hard bit. Giving your initial number. Do this well, and the rest of the negotiation will go relatively smoothly. Do this badly, and you're solely in damage control mode. Given these two options, let's make sure you're given the tools to do this well then.

First, your opening position needs to be credible in its content (that is, *what* you say). As we talked about during our previous chapter around target setting, the opening position is to be both *ambitious and realistic.* And remember, you're never going to get anything better than this number as part of the negotiation.

2. *See* G. Richard Shell, Bargaining for Advantage 144–46 (1999).

We also need to make sure the client understands what they are getting for that number. This is sometimes referred to as the package. This should cover not only the proposed fee but elements such as scope, timing, fee arrangements, and payment terms. And the number should be given *at the end.*

Why? Think back to some negotiations you've had in the past, whether when you have been buying a car, a house, a holiday, or something for your office. As the discussion progressed, you were probably waiting for one thing—the number! You have everybody's full attention until you give the number. Once you do, however, the other party immediately begins to compare that number with the one that they had in mind (is it too high, too low?), with those potentially other competing law firms (are you charging so much more or less than X), and so on; they completely miss anything you say after that point.

Many a matter has come unstuck because one party did not hear the conditions to the opening number. Don't fall into the same trap. Give the number *at the end.* Be clear what the number is (for example, if offering a percentage discount, state clearly what the final amount will be). Also be wary of giving ranges—the client will hear the number they *want* to hear, and that is always the *lower* number. What I've seen work successfully here is being clear about what the lower number covers in terms of scope, etc. first, and then being clear what the other (higher) number covers.

And then don't speak—everything after that point (that is, giving the number) will sound like apology or justification and therefore weakens the impact of what you just said.

So not only do we need to focus on what we say, but also *how we say it.*

The opening position is to be delivered confidently. It needs to be delivered in a manner that is clear, deliberate, and firm. There is no room for "ums" and "ers" when giving the number. Similarly, when giving the number, do not use what is referred to as "floppy language." Examples of floppy language include phrases such as "We were hoping for . . ." and "We were looking for . . ." and "How about . . . ."

If you do not deliver your opening number credibly, how is your client supposed to take that offer credibly? Also be aware of your body language, especially body language that appears defensive or lacking confidence. For example, don't avoid eye contact when giving the number as this gives the impression that you are embarrassed by the offer you are making. Make sure you keep the tone of your voice constant (which is not the same as speaking in monotone). This is the step, above all others, that you want to *practice, practice, practice.*

When Do I Give My Number? (Or Should I Go First or Second?)

A question people often ask about negotiation is whether they should make their offer first or second. Indeed, there is much debate within negotiation literature as to what the right approach is.

Human nature in these situations, particularly if uncomfortable or unfamiliar with negotiation, is to want to go second. This in part is because you want to hear what the other person's offer is, and hope that consequently your offer is going to look very good. By going second, you may get a pleasant surprise for your client's opening offer, but in reality this is just down to luck.

Going first has a number of advantages, particularly when negotiating any type of professional service. The key advantage is that by going first you are providing a very strong anchor. This then means that you are negotiating from your own number. An additional benefit is that by negotiating from your own number you can also then begin to influence the client's perception of what the appropriate range of fee should be for this type of work. It is much better to be negotiated down from your number, than try to negotiate the client up from its.

Certainly in my experience, I've heard of a number of stories where the client was maybe not as aware of the complexity of the project and therefore had not appreciated the potential cost of conducting the matter appropriately. By going first, you can then begin to set the more appropriate expectation, and then discuss from that point on how best to achieve your client's objectives.

My own view is that it is better to go first, not only for the reasons outlined above, but also a more practical one. The client is more likely to want you to propose a number than them providing you one at the start.

Going first, therefore, can also help avoid the awkward silence (although remember, silence is good in a negotiation), as in most businesses there is expectation that the seller (you) goes first. Although there are a couple of situations where it may make sense to go second, these are relatively few and far between, so I haven't covered them here for the sake of simplicity.

Recognizing the Difference Between Interests and Positions

As a negotiator, it's important to recognize the difference between somebody's *position* and somebody's *interest*. Interests and positions are not the same.

Interests, which are often not stated, drive people's stated positions as part of negotiation. By stating your position, you are setting out your stall from where you will negotiate from. Consequently, these are often stated early on in the negotiation, with the other party (or parties) reacting to these without finding out what underlies the position itself. Interests, on the other hand, are the concerns and motivations of those parties in the negotiation, which we really need to uncover to be able to effectively satisfy the other parties' needs, and share our own so that these can also be taken into consideration during the negotiation dance.

The most frequently told story or example used to highlight the difference between positions and interests concerns two sisters, each of whom wants the single remaining orange in a bowl. Each claims to the other that she needs the whole fruit. That is each sister's position. However, when their mother asks each sister in turn why they want the orange, the first sister replies that she wants to drink some freshly squeezed orange juice. The other sister wants to use the orange rind to bake a cake. The reasons that each sister wanted the orange—that is, their interests—in this case are not mutually exclusive. As you probably can predict, especially if a parent yourself, the wise mother merely grated off the rind from the orange, then squeezed the juice out. Each sister then gets her "whole" orange.

The moral of the story? The most effective way to address issues in negotiation is to focus on interests. We can easily identify interests just by asking some very simple questions such as "why" and "why not." Through effective questioning, listening, probing, and summarizing, we can therefore have much more mutually rewarding negotiations.

The Flinch

There is one final step to these initial, opening exchanges. It is using a technique adopted by experienced negotiators called "the flinch," so it is best to be aware of this so you know how to appropriately respond.

This is delivered immediately after they have heard the other party's proposal, and is used as a nonverbal signal that the number they have just heard is not acceptable. The reason that flinching is seen as critical is because, as Roger Dawson points out in his book *The Secret of Power Negotiating*, "most people believe *what they see* more than what they hear."[3]

Although a gross generalization, if you don't see a flinch from the other side, it generally means that the number you have just given was in line with their thinking (give or take). Also remember that the other side has also heard about "the flinch" and therefore may be using it as well, so don't assume that a flinch signals displeasure from the other side. Confused? I know I am.

But it *is* effective, and it may give you the opportunity to negotiate a more attractive outcome if you feel comfortable adopting such a technique.

The best flinches are those that are practical in tone. At first it will feel unnatural. If interested in adopting this approach—and I confess it is not for everyone—give it a go in front of a mirror and see how you feel. (If using as part of a negotiation, as a safety precaution, I also suggest that you should give a *verbal* signal when delivering a flinch. Often the person giving you the number may not be looking directly at you and your nonverbal signal may therefore be wasted.)

What to Expect at This Stage

Roger Dawson in his book talks of "negotiation gambits" (indeed, the first 25 chapters of his book focus on these different approaches[4]). These are techniques often adopted by trained negotiators to exert power during the negotiation itself.

Although there are a number of gambits that can be used during this time, the three you are most likely to see at the stage will probably be

- the *beauty contest* (where you are informed that your competitor's offer is better);

3. Roger Dawson, Secrets of Power Negotiating 31 (1999) emphasis added.
4. *Id.* at 13–123.

- the *limited budget* (that is, “we only have $10,000 for this matter”); and/or
- the *tight deadline* (that is, “we need to agree to the deal today”).

Being aware of, and more importantly being prepared for, these will stand you in good stead.

Some suggestions on how to mitigate each of these are briefly covered below. If you want to find out more, a simple search on the Internet or some of the books in the suggested reading section will also provide you with much food for thought.

The Beauty Contest

- Your clue: “Your competitor’s offer is better/cheaper/etc.”
- Suggested mitigating action or response:
  - Ensure that services or products being evaluated are *truly* comparable (that is, an apples to apples comparison).
  - Emphasize areas of service or product differentiation, and value being delivered.

The Limited Budget

- Your clue: “We only have a budget of $10,000 for this matter.”
- Suggested mitigating action or response:
  - Question what is driving the budgeted figure.
  - Ask if there is someone else who may be able to find more budget (you never know!).
  - Amend the specification of your original offer to match budget (if you still are of the view you can successfully support the matter with this reduction in scope).
  - Explore whether contingent-based fee approaches may be appropriate here, to help reduce initial outlay.

The Tight Deadline

- Your clue: “I need you to agree to the deal today.”
- Suggested mitigating action or response:

- ◦ Question what is driving the deadline (is this business driven or personal?). Note: I have been in situations where there have been tight deadlines imposed, only to subsequently discover it was because the respective clients were going on holiday and wanted it done before that time.

Moving Together: Narrowing the Gap

You reach this stage once you have established what the gap is between yourself and your client.

This could either be a specific gap between your opening position and your client's opening position, or could be between your opening position and an implied gap based on client reaction (for example, if they say something along the lines of "that won't work").

This stage is all about narrowing those points of difference—that is, narrowing the gap. It is also at this stage that most of the tactical mistakes are made by an inexperienced negotiator, yet fortunately for us are relatively easy to fix.

There are normally three approaches used to try to narrow this gap.

These are, in typical order of adoption:

- reason (that is, convincing the other party on the strength of your argument and logic);
- power (that is, bargaining with the other party); and finally,
- creativity (that is, where you seek to generate options for mutual gain and you try to solve the problem).[5]

As said above, this is the *typical order* of adoption but not necessarily the *right one*. Although those of us in the practice of law tend toward reason (or argument) as our natural mode of operation, this does not work as well in the

5. Ori Weiner, High Impact Fee Negotiation and Management for Professionals (Kogan Paul 2013). Chapter 12 covers this in a good amount of detail for those wanting to find out what Ori refers to as "the ultimate negotiation skill."

typical negotiation with our clients unless we feel we have a strong case (or rationale) and they are prepared to look at issues on their respective merits.

Don't Wait to Be Creative

Imagine the following scenario:

Both parties recognize that there's a gap in the expectation as to what the matter will cost. Each party then tries to reason with the other, trading arguments back and forth, but to no avail. One party then tries to start using the power mode, bargaining with the other, again to no avail. And only then do they consider moving to the third mode, creativity.

Now ask yourself this. If you were on the receiving end of this exchange, how willing are you now likely to be when the other party, out of sheer frustration, says that "we should see how we can make this work for us"? I would wager that "not very" is the answer.

There are a couple of other observations to make about this stage.

- Discussion at this point tends to becomes less scripted or planned, with potentially more people participating in the conversation.
- You are also likely to be still exchanging information, although this may become more detailed than in previous steps.
- You often need to adjourn during this stage to give yourself the opportunity to regroup and reevaluate your approach (more on which later).

Making Concessions: The "Rules"

Avoiding "Gifts"

The first rule to remember is quite simple. Don't "gift" your concessions. In other words, don't give something unless you're getting something back in return. Why? Because if you do, you will find that you are asked again and again for more concessions without anything in return. After all, from a client's perspective, if you don't ask you don't get.

"If You, Then We"

Language is a funny thing sometimes. Similar to what we talked about when placing the number at the end of what you are proposing, the phrase "if you, then we . . ." operates on the same principle. It is also a clear indicator of your willingness to move.

As an example, if the client is looking for a further 5 percent discount, you may choose to say something similar to the following: "if you can introduce us to the head of Department X/allow us to pitch on the next X matters, then we would be able to give you a further 5 percent discount." Whether the client agrees to this request or not, the important thing is that the demand for a further 5 percent is *clearly linked* to a concession that they need to make as well. If the client asks for a 5 percent discount and you respond differently, you are unlikely to get the chance to request, and therefore potentially receive, any concession you were looking for.

These phrases would typically be more general at the start of the negotiation trading process, but will become more detailed and specific as the discussion continues. For example, this may be along the lines of "if you consider lowering your price, then we may be able to offer you additional work" at the start of proceedings, only to develop into "if you offer a further 10 percent discount, then we will allow you to bid on the next transaction" toward the end.

Never be afraid to ask for something at this stage, but when you do, remember the extremely useful phrase "if you, then we." It makes a statement, it avoids interruption, and (importantly) it makes you think about the trade-off.

A Fair Trade?

Something else to watch for is the *flow of concessions* from one party to the other. What you're trying to achieve in a negotiation is a fair flow of concessions from one side to the other. The reason you asked for concessions is because you have placed a value or the client has placed a value on that specific item.

(Note: It is also good practice to record the concessions made during the discussion, as this helps prove a useful reminder to monitor the flow, but it also allows you to record these items as appropriate when seeking to document the agreement.)

You may never get this to be a one-to-one match (the goal of the very best negotiators), but as long as it's in the right ballpark, that's fine.

You Know You Need Them, So *Plan*

It is important to *plan for your concessions*, as you will inevitably need to make some during the course of any negotiation.

Some concessions are more important than others. Some have a clear and tangible financial value, others less so. Similarly, concessions do not have the same value necessarily for each party in the negotiation. What you value highly may be relatively insignificant to the other party and therefore one that they would willingly give if requested, and vice versa. This is known as a concept of variable value, and is something that good negotiators look to leverage as much as possible.

An Example of Variable Value

A good example of this was from some client feedback given after a proposal. This was dealing specifically around value-added features of the proposal that would be offered in addition to the discount on fees. Typically these value-added items include access to specific seminars, publications, potentially precedents and templates, and even sometimes to seconded staff.

As part of the feedback given, the client commented that "all the usual things were there." However, what it would find most valuable was actually for the law firm to be its "eyes and ears" in the market and give feedback on any insights they picked up in their attendance at conferences and similar. If you take a minute to think about it, the cost to the law firm of doing this was negligible as they are likely to be attending these conferences anyway, yet the value to the client was significant as it did not have the resources to do similar, or the insight to distill the relevant core legal messages.

On the flip side, there are also many law firms offering client secondments. As a result, clients sometimes now place more limited value on these, whereas, to the law firm, this can be at a significant "opportunity cost" to them of doing so.

In Ori's book, there is a great section on concession strategy, which addresses both the timing and the size and sequence of concessions.[6] There are pros and cons to each approach, but a good guide is to make sure that when

6. *Id.* at ch.10.

you're giving concessions, these get smaller and smaller over time. It is typically better to deal with the more substantive concessions at the start—the smaller the concession signals to the other party there is less likelihood of further substantive concessions to come.

This also brings me to another key tip that I summarize as "don't negotiate in fives." How many times have you seen a volume discount structure go from 5 percent to 10 percent to 15 percent and potentially beyond? We all tend to like round numbers. We like numbers to end in 0 or 5. (Indeed, there is a whole field of pricing psychology that discusses why items are priced ending in 99 cents rather than a round dollar.) When it comes to our fee negotiations, though, what's stopping us from going 5 percent, 6 percent, and 6.25 percent? Here the concessions are getting smaller and smaller, so we are achieving that objective. Additionally, the *more precise* the number is, the better, as this clearly conveys to your client that you are approaching the end of your negotiating range, which should be aligned with the value of the service you are offering to the client. Whilst I'm not advocating you start offering percentage discounts of 6.875 percent, you hopefully get the picture.

Maintaining Momentum

Acknowledging progress is good during negotiation. It reminds both parties you are getting closer to the agreement that you hopefully outlined as part of your three-button statement. Remember to take some time to do this.

"I Need a Break": The Power of an Adjournment

The final rule I would like to cover in this section is the appropriate use of adjournments.

For those of you who participated in eBay auctions, you will appreciate that sometimes you can get caught up in the heat of the moment and place a bid for something that is accepted, only to—with the advantage of calm reflection—realize that you bid more than you intended and that the item actually wasn't worth that much after all (at least to you).

The same can happen in negotiation, and this is where an adjournment or temporary break in the proceedings can prove extremely useful. This may be due to new information being revealed that may impact your proposal, or the other party's counteroffer that you need to digest, or it may be that you'd want to check that you've covered everything that you needed to cover.

An adjournment is merely a break in negotiations, agreed to by both parties. It may be relatively short and sweet or more lengthy, and can be used in any negotiation. Remember that it also creates an expectation that there will be new information or a new proposal to be submitted, so you need to manage that expectation carefully.

There are also a few guiding principles you should adopt when looking to have an adjournment. These are outlined below:

- State your need for an adjournment, and the reason that it is required (this may be simply because you want some breathing space to go to the bathroom).
- Suggest and agree on the duration of it.
- Gather up your materials and leave politely (any delay in doing so may provide the other party with an opportunity to try to continue the negotiation).
- When restarting, provide a summary of where you were in the negotiation before the adjournment took place so that everybody is on the same page.
- Also when restarting, avoid bringing new issues to the table initially after the adjournment (if you need to bring up new issues, it is better to do so once the negotiation is back in full swing).

What to Expect at This Stage

As in our previous section, there are a number of gambits that can be used during this time by good negotiators, but those you are most likely to encounter will probably be

- the *salami slice* (where we don't realize we have given away most of the salami sausage because it is being taken slice by slice);
- *jumbled numbers* (where the client seeks to confuse you intentionally or otherwise);
- the concept of *limited authority*; and
- *silence*.

These approaches may be used against you in your negotiation, but remember that you can also use them (and those mentioned in the previous section) too (but please use in an ethical and responsible manner). This does not need to be one-way traffic.

The Salami Slice

- Your clue: the other party seeks to negotiate and gain concessions on *each specific item* by specific item.
- Suggested mitigating action or response:
    - Note the issue and come back to it later, once you have a more comprehensive picture of what the client is actually after in totality.

Jumbled Numbers

- Your clue: the other party seems to be using a wide array of numbers, or is introducing a high volume of issues or facts with the potential intent to confuse and seek to implement a one-sided agreement.
- Suggested mitigating action or response:
    - Listen, and don't be afraid to ask for clarification.

The Concept of Limited Authority

- Your clue: the other party states that it only has the authority to agree to a certain level (funnily enough, this level is almost certainly below that at which you wish to agree).
- Suggested mitigating action or response:
    - Check the party's authority at the outset.
    - Ask to speak to the person who is able to make the decision.

As an aside, some of the best adopters of this last approach are those you'd expect to be less willing to use it. I've typically found that there are more "senior" partners who effectively utilize this technique than anyone else (ironically, those who are probably in a position to make the decision on their own rather than consulting with their fellow colleagues). Importantly, what it does do is it gives them *time to think* and come back with a reasoned counterproposal. If they can do it, what, apart from pride, is stopping you from doing it?

- There is another variant of this, which is the "call for higher authority"—that is, "I need to get my boss to speak to your boss."
    - This is used most frequently as an implicit threat to try to encourage more concessions to be given as part of the negotiation. Your mitigating approach here is to arrange for your "higher authority" person to have a discussion with the equivalent person—that is, you are calling the bluff, but you do need to be there to follow through if required! It is also very effective. If the other party believes that it is only dealing with you, it will focus all its efforts trying to convince you of its position and therefore may not try as hard to offer concessions.
    - This approach works most effectively if the higher authority is a group or entity such as your management committee or pricing committee. If a single individual, the other party may just want you to phone immediately or ask why he or she was not in the meeting in the first place!

Silence

- Your clue: silence!
- Suggested mitigating action or response:
    - Ask an open-ended question.
    - Ask whether there are any points to have clarified.
    - Propose a break for coffee.
    - Stress "disappointment" in the stall in the discussions.

Use silence, but don't be used by it. Many people when faced with silence continue to offer more concessions until they get some sort of verbal reaction. Think through how you will deal with silence in advance.

The Final Bow: Closing the Gap

When you feel that you have discussed all your key points, and sense that you are nearing agreement, there can be the temptation to rush to the close. But beware. Like the two main phases already discussed above—finding and narrowing the gap—seasoned negotiators often adopt a number of gambits here too.

Anecdotal evidence has "proved" that sometimes the majority concessions are actually given at this stage in a rush by inexperienced negotiators to seal the deal. Don't let that be you.

When should you look to close the deal then? There are a number of factors that can influence this, but normally you need at least two of the following:

- The 'gap' is narrow.
- There are no more concessions coming from the other party.
- Your client begins to ask implementation-orientated questions (note that this on its own is not enough, they may just be seeking more information).
- They are expressing a high degree of interest (for example, through their body language).
- You have reached your target price (or, conversely, you have reached your limit).

Once you think you are there, double-check to make sure that there are no outstanding issues still remaining. If no issues remain, you and your client are now able to agree to the final proposal. Although the temptation is to breathe a huge sigh of relief and then leave, don't—at least not yet.

Many a deal has come unstuck at this point, but there are four simple things you can do to avoid this.

- Summarize the agreement.
- Secure everyone's commitment (this may mean literally asking everyone in the room whether they agree).
- Record the agreement (so there is documentary proof—you may also want to offer to draft the written agreement).
- *And only then*, close the meeting (and don't keep talking, *at least not about the deal*, or else your carefully crafted deal may begin to unravel!).

What to Expect at This Stage

Unsurprisingly, there are a few gambits or tactics here too. These can feel even harder to address than the previous ones as they can play on your potential vulnerability now that you think you are near a deal and are probably mentally exhausted.

You're most likely to encounter (or use!) one or more of the following:

- the nibble
- "Yes, but" (which is closely related to our friend, the salami slice)
- Splitting the difference

One approach that you may have expected to see here but don't is the classic "Good Cop, Bad Cop" routine. The main reason I have not included it here is that in our professional environment we tend not to come across this too often, as we tend to try to focus more on developing relationships with the other party rather than adopting a potentially more confrontational approach. If you spot it (and it is easy to spot), highlight it, and they will most likely stop due to their embarrassment at being caught. (If wanting to find out more on this (or indeed others not included), check out the suggested sources in the chapter footnotes.[7])

The Nibble

- Your clue: A number of minor points or issues are raised late in the proceedings—that is, trying to get a little bit extra (either pre-agreement or, worse, after agreement).
- Suggested mitigating action or response:
  - Withdraw the concessions you have already made.
  - Make new counterdemands.
  - Play the "higher authority" card (for example, "I need to check with my pricing committee on this").

7. Dawson, *supra* note 2, is very good on this topic. Another source (which is surprisingly comprehensive) is *Negotiation Tactics*, CHANGING MINDS, http://changingminds.org/disciplines/negotiation/tactics/tactics.htm.

- ○ Make the other party feel "cheap" about the request (but do so in a good-natured manner!).

The main reason this approach tends to work is that by asking for a "small" thing (a nibble) it makes it appear mean if the other person refuses. Typically, when one party believes that a deal has nearly been (or has been) agreed, they tend to give in on small details easily.

The "Yes, But"

- Your clue: Every time you agree to a demand they make another one.
- Suggested mitigating action or response:
  - ○ Make sure that all issues are put "on the table," and check throughout with questioning.
  - ○ Withdraw previous concessions.
  - ○ Make new counterdemands.

The "Hmm, And"

If tempted to use the "Yes but . ." tactic yourself, a more positive approach on this (and one that exhibits less of a defensive reaction) is the "Hmm, and" approach. Here you raise the same concern but in a much more positive manner. For example, rather than "Yes, but we can only do this at the price quoted this week," you could say, "Hmm, and we can only keep this price this week as we have a new matter commencing next week."

"Let's Split the Difference"

- Your clue: Your client suggests to you that you both split the difference, after all agreeing a solution that is halfway between two positions appears to be fair, and hence can be difficult to refuse.
- Suggested mitigating action or response:
  - ○ Remember that splitting the difference is not necessarily fair. The halfway point can be very advantageous to one party or the other. In addition, you can do this more than once.

- Play the "higher authority" card, as it gives you some time to think whether this is fair to both parties.

It is better not to offer to split the difference yourself, but encourage the other party to do so, as it then puts them in a position of suggesting a compromise. You can then accept the proposal "reluctantly," thus making them feel that they have won the negotiation. If you are still intent on doing this yourself, try to make the situation one in which a halfway position is actually still a very agreeable solution for you.

Avoiding the Common Negotiation Pitfalls

In closing, there are a number of recommended approaches to help you avoid the most commonly identified negotiation mistakes, which I've highlighted in table 12.2.

Table 12.2: Recommended Approaches to Avoid the Common Negotiating Pitfalls

Have a plan (and don't forget to prioritize your key objectives)	Build a package for your proposal (with the elements of your proposal at the front, and the number at the end)
Make sure your proposal is clear and that you understand the basis of any counterproposal	Always use "If you, then we . . ."
Don't argue to win—listen, question, and respond appropriately	Do not negotiate (or discount) in "fives"
Put yourself in your clients' shoes; see the negotiation from their perspective	When making concessions, these should get smaller and smaller
Value concessions made by the other side (and say so), but also make sure you understand the value of your own	Summarize and document the agreement
Trade your concessions, don't give unilaterally	

Avoiding these, and implementing the approaches outlined above, will go a long way in helping you have the best commercial "starting point" for your matter.

In closing, the entomology of the word "negotiation," "Negotium" (from "Nec Otium"), means literally "not leisure."[8]

Although it will never become a leisure pursuit for most of us, hopefully applying some of the approaches highlighted in this and the preceding chapter will mean it at least becomes a bit easier and less daunting. One final comment: Do not try to adopt all the techniques outlined all at once. Try a couple of things, get comfortable with using them (or recognizing them), and then try a few more.

Good luck in your next negotiation!

Don't forget *(a summary of the key points):*

- Like a good novel, every negotiation has a beginning, a middle, and an end. Recognize what stage you are at, and react accordingly.
- Building rapport is essential to any negotiation—do not rush to the details.
- When presenting your initial offer, do so confidently—it needs to be *credible in content and in delivery* (remember, you will never get anything better than this number as part of the negotiation).
- Give your number at the *end* of your statement (and then keep quiet). It ensures your client's full attention to what the number includes.
- Skilled negotiators ask *twice* the amount of questions as average negotiators do—ask more pertinent questions when you can (you may find out something useful).
- Don't wait to be creative in how to seek agreement. This approach is often used last—use it first.
- Plan your concessions. What do you want? What are you prepared to offer? And what value do you (and your client) place on each?

8. *Negotiation*, WIKIPEDIA, http://en.wikipedia.org/wiki/Negotiation (last updated Dec. 31, 2013).

- There are a number of well-known negotiation gambits or techniques adopted throughout *any* negotiation—recognize and react to each accordingly.
- And finally, never negotiate in "fives"!

Step Three: Manage to Price

Chapter 13

The Rise of Legal Project Management

There is perhaps no other legal topic which has gathered as much attention in the legal press, blogs, and at conferences in recent years than the topic of legal project management (LPM), with the possible exception of pricing and alternative/appropriate fee agreements.

In this chapter, I'm going to give a very brief overview to the rise of legal project management to help set the scene for our subsequent chapters on this quickly emerging and critical area.

This will give us a grounding as to why such attention is being given to this topic by both law firms and clients alike, and the value to both that the successful adoption of legal project management will deliver. There are a number of excellent publications elsewhere that go into legal project management in much more detail, which I have also included within the bibliography for your information.

Why All the Fuss?

Project management has been around in its current guise at least since the mid-1950s in a wide variety of industries and professions. In 1969 the Project Management Institute was established, with its prime objectives being increasing greater communication and sharing best practices in the field. Indeed, project management as a discipline is used on a daily basis by other professional services organizations such as consultants and accountants, architects, and construction workers, to name just a few, but only recently explicitly adopted within law firms.

Even arguably in the legal world, it could also be seen as not *that* unusual, with Bruce McEwen (a noted legal commentator and president of Adam Smith, Esq.) observing that "every time you run a matter for your firm you are engaging in project management." After all, lawyers do plan matters, they do (hopefully) delegate appropriate responsibilities, and they seek to deliver their matters to the appropriate level of quality, don't they?

Another noted commentator in this field, Steven Levy, observed (in my favorite LPM-related quote of all time): "All projects are managed. Some are managed deliberately, some inadvertently. Deliberate project management is better." Again, this tacitly acknowledged that lawyers do—at least to some extent—manage their matters.

So why all the fuss? Well, in April 2010, an article in the *Canadian Lawyer* noted that "project management is so new to the legal professional that everyone is still trying to figure out what it can do and how to make it work." In some respects we still are . . . a few more years further down the line. Indeed, only as of late 2010 was there a specific group within the Project Management Institute dedicated to the area of legal project management. However, the key comes back to Steven's observation—*deliberate, and more structured*, project management is better. It is the focus on those four italicized words that is driving current attention.

Coupled with the increasing adoption of using non-hourly methods of billing (such as fixed or contingent-based fees), clients and law firms alike are now needing to determine (and execute) the most cost-effective and efficient approaches when conducting matters in a more effective fashion.

Now is therefore the right time to *take out the mystery and put back the pragmatism* as to what legal project management is. What do I mean by this? Be pragmatic in recognizing that LPM is really only a better way to manage matters—something that you do day in and day out—sometimes very well, perhaps other times less so. Although LPM brings into play more formal processes, tools, techniques, and technologies, at its most fundamental level, it is about managing your matter well. See it for what it is.

Also, don't feel as if you have to try to do everything at once—do a couple of things at a time, get comfortable with them, then introduce a few more changes, and so on. It really is like the question "How do you eat an elephant?" (The answer, in case you don't know, is "in small bits.")

Defining LPM

LPM can mean different things to different people. Indeed, in a recent ALM survey on the topic, it was proposed that the lack of a clear definition has in part contributed, at least to date, to the mixed success of LPM implementation within law firms.[1]

In one sense, this has been articulated as a process to help you define, plan, execute, and evaluate the matter that you are working on, strongly underpinned with effective communication and the setting and meeting of client expectations. This can then be further supported by specific tools, knowledge, and techniques that help you successfully achieve the matter objectives agreed upon.

The definition of LPM used in the ALM survey itself was very similar in nature, with LPM defined as "the discipline of planning, organizing, securing, and managing resources to achieve specific goals related to the control and management of legal cases and matters."[2]

In another sense, and perhaps more simplistically, it is doing what's right for the matter in the most effective manner. It is doing so in a *proactive and deliberate* fashion, using the most appropriate "tools" that the legal project management "toolkit" can provide.

LPM itself involves a number of key elements:

- more upfront discussion of your client's objectives and the expectations at the outset of the matter
- a more detailed definition of scope to be addressed (and how to address any subsequent changes)

1. ALM Legal Intelligence, Legal Project Management: Much Promise, Many Hurdles 8 (2012).
2. *Id.* at 8.

- better and ongoing communication with the key stakeholders (or influencers) within your client's team (within your own team)
- a more structured approach to budgeting work
- better and ongoing management of the matter throughout (including progress of budget cost to the actual cost for key phases or sections of the work)
- (and the often forgotten) evaluation of the matter at its conclusion to identify potential lessons learned (which may be applied to future matters)

When I was reflecting on what LPM means to me, ultimately (and as Jim Hassett has also pointed out), it is the adoption of a range of existing management approaches[3] that help you deliver appropriate client outcomes, client value, and client business objectives, whilst also protecting your own profitability.

Don't Forget the L in LPM

Why *legal* project management? How is this different from the "plain old vanilla" project management used in other industries?

There are probably a couple of key differences. The first is around the ability to schedule resources effectively. Lawyers by nature are relatively autonomous and as such prefer to act on their own rather than be directed in what to do. There's also the issue of changing timelines, with these often being changed by clients, courts, aggressive opposing counsel derailing your well thought-through plan, or even external events impacting the matter.

Second, whereas in typical project management there are specific outcomes—that is, something is either completed or it is not—in legal project management, that is not necessarily the case. On a matter, you may have completed all the activity even if the eventual outcome was not the one that was hoped for at the beginning (for example, where you suffer an adverse ruling in a litigation matter).

There is one final key difference, especially when reviewing the Project Management Institute's definition of what project management entails. There is a greater, and *more explicit*, emphasis on the role of

3. Jim Hassett, Legal Project Management, Pricing, and Alternative Fee Arrangements 13 (2013).

communication,[4] a key element of legal project management and its role in ensuring a more "predictable delivery of valuable work." (This is typically addressed in project management through rigorous documentation, as it is recognized that many projects fail through poor communication.)

Many of the elements *are*, however, the same regardless of whether this is project management or legal project management. The activities are similar, and both clearly focus on the commercial or business-related components of a project (for example, cost, scope, resources, and timeline). But don't forget the L—there are important differences!

The Key Drivers Behind the Rise of LPM

The key drivers behind the need for legal project management, I believe, may be grouped into three overall themes: those that are client centric, those that are market driven, and those internal to the law firms themselves.

Increasing Client Demands and Expectations

The first driver is *client centric*, with the increasing level of client demand and expectations. Clients, particularly after the global financial crisis of 2008, recognized the shift in the balance of power from law firms to themselves. There was "oversupply" in the market and the clients now had the luxury of choosing and then negotiating aggressively with their preferred provider.

We've already talked about the client requests for alternative fee agreements, but there is an increasing expectation that law firms also begin to stick to the agreed budgets, with this budget now effectively becoming a cap. (Given how some law firms actually manage their matters, this for some has come as a shock.)

There was also the fact that clients began to be more aware of *perceived inefficiencies* in how law firms actually executed and conducted their matters. For many of these clients, they had already begun to identify ways

4. Steven B. Levy, Legal Project Management: Control Costs, Meet Schedules, Manage Risks, and Maintain Sanity 45 (2009).

that they in their own organization could reduce costs and inefficiencies through the adoption of project management techniques given the increasingly constrained economic climate, and they began to question why they were paying for perceived law firm inefficiencies rather than law firms changing current behaviors. Firms such as Cisco, FMC Technologies, Caterpillar, and DuPont were at the forefront of driving this approach and encouraging better project management (and therefore accountability for the overall matter outcome) within the legal community.

Another parallel development was the growth in in-house legal teams, with many organizations recruiting lawyers from private practice to head up or play key roles in their in-house teams. These individuals had a clear understanding of how law firms worked and therefore were acutely aware of where there was potential to improve the delivery of legal services from outside counsel. This led to an increasing expectation that law firms would be able to create their own "economies of scale" or greater efficiency to their expertise in handling similar matters, and that this benefit should now be shared with (if not fully passed on to) themselves. Although undoubtedly some matters will be unique, clients now recognize that the vast majority are not and therefore are of the view that potential efficiencies should already exist within the law firms concerned.

One other increasing and interesting trend over the last 12 to 18 months has also been in the manner in which companies select their outside counsel. A recent survey from Acritas highlighted this change of criteria. As part of their Global Elite survey, they asked participants about the relative importance of key themes they considered when evaluating a tender or panel selection. For each, they were rated as being either essential, nice to have, or irrelevant.

The quality of a law firm's project management system ranked second (with 60 percent), only being denied the top spot to the theme of "taking time to understand your business" (with 81 percent). In almost an exact mirror of the results, it also had the second lowest score for being seen as an "irrelevant" criteria, with only 11 percent of respondents saying this did not impact their buying decision (again the lowest was demonstrating an understanding of the client's business with 5 percent).[5]

In addition, questions specific to how law firms approach the question of legal project management are now becoming increasingly commonplace in client requests for proposal (RFPs). Whereas previously questions focused on the theme of efficiency and cost control would be evident in such documents, we are now beginning to experience (for example, in a late-2012 RFP from a global investment bank) questions specifically addressing the number of legal project managers in place within the firm, the number of those deployed on the client's matters previously, value these resources have delivered, and the associated tools and training available within the firm.

In my mind, there is now a very strong parallel emerging here between how questions on alternative fee arrangements within the commercial section of an RFP have shifted from being a differentiator to a *hygiene factor*, with a similar trend continuing (in my humble opinion) with legal project management within the next 12- to 18-month period. Therefore, if you haven't started your LPM initiative yet, you have a small, but rapidly declining, window of opportunity.

The Legal Market and Increased Competition

The second driver is more a function of the legal market and the *increasing competition for legal work*. This was particularly acute during the height of the financial crisis when stories abound of law firms being undercut by more expensive rivals, but continues today. One example is when a midsize law firm was under bid for work by a major New York–based firm by between 40 percent and 60 percent within the midsize firm's "home market" (despite the New York firm having a higher cost base) in an attempt to secure key mandates and clients.

As we discussed during our chapters focused on value, many of the services offered are ones that have historically been at a premium, or at least a higher rate, but are now beginning to become viewed by clients as more commoditized or routine. For firms to be able to conduct those matters

5. ACRITAS SURVEY PREVIOUSLY MENTIONED

effectively, they need to focus not only on *managing the delivery of the matter* but the means *by which* they deliver the matter.

The Nature of Law Firms

The third and final driver is more *internal to law firms' themselves*. This relates to the main way in which law firms maintain their profits per partner (PPP), that of increasing the standard billing rates to their clients.

During the period 2000–2007, while standard billing rates increased dramatically (with typical increases ranging from 5 to 10 percent per annum), many of the other key metrics of law firm profitability were in decline. For example, overhead costs were increasing, lawyer productivity was declining, realization declined, as did leverage. In effect, the ability to increase billing rates masked a more fundamental problem, which became increasingly evident as of the global financial crisis, as we explored in our introductory chapters.

Through the increasing circulation within the legal press of law firm financial metrics, such as PPP rate increases and the like, through the tables, such as those produced in the *American Lawyer* and other legal magazines, clients began to question whether they were receiving value for money and experiencing the most efficient delivery of services.

In addition, the vast majority of law firms have already identified where they may be able to further reduce costs or improve revenue with many of these initiatives being undertaken during 2009 and 2010. For many, this did not result in any significant change to their business model (as they perceived more immediate and pressing priorities).

With these avenues now exhausted in most instances, and law firms once again need to look for initiatives that will help drive (or at least sustain) acceptable levels of profitability, LPM has come to the fore as a potential solution.

The Law Firm View: The Key Drivers of LPM

When asked in the ALM survey[6] what were some of the key drivers that had led law firms to pursue project management initiatives (with participants able to check all that applied), these were the top five responses (out of the 108 eligible responses):

- increased efficiency and productivity for specific matters or cases (72 percent)
- reduced costs (65 percent)
- more productive relationship with clients (64 percent)
- increased efficiency and productivity with the law firm (62 percent)
- improved communication with clients (60 percent)

The Benefits of LPM

The beauty of LPM is that when done well this benefits both the law firm *and* the client. Table 13.1 outlines some of the most commonly identified benefits of LPM.

Table 13.1: The Benefits of LPM

Sample Client Benefits	Sample Law Firm/Client Team Benefits
Greater predictability of cost, both by phase and for the total matter	Greater client satisfaction
Enhanced communication and better management of expectations (the concept of "no surprises")	Improved profitability (and realization), through minimizing write-downs/write-offs
A more managed approach to legal work	Better risk management
Better predictability of (and improvement to) the eventual outcome (especially true for litigation-related matters)	Differentiation from competitors (although, arguably, this is now beginning to decline as more firms begin their own LPM efforts)
Work delivered "on time, and on budget"	Better consistency across the firm's offices and practice areas

6. ALM LEGAL INTELLIGENCE, *supra* note 1, at 10.

Sample Client Benefits	Sample Law Firm/Client Team Benefits
Greater efficiencies (for example, the reduced need for "reinventing the wheel" on client matters)	Better teamwork/effectiveness among matter team members
Better quality and greater consistency of work product	Better morale/improved retention (due to the associated investment in training and personal development)
	Protection of business with current clients
	Delivers better know-how, precedents, and training

When participants of the ALM LPM survey were questioned as to which benefits their firm had realized from their LPM efforts, nearly two-thirds identified having a "more productive relationship with clients" as being the main benefit realized.

Interestingly, the top five benefits (of the 13 offered) mirrored very closely the top five key drivers outlined a few paragraphs ago. The only change in theme was the inclusion of "greater predictability of cost" as the fifth most popular (at 48 percent) replacing "reduced costs," which was seventh (at 42 percent). Whether by luck or design there at least seems to be some consistency.

So, to sum up, in an effort to remain competitive, to be able to meet client requests, and fundamentally seek to reconnect the cost and value of legal services, LPM has a critical role to play.

When revisiting one of the themes we talked about in one of our earlier chapters, that of the "lost profit to unintended discounts," LPM is key. Whereas better pricing (and negotiation) can help us begin to "close the gap" between our discounted cost and the appropriate price for our services (the "conscious discount"), better project management is instrumental in closing the gap between our realized cost and our intended discounted cost (the unintended discount).

For those firms that have already embraced LPM in the current market, the very presence of this capability may continue to act as a key market differentiator in the immediate term, and stand them in good stead for the times ahead. However, as the rest of the legal industry is beginning to catch up and the level of differentiation that LPM provides continues to erode (except for those who remain at the bleeding edge), LPM will become to be viewed more as a "hygiene factor" when clients seek to select their external law firms that will dictate whether a firm becomes appointed or not.

Now is not, therefore, the time to rein back on these efforts, but to move full steam ahead.

With this in mind, our next chapter looks at how you can either get started with your first set of LPM initiatives, or kick-start and revitalize your existing ones.

Don't forget *(a summary of the key points):*

- It is time to take out the mystery of legal project management and put back the pragmatism.
- Although sharing many similarities, *legal* project management is not the same as more traditional project management—the L matters.
- The rise of LPM is being driven by three key themes—those of increasing client demands and expectations, the legal market and increasing competition, and the nature of law firms themselves.
- LPM has a critical role to play in how today's lawyer can remain competitive, become more efficient and effective in the delivery of services, and in the ultimate delivery of value to clients.

Chapter 14

Thinking Big, Starting Small

I Know I Need to Do Something, but What?

If you are reading this book, you are probably already thinking about either how to start your firm's legal project management (LPM) initiative or how best to sustain it.

If you are not, but struggle with things such as missed client deadlines, poor communication or miscommunication on your matters, and late time entries (some of the acknowledged project management warning signs), you probably should be.

A Potential Path Ahead

Through a combination of learning from others who have already started with LPM initiatives, and by also taking advantage of what you already know, you should be in a great (starting) position.

Learning from Others

We're fortunate in that there is a general consensus among legal commentators to those factors that lead to a successful LPM implementation.

The 10 key themes identified may be summarized as follows:

- Spend a lot of time at the "front end" (a theme we will return to when we look at LPM itself).

  - Here it is important to work out from the outset *what you are trying to achieve*, and then focus only on these elements. For example, will this be for all lawyers or just some? Is the intent to educate so they can "talk" LPM in client conversations or also actually *do* LPM? As some of the pioneers who drove the initiative at Dechert (Ben Barnett and Colleen Nihill) aptly put it (admittedly in the context of a single matter), "You can't do what you don't define."[1]
- Your LPM approach should be designed to live with your firm's culture, your firm's strategy, and your firm's clients (and their priorities).
- Identify powerful (and credible!) champions, and secure *visible* commitment from leadership for the short term, midterm, and long term (it is also good to make sure that all the key players *understand* what is being done and are committed to it).
- Focus on those areas where you can make a real difference—for example, driving improved realization or minimizing write-offs. This may mean initially limiting your initiative to specific practice areas (where adopting LPM approach's techniques could improve efficiency and overall profitability) or client teams (as before, plus the factor of client "pressure").
- Any approach needs to focus on lawyers' "right now needs." It needs to deliver immediate benefit or else it will not be adopted (so training should go short on the theory, long on the hands-on practice).
- *One size does not fit all*—any training or approach needs to be tailored to the relevant practice group, client team, or specific matter (but along some common principles).
- Training needs to be done in parallel with developing the appropriate tools and infrastructure, otherwise expectation surpasses reality (and that is where frustration typically kicks in).
- Get some *quick wins* on the board and actively publicize the success (this helps build a healthy degree of competition among participating lawyers).

1. BARBARA BOAKE & RICK KATHURIA, Project Management for Lawyers 80 (2011).

- Don't be frightened of technology, but do adopt it appropriately (see "The Danger of Putting the Cart Before the Horse" sidebar).
- Above all, *keep it simple.*

One other key theme I have noted (and subsequently have had confirmed with colleagues in other firms) is *don't try to push water uphill.*

Those who want to do it, and those who don't, will soon enough. As the previously quoted ALM survey noted: "Partners most willing to adopt LPM should lead efforts in an incremental manner. The quicker there are demonstrable positive benefits, the faster other partners will take notice."[2]

Taking Advantage of What You Already Know

If being honest with ourselves, much of what LPM is about is doing what we already do (*or should be doing*) better. There doesn't need to be any rocket science behind this (although you may want to add your own).

By taking some of the perceived pain (and jargon) away from this area, you will find adoption significantly easier. Therefore, the key to gaining buy-in is to first acknowledge that the lawyers possess the basic skills, and project management techniques really provide structure around what they are already doing and refine these further.

When getting started, begin working from what you know rather than trying to work out all you don't. Changing the way you do just one thing can make a big difference to you and your client.

Remember: take all the mystery out of LPM and put back the pragmatism. Focus on what matters.

2. ALM LEGAL INTELLIGENCE, *supra* note 1, at 17.

The Question of Training

The training question is a tricky one. Yes, you certainly need it, and for many it will be the cornerstone of your LPM efforts, but there are a couple of key considerations it's useful to bear in mind from the outset.

- These types of sessions are typically covering key concepts (particularly if you are just embarking on the LPM path). Susan Raridon Lambreth observed (and I agree) that "You're actually not 'training' in project management but more typically (providing) *education* about project management."[3]
- "Passive" learning is not effective for teaching new skills or building specific skills—the greatest success occurs when it is around real, practical training. Indeed, according to some recent research, around 40 percent of the knowledge acquired in training is lost after a break of one month, rising to 90 percent after 6 months.[4]
- Not all people attending your training need to be project management experts—recognize this from the outset and tailor your approach accordingly. (This is something we have done at Baker & McKenzie, where we have developed a number of distinct levels of training, ranging from the "essentials"/must-haves all the way through to certification.)
- Don't forget the associates and professional staff either! This is not just for partners. Indeed, some firms (for example, Winston Strawn) have actually started at the associate level first. Similarly, remember to also include your key professional staff, as many of them will also have a role to play (think of business development, marketing, finance and pricing, the knowledge management team, and so on).

---

3. SUSAN RARIDON LAMBRETH, Legal Project Management: Transforming Legal Services (2011). Susan, in partnership with David A. Rueff, has authored a book more broadly on the topic of Legal Project Management, entitled *The Power of Legal Project Management: A Practical Handbook* and published by the ABA, http://apps.americanbar.org/abastore/index.cfm?section=main&fm=Product.AddToCart&pid=1620600.

4. Jim Hassett, Legal Project Management: Quick Reference Guide 133 (2nd ed. 2011).

Managing Change

Legal project management *is* driving a change in the way that lawyers currently do business, and change is difficult for everyone. Just ask the management consultancy firms that continue to make significant revenues from change-management consulting.

Following on from our theme above, educating is easy (relatively), but changing behavior is much harder, and this change is especially difficult for lawyers. Lawyers need to buy in to the idea that LPM will help them, and it will take some investment—both via their participating in training (the easy bit) and in their willingness to make changes to their behavior (the difficult bit).

Whether you have demystified legal project management or not within your firm, you cannot underestimate the importance of change management when embarking on this process. The truth is that there *will be* grumblings from the troops as you progress (common grumbles being lack of resources, lack of time, lack of applicability, and lack of infrastructure).

Having a strong change management approach will make a big difference. Helpfully, the Association of Corporate Counsel as part of their Legal Project Management Primer (issued in October 2011)[5] provided the following practice tip on change management (which I have only slightly amended and many of which we have already covered), as shown in table 14.1.

5. Ass'n of Corporate Counsel, Legal Project Management Primer 18 (2011).

Table 14.1: Effectively Using Change Management to Support Your LPM Initiatives

Change Management Framework	Suggested Tips for Success
Set the scene Establish a sense of urgency Form a powerful guiding coalition	Clearly define why the change is needed Establish clear success metrics for the project and incorporate them into the individual's performance goals Establish a project steering committee with leadership from affected areas Identify an internal project leader Supplement with an empowered core team Raise awareness of who is part of the project team Make the vision for change clear, desirable, and feasible—have an elevator speech
Decide what to do Develop the change vision and strategy	Identify an important business driver and keep that message consistent throughout the project Evaluate your organization's readiness for change and organizational culture Acknowledge that there will be change and that there will be resistance
Make it happen Communicate Empower others to act on the vision Plan for, and create, short-term wins Consolidate improvements and keep momentum	Communicate early and often, using multiple methods Encourage consistency in senior leadership behaviors to support the vision Provide a mechanism for feedback/suggestions and the freedom to challenge the status quo Plan checkpoints to stop and recognize progress Make the celebrations public and reward contributors Don't declare victory too soon
Make it stick Institutionalize the new approach	Make sure that senior management continues to "walk the talk" Conduct a structured "lessons learned" session and be willing to discuss the good, bad, and ugly of the change effort Recalibrate success metrics once improvements have been made

The Danger of "Putting the Cart Before the Horse"

Many of the initial legal project management efforts failed. Why? Well, in part due to them not having the guiding themes listed above, but also due to an initial focus on technology.

Some of the early efforts at developing LPM-specific software were too complex to those that were expected to use it. It was frequently difficult to learn and then apply to matters (pun intended) at hand, leading to lawyer frustration and limited adoption. Pam Woldow neatly summarized the issue when she said, "you can't make lawyers talk IT, IT has to learn to talk lawyer"[6] (the blog this appeared in also had a number of other great observations too). What many at the time didn't realize was that technology wasn't the (main) solution to the business problem at hand. Change management was—and still is!

Not all who went down this path were unsuccessful, however. A (very small) number, such as Baker Donelson and their BakerManage platform have been very successful. They and others have built their solution incrementally, recognizing that needs were going to evolve over time. Many were (and remain) "homegrown" solutions that more clearly addressed their firms' specific needs (although a number of newer tools are available that better fit this need, this topic being covered more fully in Chapter 22). This approach is certainly not for the fainthearted, though. Don't say you haven't been warned.

My suggestion to you is to focus on trying out some of the themes mentioned here (and also in the other chapters of this section) rather than looking to put in the perfect system that will drive greater long-term efficiency and reporting, takes significant time to implement, and then gain adoption. Don't "build then *do*," "*DO then* build."

6. Pam Woldow, *You Can't Make Lawyers into Techies: 3 Lessons About Legal Project Management*, AT THE INTERSECTION (Feb. 14, 2012), http://www.pamwoldow.com/2012/02/14/you-cant-make-lawyers-into-techies-3-lessons-about-lpm-tools-technology/.

The Baker & McKenzie Approach

The approach we have taken at Baker & McKenzie is a combination of a number of the themes mentioned above, perhaps not surprising given the geographic reach and number of attorneys in the firm. I have previously referred to this (while at conferences) as our scatter-gun approach, but that phrase does the approach a gross disservice.

What we were doing was seeing what worked best in different situations. Over a period of time we have tried a combination of activities. Some of these have included third-party training (including initiatives around certification in LPM), external coaching, and use of dedicated legal project managers (which we have had in place since January 2010). Many we still continue with, but all have had strong and visible sponsorship from our executive committee and other key members of the firm, and all strongly align to our LPM vision and strategy.

Through being able to experiment, we now know what works well for us as a firm and for our firm's culture, and what works less well. I am not saying that we have always got it "spot on," nor that we are close to finishing our journey, but the moral here can probably be summed up as follows: *Try what feels right, do something, and adapt as you go.*

Keeping Momentum

Once you have got your LPM initiative underway—whether this be firm-wide or in selected pockets—you need to have a plan to maintain the momentum.

Many of the earliest adopters are also here. The Decherts, Eversheds, and Sutherlands of the world still have the challenge of making their impressive changes sustainable. For those who were at the vanguard of LPM four or more years ago, they are now refining the process and tools they put in place, taking advantage of the technical and process improvements that have been made.

However, the ALM survey noted that 58 percent of respondents admitted to encountering "snags" in their implementation. Reasons noted ranged from the lack of perceived need (either at an organizational or individual level), the lack of skills and necessary training, to inappropriate governance.[7]

7. ALM Legal Intelligence, Legal Project Management 15 (2012).

But a number of core themes remain to all, including

- reviewing and adjusting your strategy and vision (after all, the early mover advantage is fast disappearing as competition becomes more intense). Once you are past the immediate euphoria of your successful initial stage, it is useful to revisit the strategy and "kick the tires" a bit, before moving on;
- ensuring that LPM maintains *appropriate* organizational visibility—for example, at regular partner meetings or events and through the capture, and communicate your success stories and convert the remaining skeptics (however few remain);
- continually adapting and refining what is being done at a practice group and client team level (that is, encouraging experimentation); and,
- ensuring that your LPM infrastructure remains in step (as a minimum) with the demands of your lawyers and professional support staff.

Daunting a list as that may sound, even by simply introducing *one element of change at a time* allows you to keep the momentum. You do not need to rely on grand sweeping gestures—at least not yet.

Don't forget *(a summary of the key points):*

- Keep it simple—initially focus your efforts around the people, then processes, and only then the systems. You may not even choose to call it legal project management—it is, in many respects, doing what we already know as lawyers (but better!). Take the mystery out of LPM and put back the pragmatism.
- Don't over analyze it—it is better to do something, try it, refine it, and then do something else. One step at a time is fine, as long as there is a key path ahead. Do, *then* build.
- Find your champions. These should be at a senior or executive level within your firm who can credibly champion the LPM vision and strategy, but also find your champions at the practice group level—this is really where the rubber hits the road, but is also where the benefits derive! The need for the change needs to be led, not mandated.

- One size does not fit all—just like in pricing (when discussing appropriate fee alternatives with your clients) what works in one practice group or client team may not immediately transfer to another, both in terms of real-life experiences and in training.
- Remain positive—it is a marathon, not a sprint. That is why you have a vision and strategy to guide your way.
- And finally, "Think big, start small."

Chapter 15

Getting It Right from the Start

One of the key challenges of legal project management is making it meaningful and accessible to those who are unfamiliar with project management approaches.

Much of the existing literature focuses on key project management terms (for example, project planning, stakeholder analysis, communication planning, and risk registers). For many lawyers (most of whom are unfamiliar with this terminology), the thought of conducting legal project management activity can therefore feel intimidating, to say the least.

One of the key themes I have seen emerge time and time again during my discussions with colleagues in other law firms is *the need to keep legal project management simple.*

For the remainder of this section (Chapters 15–18) I am going to try to achieve this on our joint behalf. What works best in this situation are approaches that are simple, able to be clearly understood, and directly relate to the way someone performs a matter.

Recalling Steven Levy's quote from a few chapters ago, "All projects are managed. Some are managed deliberately, some inadvertently. Deliberate project management is better." Indeed, for all lawyers who lead significant matters, there are two key roles that they must play. The first is to perform the legal work required itself (the "technical" stuff). The second is managing the project itself (something that is becoming increasingly and more explicitly required).

Wearing your project manager hat, having a good understanding of the likely matter lifecycle is key. Although all matters vary in both their size and their complexity, figure 15.1 shows a generic matter lifecycle that all matters can be mapped to.

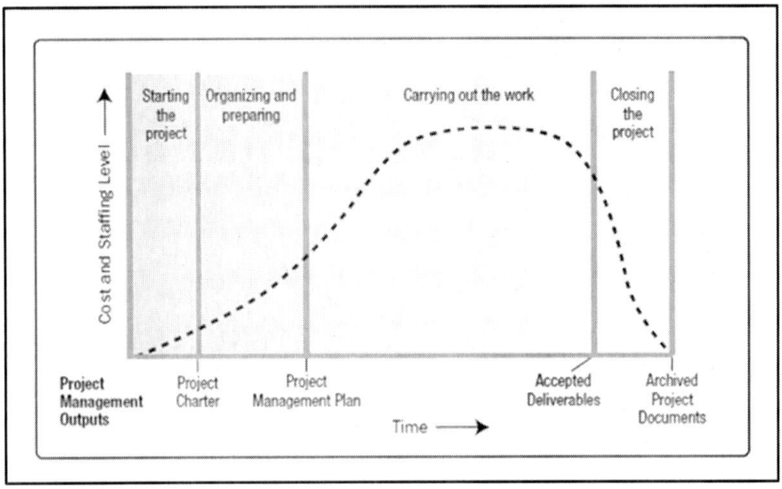

Figure 15.1
Mapping a Typical Project Lifecycle
Source: PROJECT MANAGEMENT INSTITUTE, A GUIDE TO THE PROJECT MANAGEMENT BODY OF KNOWLEDGE (PMBOK GUIDE) 39, fig. 2.8 (5th ed. 2013).

After all, all matters really do have a beginning, a middle, and an end. They start; there are a number of activities involved in getting organized and prepared; there is the actual legal work related to the matter itself; and then finally, there is the matter closing. What will differ is the matter's *rhythm* once the hard work begins, specifically the profile of effort (and associated costs) throughout.[1] For example, think through the typical matter staffing profile and hours/cost expended when conducting a mergers and acquisitions deal with significant effort required to conduct due diligence versus preparing a visa request or conducting tax planning.

It is also good to remember that risk and uncertainty are greatest at the start of the matter (although I know it sometimes does not feel like it!). As

1. Project Management Institute, A Guide to the Project Management Body of Knowledge (PMBOK Guide) 39, fig. 2.8 (5th ed. 2013).

shown in figure 15.2, risk and uncertainty *decrease* during the matter's lifetime as we reach agreement and decisions with our client how to proceed, and as our legal "deliverables" or documents are accepted and approved.

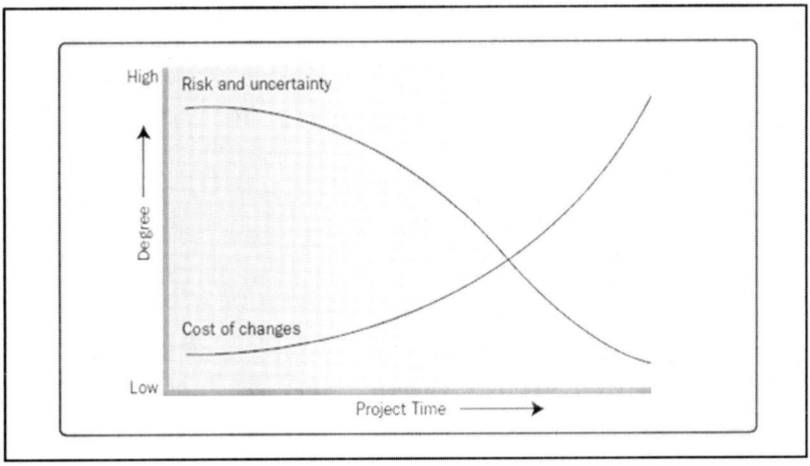

Figure 15.2
The Typical Project's Risk Profile
Source: *Id.* at 40, fig. 2.9.

Many of the challenges faced when conducting a matter can often be directly linked back to what we did (or did not do) during these initial stages. There is a tendency in lawyers that, although admirable, sometimes means that the early preparation is overlooked in eagerness to address the core legal problems at hand. However, spending slightly more time at the front end will save significant "noise" both during, and at the close, of the matter. By having this more holistic perspective from the outset, this allows you, as the lead on the matter, to work out what really are the key activities you need to pay attention to.

In the more typical "project management speak," this would be the Defining and Planning phases of a project. In our version, this is simply "getting it right from the start."

Before moving onto the rest of the chapter, consider the following:

When you are structuring a legal agreement, what is typically one of the first key sections? A definition of terms, right? As a lawyer, you recognize the importance of having these terms defined at the very outset to ensure that all parties understand what is about to follow, or what we are agreeing to. We spend a lot of time clearly defining what we mean in our legal documents, yet seldom do this when about to commence a new matter (remember, the matter's engagement letter serves as a form of agreement). We should take some of our legal contractual mind-set and follow the same principles when starting a matter.

Ok, *now* it is safe to proceed.

Getting It Right from the Start

When getting started on a project or matter, there are three key themes it is important to address at the outset. These are the themes of better communication, greater clarity, and easier review. These break down into 10 key elements that a lawyer tasked with leading a matter should consider at this stage, but each relates explicitly to one of more of these three themes.

For the remainder of this chapter (and the next one) we will go into each of these areas in a bit more detail.

The 10 key steps for those responsible for leading a matter are

- confirming what the client wants and expects, and identifying any potential risks to matter success;
- grouping the work into the main areas of focus;
- *agreeing how to address changes in scope up front*;
- developing and agreeing on the matter plan;
- agreeing on the fee and the fee approach;
- *agreeing on the engagement letter*;
- agreeing the reporting format and schedule;
- *establishing your matter phases and tasks*;
- *approving new timekeepers*; and
- staffing the core team and agreeing on the client responsibilities.

There is nothing in this list that should appear unfamiliar to many of you. Some of the terms may be different, but if you were asked to list what you think you would need to do at the start of any matter, your list, I'm sure, would be pretty similar. There really is no rocket science in the above . . . *but there is a structured approach.*

Table 15.1: Our Ten Key Steps: Where They Sit and What They Support

Step	Step Description	Theme(s) Addressed	Traditional Project Management Stage
1	Confirming what the client wants and expects, and identifying any potential risks to matter success	Greater clarity	Define
2	Grouping the work into the main areas of focus	Greater clarity	Define
3	Agreeing how to address changes in scope up front	Better communication	Define
4	Developing and agreeing on the matter plan	Greater clarity	Plan
5	Agreeing on the fee and the fee approach	Better communication	Define
6	Agreeing on the engagement letter	Better communication Greater clarity	Define
7	Agreeing on the reporting format and schedule	Enabling easier review Better communication	Define
8	Establishing your matter phases and tasks	Enabling easier review	Plan
9	Approving new timekeepers	Better communication	Define
10	Staffing the core team and agreeing on the client responsibilities	Greater clarity	Plan

In reality, a number of these key stages are often skipped completely in the rush to start the matter as quickly as possible. Whereas many of these activities are frequently done, those highlighted in *italics* are often done in a piecemeal fashion. Or worse, they are completely forgotten until requested by the client or required to address an issue on the matter itself (which is worse as you are often then fully engaged in the matter itself and have less time and are more reactive—it is also potentially damaging to your longer-term client relationship!).

Is it not better to spend some time up front (when time is less pressured) to think these issues through and develop and agree on a pragmatic way forward?

Assuming that you agree, how do we get started?

Step 1: Confirming What the Client Wants and Expects

Confirming what your client's expectations are on the matter is key. It is important to understand the expected scope of the matter and the legal and business issues being addressed, and discuss potential outcomes.

It is at this stage where you can gain a better understanding of what the client is looking for, and start to distinguish between a client's wants and needs.

During this initial discussion, you are actually playing two roles. The first role is a lawyer. Here you're looking to use your professional experience to guide the client in addressing the legal problem at hand in an appropriate manner. However, you are also playing the role of the project manager. Here, you are looking to identify your client's overall expectations, objectives, and the associated impact on scope, timing, and cost.

Often clients may not be exactly sure of the legal issue to be addressed, perhaps due to lack of familiarity with similar matters previously, this being especially true in some of the more emerging economies that are needing to address more complex legal issues. By having this discussion, this allows you to both demonstrate your expertise and understanding of the issue at hand but also make sure the client is aware of what each "want" or "nice to have" will cost.

It is also good to understand what success will look like for both the client's organization, the client's leadership team (however defined), *and* the client itself, as these are very unlikely to be the same. It is here that you can gently probe to find out what they liked about how other firms have conducted matters for the client (and ones that you would be keen to also adopt), and also what they didn't like (and you want to avoid at all costs).

One area you may also want to address here is what level of quality is required. What I'm not advocating is the delivery of substandard work:

it is really making sure the client does not receive a Ferrari when you're expected to give them a Fiat or pickup truck. One example of this is during due diligence when a client may be perfectly happy to accept (or actually prefer) a "red flag report" rather than a full due diligence review. Depending on the quality required, this has an impact on a project's scope, timeline, and overall cost.

The Issue of Risk

Finally, it is also at this stage we should explore any potential risks to the overall success of the matter. I know that some other guides to legal project management may include these at a later step (and that is okay); however, my own view is that the earlier risk is discussed, the easier it is to mitigate and manage. It also helps manage your client's expectations from the start.

There are legal risks but also risks that are specific to the matter itself, irrespective of the finer points of law being discussed. Risks could be those identified within the client's business (for example, business reorganization, changing stakeholders, etc.), those within your own firm (for example, availability of the necessarily skilled resources), and those that are external (for example, the introduction of new legislation, identification of expert witnesses, etc.). More typically, they are our ability to meet budget and timeline.

In my experience, the rigorous management of project risk is something that is lacking on many legal matters. Indeed, more generally, one of the least used documents on many projects is the risk log, register, or worksheet. The approach adopted doesn't need to be complex, but there *does* need to be one.

These can easily be prepared in Microsoft Excel, PowerPoint, or similar types of applications (I personally prefer spreadsheets as you can add some degree of functionality and weighting to potential risks more easily).

When assessing a risk, there are seven key elements to consider or track:

- These start with the risk itself.
- But you should also consider what happens if the risk occurs.
- The probability. (What is the likelihood of this happening? Is it high, medium or low—or even better, can you assign a value to it? Will the degree of risk change over time?).

- What is the risk's impact (either expressed as a financial value/loss, or your "exposure")?
- How can you help mitigate the risk (that is, trying to help minimize the change of the risk actually occurring)?
- What is the contingency approach (which is what is needed once the risk actually happens)?
- And finally, you should also be aware of how time can affect the likelihood, and potential impact, of a risk.

Spending time to identify and understand the potential risk at the outset of a matter will stand you in good stead. It will allow you to address these issues explicitly within your matter plan (see Step 4), when providing status (covered in Step 7) and when documenting the matter more formally within the engagement letter (covered in Step 6).

Regularly reviewing these (and adding or removing risks as necessary) on a weekly or biweekly basis will allow you to keep a strong hand on the matter's potential "danger areas." Also, remember your role when it comes to risk management. As the lead attorney, your role is to help *mitigate* the risk where possible. Remember, it is the client's role to *own the risk* and determine what level of risk they are prepared to accept (based on your advice).

Going through this exercise as part of the first step can also provide a very early flag whether this matter is one you are comfortable to undertake and, if so, on what fee basis. On reflection, are you now being asked to take on more risk than originally envisaged, and, if so, do your current commercial terms reflect this?

An Unexpected Benefit?

One potentially beneficial side effect of explicitly being seen to manage (and having a strong track record *in managing*) risk may be the reduction in your associated costs of professional liability insurance. This is typically one of the larger operating-cost elements for a law firm, others being compensation and real estate. When coupled with the wider themes of LPM (for example, the ability to meet deadlines, have a clear understanding and basis of any fee, and having regular, ongoing client communications), the level of professional liability risk can sometimes be reduced.

Stuart Pattison, a vice president of Chicago-based CNA (one of the largest commercial insurers in the United States), quoted in an article by Julie Goldberg, "The Evolution of Law Firm Risk,"[2] talks about the importance of clearly defining scope (and management of risk) as follows:

"Lawyers can significantly minimize risk at the onset of an attorney/client relationship. A well-drafted engagement letter can also spare future turmoil by spelling out the precise nature of professional services including the attorney handling the matter, specific duties that are not covered, a time-frame and a definition of who the firm will and will not be representing."

Pattison manages CNA's large-law-firm group for lawyers' professional liability insurance, so he knows what he is talking about.

Step 2: Grouping the Work into the Main Areas

Once you have a clear idea of scope through your discussion with the client, you can now start to group the key parts of work into main areas. This is often referred to as developing the "work breakdown structure" (or WBS), but remember that this is merely a fancy term for the list of matter tasks required (to varying degrees of detail).

Going through this step is helpful, as it gives you a very good overview of what you need to do. Typical benefits of having a WBS also include making you think through all the aspects of the project, helps prevent work "slipping through the cracks," encourages you to focus the team's experience to where it will add the most value, and provides a solid basis for estimating staff cost and time (which we will get to shortly).

It can be difficult, if starting out implementing legal project management, to bring a lot of specificity to your legal work. However, even if you don't develop a detailed plan of work breakdown structure initially, just taking time to verify all the key phases and sub-phases of your matter will go a long way to helping you build a better budget from which you can manage and improve the overall profitability of the work you do.

2. Julie Goldberg, *The Evolution of Law Firm Risk*, RISK MGMT. MAG., Aug. 2008, at 48, *available at* http://www.kornferryinstitute.com/reports-insights/evolution-law-firm-risk.

This can be done to varying degrees of detail at this stage, as outlined in figure 15.3. For example, I have seen some examples drill down as far as Level 4 in the level of detail provided, whereas many others are typically either at Level 2 or Level 3.

Bear in mind what you are trying to accomplish at this stage. You are going to use this to confirm with the client that the key activities are being addressed, to ensure that there are no obvious gaps, and then use this as a basis for more detailed planning. Given this objective, providing detail to either Level 2 or Level 3 feels a more pragmatic way forward.

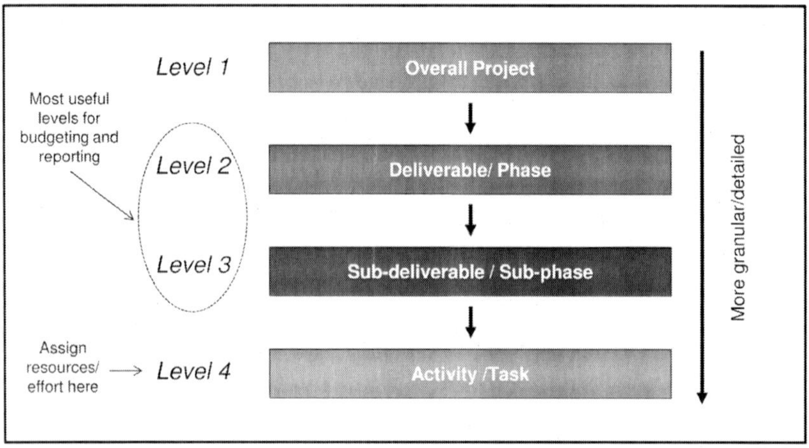

Figure 15.3
A Typical Legal Matter Hierarchy or Breakdown

Defining the Main Areas

You may choose to define the key areas either by matter phase or stage, or even by the key deliverables that will be produced (although these are likely to relate closely to your phases anyway), as we saw in figure 15.3 on the previous page. Choose the approach that is best for you and your client to provide *clarity*.

The Project Management Institute has identified two key tools and techniques when doing this task. These are decomposition and expert judgment.[3] We will return to the concept of decomposition later (during Step 4), although it is really just the concept of breaking down activities into much more manageable parts.

The second technique, that of expert judgment, is more relevant here. In this context, this is either using previous examples from similar matters or exercising your (and others') professional judgment. Being able to capture and have access to these previous examples is invaluable, and yet many law firms have yet to put in place a way to make this information readily accessible and usable. (If using a previous example, it is also sensible to check whether the matter phases turned out as planned. You don't want to set off down the wrong path.)

A good example of a work breakdown structure is shown in figure 15.4.

I would be lying to you if I were to say that this step is easy. It is not. *But it does become easier* with more practice and familiarity (especially if you are working on similar types of matters).

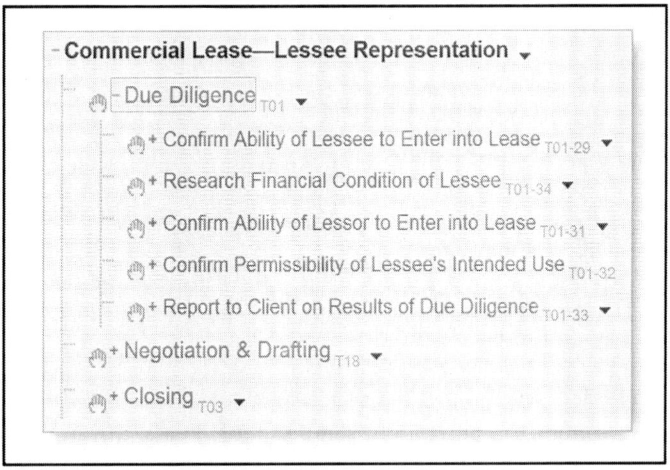

Figure 15.4

An Illustrative Example of a Good WBS

Thomson Reuters, Engage: Legal Project Management Brochure, 9, *available at* http://www.elite.com/files/Publication/768f8caf-b553-4481-bcfc-0705fb6e86fd/Presentation/PublicationAttachment/48d6f630-01ab-4eae-8760-1fa911ae474a/Engage_Brochure(L-373380)11-12.pdf.

3. Project Mgmt. Inst., *supra* note 1, at 128–31.

Eric Verzuh, author of *The Fast Forward MBA in Project Management*, summed up the challenge of creating a good WBS where he said "because a good work breakdown structure is easy to read, people often assume that it's also easy to write. This, however, is a false assumption."[4]

Remember that the simplest processes are often the best. Don't overcomplicate matters on your matter!

Step 3: Agree How to Address Changes in Scope *Upfront*

As part of the very first step (confirming the client's wants and expectations), we should have already gained a clear picture of what is required to successfully deliver the project. This should include a clear definition of the initial scope required.

However, in the real world, the initial scope is very rarely that which is executed by the end of the matter. This could be due to either additional complexity, parties, or change in overall business intent and objective when compared with the start. Indeed, the ever-changing scope is one of the key differences between legal project management and project management (at least in my view).

Don't get me wrong, it is important to have scope clearly defined and the overall goal understood by both parties at the outset. Otherwise, as Steven Levy noted, "if there is a lack of clarity . . . every action becomes a question."[5]

Where I have seen or heard many projects fall down is not through lack of a clear scope at the outset (although this certainly has an impact), but rather *ineffective management of scope* during the lifetime of the matter. This is, in part, due to the lawyer's reluctance to have "the difficult conversation."

So, let's assume that we *do* have a clear scope to work from. What then?

A recommended approach is to agree at the *outset* of the matter how any changes in scope should be addressed. Sounds obvious, but this is very rarely done—and the benefit gained during the lifetime of the matter can

4. Jim Hassett, Legal Project Management,: Quick Reference Guide 35 (3d ed. 2013).

5. Steven B. Levy, Legal Project Management: Control Costs, Meet Schedules, Manage Risks, and Maintain Sanity 27 (2009).

be extremely significant, both in additional revenue generated and also in terms of the client relationship.

Given that some degree of change inevitably happens on a matter, you should seek to implement a couple of very simple steps.

The process you put in place should cover

- an agreed approach on how to communicate potential changes in scope (for example, agreeing on a meeting to go over change requests as required, or e-mail when potential "scope creep" is identified);
- defined criteria, which should be considered when looking to decide which changes to implement, enables you to both understand and determine its potential impact on the matter;
- confirmation that a change is actually required to the current plan;
- an appropriate "escalation path" if needed; and finally
- communication to the appropriate individuals (for example, your team, key stakeholders, etc.) that a change has occurred.

Some approaches I've seen adopted in the past have included the lawyer sending a quick e-mail to the client outlining the potential change and suggesting a course of action through to drafting an addendum to be added to the original engagement letter outlining the additional scope and potential cost for client review and signature.

What is important for you as a lawyer (and also for the client) is that *any scope change is documented* and *any agreed action similarly documented*. What I have seen used by some legal teams is a very simple table (or spreadsheet) that captures the potential change, outlines the potential impact, and then captures the agreed action.

In summary, there are two key messages here: one, don't commence work until approved, and the second, be pragmatic and don't overcomplicate the scope change process (the conversation can be hard enough!).

Step 4: Developing and Agreeing on the Matter Plan

This is the stage where there tends to be the greatest degree of skepticism among lawyers. Many are of the view that they are unable to plan for the matters given, that there are so many variables at play and therefore the progression of the matter is out of their specific control. Whilst having a degree of sympathy with this, this view is not one that I would subscribe to.

The project plan is a *living* document. It is something that acts as a guide (based on all available information) rather than being imbued with Nostradamus-like predictive qualities. As Barbara Boake and Rick Kathuria commented in their book *Project Management for Lawyers*, "A project plan is not a strict playbook; it is a path to follow."[6]

The majority of work at this step revolves around our legal project management milk stool™ (sometimes also referred to as the iron or resource triangle), and as shown in figure 15.5 which seeks to manage the balance between scope, timeline, and resource (which can mean either physical bodies, financial, or other).

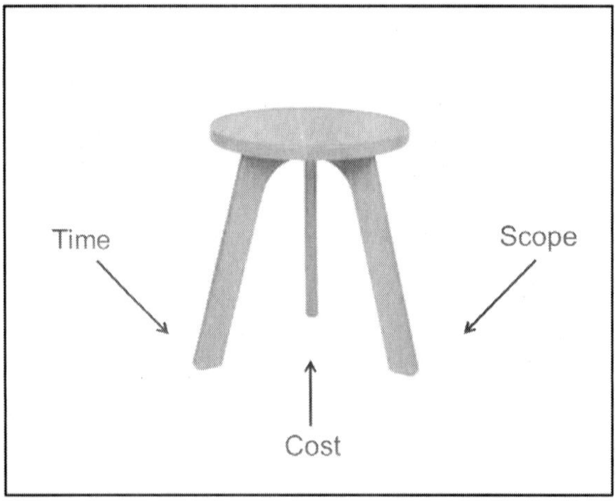

Figure 15.5
The Legal project management milk stool™: Maintaining the Right Balance

6. Barbara Boake & Rick Kathuria, Project Management for Lawyers 27 (2011).

Changes in one of these elements have a direct impact on the others. If we increase one of the legs of the milk stool, think about what happens to the person who happens to be sitting on it at the time! In the end something has to give, whether that is the impact on scope, the need for more or fewer resources, or the need for more or less time. You need to maintain the appropriate balance among all three legs.

When developing the matter plan, there are a number of factors that need to be considered. These include the tasks themselves, estimated costs, the resources/staffing required, the assumptions built in to the matter, and any associated project risks. Understandably, this can be a little daunting to those who haven't done this before.

The first step is to take those key activities identified during Step 2 of this process (that is, grouping our work into the main areas), and breaking these into a number of smaller related activities (remember the Project Management Institute concept of decomposition?). What I used to find helpful when developing project plans as a consultant was to start with the end deliverable of work product in mind and work back from that point. Try it, you may do so too.

By doing so, this allows us to more clearly assign resource timings and improve our ability to track progress. Although these are more traditionally viewed as a list of detailed task activities, as Jim Hassett has pointed out, they can also sometimes be simply a to-do list or shown in a flowchart.

Too Much or Too Little: Determining the Appropriate Detail

One challenge when planning the tasks is to what level of detail is appropriate. Ultimately the plan has to be detailed enough to be understood by the lawyer tasked with completing the work. Another good rule of thumb is that tasks should be no longer than two weeks in duration and no shorter than four hours. More often than not, plans often cover activities that spanned between one day (8 hours) to one week (40 hours).

Like everything, there is a balance. And remember that here time has *two* meanings—there is the *actual effort* required (that is, the amount to be billed) and the *elapsed time* (overall duration). Don't confuse the two. You should primarily focus on one or the other depending upon the agreed priority for the project—for example, if there is a greater emphasis on completing on time you need to focus on *duration*, and if on budget, on expended *effort*.

If there is insufficient detail, this can drive poor estimates and increase the level of inefficiency due to confusion or misunderstanding of what was required. On the flip side, don't overplan. If there is too much detail, there is the key danger of conducting micromanagement as you try and allocate tasks to very specific levels of activity and as such risk the danger of missing the bigger picture. Remember the plan is merely a recommended path to follow (based on the available information) but you may need to make adjustments as events unfold.

Do what you can, and to the level you feel most comfortable with. For those activities you are less sure about, use a SWAG. I came across this courtesy of Steven Levy, who refers to this as a "sophisticated wild-a–guess."[7] For these items, include them in your plan (ignoring the timing rule of thumb above just for a moment) until you have a better understanding of what these activities are. Once you do, they can then move from being a SWAG to an estimate (at which stage the timing rule of thumb should apply).

Build in a number of internal and external reporting or status meetings in your plan. (This will be further addressed in Step 7 and covered in the next chapter). There is a tendency to focus purely on the legal activities required to be performed during a matter, rather than thinking about how to successfully deliver the matter overall, a key component of which is *ensuring appropriate communication* within the project team and to the key stakeholders of the matter within the client. A tip I used to find helpful here was to actually have these key activities as the very first key section of your matter plan, therefore acting as a visible reminder to address these elements throughout.

7. LEVY, *supra* note 5, at 193.

Building Your Reference Library

As an aside, it is often useful to keep previous examples of matter plans handy when looking at conducting similar matters. If nothing else, this gives a strong baseline from which to develop the new matter plan. However, it is important to understand how realistic the initial plan was and adjust accordingly (despite stating the obvious, it is amazing how many times people "lift and drop" previous plans without any review). We will revisit this topic during our Review the Price section, as the review of previous performance can help identify a number of key process improvements when conducting similar matters if done in an appropriate way.

Remember, too, that there is a point when doing more planning becomes counterproductive in terms of the time spent and the level of value being added. As we said a few pages ago, "a project plan is not a strict playbook; it is a path to follow." Things will change. You will deal with it.

To Add or Not to Add: The Question of Contingency

I am often asked about whether to include contingency as part of a matter plan and, if so, how much? Although there is no hard-and-fast rule here, my suggestion when conducting fixed- or capped-fee arrangements, it is recommended to have an element of contingency built in (this being typically between 5 percent and 10 percent of the total effort estimated, although this will vary based on the complexity of the matter to allow for the coordination effort required throughout).

Similarly, if developing a matter plan jointly with your client, it is sometimes useful to include some contingency, as this provides the client with an appropriate level of cost that should be budgeted, based upon the scope and assumptions agreed.

Presenting the Plan

Once the hard work of thinking through the detailed activities of the plan is done, we sometimes find ourselves in a quandary as how to best present the plan in an easy format. Given its importance to the successful completion of the matter, it is vital that people can *easily understand* what they need to do.

However, in this day and age, there are a number of software applications that can help present this information in a number of visually appealing ways. I have seen matter plans presented as a simple spreadsheet, as a Gantt chart (which can be done via Microsoft Project and similar programs) or (less commonly) as a process flow.

Each has its strengths and weaknesses. Gantt charts can show tasks and deadlines in series so you are able to see the order more clearly, but can be more complex to prepare. Excel charts are less visually appealing, but are more commonplace and easier to pull together. Process flows sit somewhere in the middle, but are (currently) less commonplace. Milestone charts, although similar to bar (Gantt) charts, contain less detail—for example, the scheduled start or completion of the key matter deliverables and any external dependencies. Depending upon the complexity of the overall matter, tracking and reporting at this level of detail may be sufficient for your purposes.

Whatever you do, show only the level of detail that you need to get your message across. When it comes to matter planning, the *Keep It Simple* approach wins every time.

Timing

Schools of thought differ as to when to do this task—should it be before or after agreeing on the engagement letter? There are pros and cons to both. You may only need to include the key work areas (and associated deliverables) outlined in Step 2 within the engagement letter. If so, you can do this part after, although sometimes it helps to also include a graphical view of the proposed matter plan.

However, in order to have a good idea of potential cost, schedule, and required resourcing, I would suggest that you need to do this step *before* the engagement letter, as this gives you greater clarity and certainty of estimates. Ultimately, though, do what feels best.

Step 5: Agree to the Fee and the Fee Approach

We have already discussed at length how we can set and get an appropriate price for the work we do for our clients.

Indeed, in the real world, the fee has often been agreed to *prior* to the matter commencing, and therefore your challenge here when wearing your project management hat is striking the right balance between what needs to be done and how you do that within the constraints of the agreed fee.

To that end, I would like to cover some key areas you should consider when developing your budget and also that you should seek to include in any subsequent fee agreement.

The Estimating Challenge

Lawyers who are less experienced in managing matters often underestimate the time required to complete a specific task or activity. As humans, we tend to be overly optimistic that we will complete a task in record time (and then forget it actually takes two to three times as long!).

We also have to be honest with ourselves in other ways too. In some cases, estimates derived are no better than "guesstimates," either at the proposal stage or when developing a more detailed and robust budget.

However, there are a number of approaches that can be taken here to bring greater certainty into the budgeting process. For example, this may be as simple as giving an estimated percentage factor to the estimated duration of a task, with those with a 100 percent rating being those where you have the highest level of confidence in the accuracy of the estimate. As you go through this exercise for the remainder of the tasks on the matter, you will get to a stage where you are in a position to estimate the overall certainty of the entire matter. This information can then be used to give a more appropriate budget estimate to the matter.

Going through this exercise can help you have better discussions with your client on where there are potential risks to the matter. Those tasks that have the lowest percentage ratings are those where the degree of risk is potentially highest to the successful completion of the matter (note that this is distinct from *legal* risk). These are the areas that you should focus on in your discussions with your client, and where they hopefully can shed more light so you can improve your levels of certainty.

If there is still a high degree of uncertainty for the duration of the matter, you may also want to consider budgeting by phase. In this scenario, you would set an agreed price for the first phase, but provide a range for subsequent phases until more facts are known and the level of certainty improves. (Giving a range is often better at this stage, as this allows you to refine as you progress through the matter but also allows your client to ensure that appropriate budget expectations are set internally within their organization. After all, no one wants to go over budget.)

Other factors to consider when developing your budget include being realistic about your team's overall productivity (although we would like everyone to be 100 percent productive all the time, in reality that is often not the case), what additional tasks they will be required to support (for example, team meetings, ad hoc requests). And remember any contingency that you may have included!

Beware of the Potential Pitfalls to Profitability

There are a number of potential pitfalls that it is useful to address during this stage if you have not already done so. Some are appropriate to all agreements and other specific to the type of fee approach adopted.

In summary, typical areas you should consider are

- for hourly based work:
  - What is the period that these rates have been agreed? Are these rates agreed for the complete duration of the matter or a defined period of time (for example, if the matter may run for many months, or where agreeing rates as part of a broader client panel relationship, which are often multiyear)?
  - Are there any exceptions to these rates that may be permitted (for example, for specific subject matter experts)?
  - Do these rates allow for any promotional related increase for timekeepers on the matter (for example, moving from an associate to senior associate level)?
- for discounts based on volume:
  - Is the volume discount determined by the total amount of fees when calculated based on your standard rate or your agreed client billing rate (where a discount may also be implied)?
  - Is the level of discount determined once the threshold of fees is passed at point of billing or at point of collection?

    - Consider how many of your clients actually *do* pay within your agreed standard terms. If they don't, and you're adopting a volume-based discount driven by billings, not only are you giving them a bigger discount once the relevant fee threshold is passed, but you are also potentially carrying the cost of money/late payment!
- for performance- or contingent-based arrangement:
    - Have we clearly defined what constitutes success? This may be very tangible (for example, a trial decision) or be more subjective (for example, client feedback on a number of agreed criteria). These need to be defined from the outset to ensure a clear alignment of goals expectations.
- more generally:
    - Have you clearly defined the agreed payment terms?
    - If working on an international matter, have you agreed on the billing currency? Remember, exchange rates do have an impact—have you considered this?
    - Be specific about exclusions to your quoted fee. For example, typically these include sales tax (or VAT and equivalents) and other disbursement charges (such as additional outside counsel, expert witnesses, permitted travel, etc.).

When looked at separately, each of these items on its own may not appear too significant. However, I'm sure you can quickly see the potential impact on profitability of two or more of these combinations if not addressed appropriately.

The key message here is not forget to be specific around the fee approach *before* the matter commences. It will save potential frustration later. Having a clear understanding of the fee and approach from the start is *always better* for both our client and ourselves.

Sharing Budget Information with Clients

It may also be sensible to exercise a degree of caution in what level of fee (or budget) information you decide to share with your client, both during this step and in subsequent reporting (see Step 7).

What I am not advocating here is not being transparent with the client in what we do (which we should be), merely to what level of detail we provide. The more details provided can mean more scrutiny, more questions on specific detailed estimates, and more time spent managing these issues than conducting or performing work required for the matter.

This can come down to the difference between what is seen as an estimate, a proposal, or a budget. My own view is that it is appropriate to share some level of detail with the client—for example, budget by phase or even sub-phase, but that it can become counterproductive to the overall relationship if taken down to the task level.

One related recent development has been the launch of a number of recent software tools developed for this very purpose. These tools can often allow the client to see the exact progress of the matter by activity and timekeeper, prior to, and at point of, billing (for example, Viewabill). Some law firms also offer similar functionality (for example, DMH Stallard in the United Kingdom).[8]

In the aggregate this information can be useful, and even at the detailed level it can be helpful when seeking to conduct similar matters in the future, but that needs to be viewed in that light.

If it means that every estimate or time entry is challenged, it has failed in its objective, and unfortunately you have also failed in keeping the client's expectations met and overall relationship on track.

Adopting the five key steps outlined in this chapter will give you a solid foundation for your matter. Our next chapter looks at how we bring all these elements together, prior to the start of the matter itself and help you down the path of *easier* project management.

Don't forget *(a summary of the key points):*

- You wear two hats on your matter—your legal hat and your project manager hat. Each requires different skills and a different focus.
- Spending time up front helps establish a solid foundation for the rest of the matter—resist the temptation to rush in.

8. *See* VIEWABILL.COM, https://www.viewabill.com/pages/home (last visited Jan. 3, 2014); *Fee Transparency*, DMH STALLARD, http://www.dmhstallard.com/site/about/fee_transparency.

- Better communication, greater clarity, and enabling easier review should be your key themes from the start of your matter.
- There are 10 key steps recommended when starting your matter—many we typically do, but a few get forgotten. Make sure you do all 10.
- Remember our legal project management milk stool™ of scope, time, and cost. Changes in one impact the others—try to maintain balance at all times.
- Ineffective management of scope is the biggest cause of lower profitability and realization once a matter starts—agree up front how you will address any changes to the originally agreed scope.

Chapter 16

Bringing It All Together

We looked at 5 of our 10 key steps required before you dive into the matter in our previous chapter. Now let's take a look at how we bring some of these steps together, and get better prepared for conducting the legal work itself.

As part of this chapter we will look at the remaining five steps, as outlined below.

- *agreeing on the engagement letter*
- agreeing on the reporting format and schedule
- *establishing matter phases and tasks*
- *approving new timekeepers*
- staffing the core team and agreeing on the client responsibilities

As stated previously, whereas many of these activities are frequently done, those highlighted in *italics* are often done in a piecemeal fashion or skipped completely.

So let's start with our engagement letter, something that really should bring our previous five steps together into one clear, yet comprehensive document.

Step 6: Agree on the Engagement Letter *and* Share with the Team

While working as a management consultant, *no* project was undertaken unless an engagement letter was in place. I never used to think much of it. However, even in my brief time working within the legal sector and speaking with colleagues in other firms, I've come to acknowledge and recognize that this tenet does not always hold true on legal matters.

At the start of any new matter, a lawyer may specify the matter scope and the agreed fee in an engagement letter. This document is also sometimes referred to as a project charter or statement of work (although each is slightly different).

Regardless of its name, the document has three key objectives:

- to improve and enhance our understanding of our clients' situation, their business objectives, and their business (and sometimes personal) expectations (this was explored in Step 1)
- to clearly define, and create a mutual understanding of, work that is in scope and also the work that can be defined as out of scope (as explored in Step 3)
- to create more realistic expectations for both the lawyer and the client side

The benefits of having one are multiple. Apart from clearly setting expectations at the beginning of the matter, it can encourage more regular conversation throughout the matter, it can provide a useful basis when creating checklists on this matter and similar (in the future), it can be used to prevent potential billing queries due to the elimination of any confusion that may arise on scope and price, and finally, it can be used to improve communication both across the project team and when integrating new members of the team when seeking to bring them up to speed.

Although I would strongly recommend that you use an engagement letter for *all* matters when you can, it is *particularly important* when doing work on a fixed-, capped-, or contingent-fee basis.

So, what does a good engagement letter or statement of work look like?

Whereas some jurisdictions (for example, New York) clearly specify what must be included within an engagement letter, there is a wide variety of what can pass as an engagement letter within many firms. There are probably eight key themes within an engagement letter that should *always* be considered. These are outlined below, although the order can sometimes change (especially for the last four items):

- a brief overview of the matter and the business objective that the matter is seeking to support
- the key deliverables, or measurable objectives, of the matter itself (for example, the number of depositions required, number of pleadings, key documents required, etc.)
- an overview of the services that will be provided to the client as part of this matter—that is, those services in scope, and also specific mention of those key areas regarded as out of scope for the purposes of this matter
- any key milestones of decision points
- the agreed fee for the matter, including the fee approach agreed on (for example, whether this is fixed, contingent, or hourly fee based) and billing schedule
- an overview of the key resources on the project
- any identified risks (and the potential likelihood of them occurring)
- any key assumptions and constraints that impact both price proposed and scope outlined

When in consulting, engagement letters always included those elements identified above. However, I have sometimes seen a number of these missing when reviewing legal engagement letters in my experience (either when acting as a consultant or when working in a law firm). These documents do not need to be long—indeed, the more concise and simple the better (as long as there is clarity around budget and scope). Similarly, this can either be a stand-alone document or e-mail. But what is key is that both the responsible client and law firm partner "sign" and agree to its content.

One other useful area to incorporate is the agreed scope change process (which you hopefully defined as part of Step 3).

A hypothetical example of what *not to do* is shown in figure 16.1.

Dear < Client >

Re: Engagement of Services

This letter confirms our agreement that the Firm will represent < Client > in connection with general corporate matters in < Country A and Country B >, and other jurisdictions as instructed.

< Law Firm responsible partner > will have the main responsibility for representation, and will use other Firm lawyers and paralegals as deemed appropriate.

Unless agreed otherwise, our fees for services will be based on the time spent on the matter, determined at our hourly rates for the person(s) performing the agreed services. Rates and charges are subject to change. Our rates are exclusive of, and are subject to, all applicable taxes in the jurisdictions concerned.

If you have any questions, please do not hesitate to contact me. Otherwise, please sign and return the enclosed copy of this letter.

Regards,
< Law Firm responsible partner >

Figure 16.1
A Hypothetical Example of a Poor Engagement Letter

This illustrative example is one extreme, but it is always useful to consider when drafting engagement letters the impression that it may leave with the client. In my previous experience, I have seen a number of engagement letters that have four or five items defined as being in scope and then pages of items be defined as out of scope. You can imagine the potentially negative impression that would leave on someone objectively looking at the engagement letter! If possible it is therefore better to identify clearly what is defined as in scope, and then briefly but clearly summarize the key themes of areas to be out of scope.

It is also good practice not to develop engagement letters in a vacuum. It should be developed *jointly* with yourself and the client, or as a minimum with client review and input.

Once agreed, don't put the engagement letter in a drawer and then forget about it.

I can recall facilitating a project management workshop earlier in my career during which I asked the audience of about 50 attendees how many had seen the engagement letter for the matter that they were working on currently. At the time the response was not encouraging, with less than

25 percent confirming they had seen the engagement letter (if I was to ask the question to the same audience today, I would estimate the number would be closer to 85 percent).

An engagement letter can act as an extremely powerful communication tool. It can also help the client's internal and legal team understand what is in and out of scope. Without this we sometimes rely on our associates being mind readers in terms of what we can and can't do on a matter and then wonder why our costs are escalating, apparently, randomly.

Step 7: Agree on the Reporting Format and Schedule

The Basic Premise: No Surprises

One of the keys to successful project management is making sure there is regular (and effective!) communication throughout—there really should be no surprises.

There *will* be a number of difficult or awkward conversations that need to be had during the course of a matter. By having regular communication with your client through a combination of ongoing dialogue and *proactive* status reporting, these conversations become a lot easier and have a more solid foundation.

It pays to remember that "unlike wine, bad news does not get better with age."[1]

You should *proactively* suggest status reporting with your client (and ideally have an example of what a report could look like).

Agreeing on the Format

Whatever format you agree on with the client, this should be consistent time after time. It is amazing how quickly someone can scan a status report when familiar with the context and format, as they know quickly what to

1. Steven B. Levy, Legal Project Management: Control Costs, Meet Schedules, Manage Risks, and Maintain Sanity 216 (2009).

look for. Make it easy for yourself and your clients to see the key points. And keep the report clear, focused, and concise.

The format should also allow you to provide not only the tasks that are being conducted but also provide some commentary and insight around what is happening on the matter. Some typical models used in status reporting are highlighted in table 16.1.

It is also important to agree up front what *type* of information the client wants to see. Are they more focused on progress against budget, or by timeline? Do they want the report to highlight potential issues in some detail, and only give a summary of other key themes?

Table 16.1: Typical Reporting Models

Approach	Overview	Pros	Cons
"Traffic Light" report	Red, yellow, and green traffic light indicators are frequently used in status reports as they summarize performance information and allow the audience to focus on expectations Traffic lights and their thresholds need to be - specific to meaningful areas of control for the business; - assigned on the basis of clear rules for those areas; - tailored and relevant to the nature and timing of the project undertaken If status is yellow or red supporting comments should be provided	Easy to produce Potentially the easiest to understand (see cons)	It is common for reports to show the status as green when the reality is yellow *or worse.* Setting aside cultural reasons why this may be so, there are often two overlooked facts about using traffic lights—what they *mean* and *when they should change*

Approach	Overview	Pros	Cons
3 x 3 x 3	Provides the top three areas of progress (or accomplishments) since last report The top three areas of progress (or accomplishments) expected to be completed as part of the next report cycle up to three potential issues/risks (*and* any potential mitigating approach)	Easiest to produce Concise Allows easier comparison with previous status report	Can be difficult to get key messages clearly across to clients
Tabular	These reports have a series of regular items in left-hand column of the table on which you report progress (see figure 16.2 for an example based on fees) The next column reports progress made You can add columns to show variance by reporting period (for example, report by report, month on month, etc.)	Easy to maintain once reporting items agreed Can align to the agreed phase and task structures (see Step 8 for more details)	Can distract focus as table will include items where no progress made
Narrative Reporting	Typically short (up to a few paragraphs) Needs to be significantly tailored each reporting cycle	Most effective on short-duration projects	Hardest to write (as each is basically tailored each time from scratch) May need to use additional communications to further detail specific problems or issues being faced

Source: STEVEN B. LEVY, LEGAL PROJECT MANAGEMENT: CONTROL COSTS, MEET SCHEDULES, MANAGE RISKS, AND MAINTAIN SANITY 216 (2009) (table adapted from the key themes mentioned).

How Often?

There is a fine line between under- and overreporting. Agree to the frequency up front. It can always be amended later. Weekly or every two weeks is recommended. Monthly is too infrequent, especially given the duration of some matters. It can also give the impression that you are reporting reluctantly and are being secretive. Neither is good.

< Client > Matter : Status Report to < Date >

Phase of matter	Original fee estimate	Dollar value of time worked (summary of previous periods)	Dollar value of time worked (current period)	Dollar value of time worked (Total)	Original fee estimate remaining
SPA	$40,000		$10,000	$10,000	$30,000
Ancillary Documents	$10,000		$2,000	$2,000	$2,000
Due Diligence	$30,000	$15,000	$5,000	$20,000	$10,000
Labor & Employment advice	$10,000	$3,000	$1,000	$4,000	$6,000
Transaction Management	$40,000	$5,000	$10,000	$15,000	$25,000
Tax advice (Out of Scope)		$3,000	$3,000	$6,000	
Total in scope	*$130,000*	$23,000	$28,000	$51,000	*$79,000*
Total out of scope		$3,000	$3,000	$6,000	
Grand total		*$26,000*	*$31,000*	*$57,000*	

Figure 16.2
A Sample Status Report

Step 8: Establishing Your Matter Phases and Tasks

One area often overlooked, but invaluable throughout the lifetime of the matter (and after!), is the setting up of *appropriate* phases and tasks to capture time spent.

Although law firms and clients alike have developed a number of approaches to help capture this information since the 1990s and the introduction of e-billing, adoption to date has been relatively limited.

With the rise of legal project management, a renewed focus has returned to this concept, with the increasing realization that valuable information can be captured and used to not only help improve overall matter management but also encourage greater client communication and ultimately drive further process improvement initiatives within the law firm.

One of the biggest challenges frequently raised about using these codes (commonly referred to as task codes) is the sheer number of actual codes and variations included. Although a number of organizations have sought to help "formalize" these (more on this later), codes not only vary by practice area but also by client. You potentially could have a scenario in which a lawyer working on multiple clients and multiple matters is having to use multiple variations of the same task code. As a result, and despite the initial intent of those who were advocates of this approach to capturing time, the reality was that very few firms began tracking time at a phase or task-code level, and that it became more the exception rather than the rule.

However, capturing this information *is* valuable. The key to making this work is a number of very simple principles. First, are they easy to understand, and second, do we only have what we (or the client) really need and is of use?

Before discussing how to determine the right level of codes to use for you, first, it's useful to have a short history lesson.

E-billing and the Rise of UTBMS Codes

One of the very first attempts to create a classification approach was the development of the UTBMS task codes. You may have already come across UTBMS codes when working with your clients (UTBMS stands for the Uniform Task-Based Management System—catchy it isn't).

What these codes were intended to achieve was to establish a budgeting and billing system designed to provide clients and law firms with meaningful cost information on legal services, primarily with electronic billing.

These can also be very useful when budgeting and planning matters. From a legal project management perspective, they can be also extremely helpful in identifying where time is being spent and where potential process improvements may be made.

A note of caution, however: Adoption to date has been mixed. First, not all law firms and clients use e-billing, and therefore familiarity with these codes varies. Second, the scope of the codes that exist are limited, with the defined codes falling into four main categories—Litigation, Projects/Transactional, Counseling, and Bankruptcy. As such, some law firms and clients have sought to define their own codes and varying levels of granularity.

The original codes were developed by the American Bar Association, the Association of Corporate Counsel with support from Price Waterhouse LLP, and have gone through a number of revisions since. There is now a permanent group, the LEDES Oversight Committee, that reviews and maintains standards. (The LEDES acronym stands for Legal Electronic Data Exchange Standard).

Codes fall into two main areas: those for time entry and those for expenses. The time entry codes are then broken down into one of three levels:

- phase codes:
    - These describe the phase of the work performed, and begin with a letter to distinguish the code set used and are always numbers in multiples of 100.
    - For example, all Litigation-based codes start with the letter L, Projects, P, etc.
    - L100 indicates the Assessment, Development and Administration phase of handling a litigation matter; L200 indicates the Pre-Trial Pleadings and Motions phase, etc.
- task codes:
    - These describe the task performed. Here the Phase of work performed is inferred from the first two characters of the task code and are followed by numbers that are (at least as originally developed) multiples of 10.
    - L110 indicates Fact Investigation/Development tasks; L120 indicates Analysis/Strategy tasks, etc. Both of the codes in this example associate to Assessment, Development and Administration phase of the Litigation Code Set because both begin with L1.
- activity codes:
    - These describe the actual work performed by the timekeeper. Activity codes always begin with A1 and there are 11 codes in total. The activity codes are exactly the same across all of the original UTBMS set, and are the most granular when used in conjunction with the associated phase and task codes.
    - A101 is used to indicate that the timekeeper performed work associated with Plan and Prepare for, A102 indicates that Research was performed, A103 indicates Draft/Revise; etc.

A completed example would therefore look similar to the following:

- Phase: L300 Discovery
    - Task: L310 Written Discovery
        - Activity: A101 "Plan and prepare for"

If you think back to the work breakdown structure of phases we discussed during Steps 2 and 4, you can probably quickly see how these codes relate to both the same levels but also how one can be used to drive and inform the other.

To bring this a bit more to life, let's take a quick look at what these actually look like. Table 16.2 shows the current UTBMS codes for Litigation.

Table 16.2: Sample UTBMS Litigation Codes (Litigation)

L100 Case Assessment, Development and Administration	
	L110 Fact Investigation/Development L120 Analysis/Strategy L130 Experts/Consultants L140 Document/File Management L150 Budgeting L160 Settlement/Non-Binding ADR L190 Other Case Assessment, Development and Administration
L200 Pre-Trial Pleadings and Motions	
	L210 Pleadings L220 Preliminary Injunctions/Provisional Remedies L230 Court Mandated Conferences L240 Dispositive Motions L250 Other Written Motions and Submissions L260 Class Action Certification and Notice
L300 Discovery	
	L310 Written Discovery L320 Document Production L330 Depositions L340 Expert Discovery L350 Discovery Motions L390 Other Discovery

L400 Trial Preparation and Trial	
	L410 Fact Witnesses L420 Expert Witnesses L430 Written Motions and Submissions L440 Other Trial Preparation and Support L450 Trial and Hearing Attendance L460 Post-Trial Motions and Submissions L470 Enforcement
L500 Appeal	
	L510 Appellate Motions and Submissions L520 Appellate Briefs L530 Oral Argument

We also have "activity" codes. These are the same for all four categories.		
A100 Activities		
	A101 Plan and prepare for A102 Research A103 Draft/revise A104 Review/analyze A105 Communicate (in firm) A106 Communicate (with client) A107 Communicate (other outside counsel) A108 Communicate (other external) A109 Appear for/attend A110 Manage data/files A111 Other	
And finally, we have expense codes. These are also the same for all four categories.		
E100 Expenses		
	E101 Copying E102 Outside printing E103 Word processing E104 Facsimile E105 Telephone E106 Online research E107 Delivery services/messengers E108 Postage E109 Local travel E110 Out-of-town travel E111 Meals E112 Court fees	E113 Subpoena fees E114 Witness fees E115 Deposition transcripts E116 Trial transcripts E117 Trial exhibits E118 Litigation support vendors E119 Experts E120 Private investigators E121 Arbitrators/mediators E122 Local counsel E123 Other professionals E124 Other

It is important to use these codes with caution, however. To paraphrase the ABA's own guidance notes for the Litigation code set:

> The intention of the Litigation Code Set is to minimize multiple interpretation and options for coding time. It is recognized that not all litigation work will fit neatly in a particular category. Work can overlap tasks, categories may be imprecise, or time may be expended on the truly unusual. Users should categorize the work to its primary purpose. Definitions are provided for guidance. Where uncertainty envelops substantial or repeating work, it is best for client and counsel to agree in advance on the category to be used.[2]

The same caveats and considerations hold true for the other defined code sets, probably more so given that these are typically *less* granular.

It is important to note that there are some differences based on jurisdiction. For example, there is a slightly different Litigation code set used in Canada, with them also having minor changes to the Project and Counseling code sets made, and not adopting the Bankruptcy code set at all (as this was seen to be inapplicable and was therefore discarded).[3]

Regardless of what is actually used, these codes can still provide a *good starting point* when developing your respective matter phases and tasks.[4]

Adopting the Right Approach for You

Some of you when reading the above section may have been wondering how you will be able to implement these with your respective firm.

Some of you (certainly those of you who already may have a number of e-billing clients) may not be aware that you are actually doing this already and have your matter billing information captured at this level of detail (and, potentially even worse, are probably doing nothing with the information it provides!).

And some of you may be just plain befuddled about what to do.

2. http://www.americanbar.org/content/dam/aba/migrated/litigation/utbms/utbms.authcheckdam.pdf

3. *See Uniform Task-Based Management System (UTBMS)*, Canadian Bar Ass'n, www.cba.org/cba/PracticeLink/MF/utbms.aspx (last visited Jan. 3, 2014).

4. For a comprehensive list of all the UTBMS codes used, check out www.utbms.com or www.ledes.org.

When trying to work out what is right for you, there are probably two main questions you need to ask yourself:

- How detailed should these codes be?
- Should you use the existing UTBMS recommendations or adopt another approach?

(There is also, according to Jim Hassett, a third question, which is, When estimating future costs, how much weight should firms put on past experience? In sum, my view is focus on where the effort is being expended rather than the cost, and ask whether you could do it more efficiently—market conditions change and therefore any cost information is merely a guide at best. It can also be time-consuming and costly to try to reclassify past matters, which some firms have done).

Each firm approaches this challenge in a different way. Even within a firm it can also vary by practice group, and the complexity of the matter in question. (For example, those who are more involved in litigation-type matters are typically more accustomed to managing by phase or milestone, and may therefore be more familiar with this type of detail. Given the focus of the UTBMS code set, this theme is further consolidated. But not all would go much past the task level of detail).

How Detailed Should I Be?

The guiding rule here should be, What is likely to get greatest adoption within your firm and will provide you with the information you need?

Given that many firms are still trying to get a better grip on this area, you want a set of codes that cover what you need *and are meaningful*, are easy to find (and *therefore properly used* when charging time), and are relatively limited in number (by which I would typically recommend fewer than 20 at the task level). Anything else will be too much.

An example of a potential mergers and acquisitions simple task code list is shown in figure 16.3.

Using this as an example, there are a couple of themes it is helpful to point out.

DD	Due diligence
SPA	SPA & deal issues
STRU	Structuring
TANTI	Antitrust
DANC	Ancillary agreements
CLOS	Closing
PROJM	Project management
OOS	Out of scope

Recommended to include for all matters to aid better reporting and budgeting → PROJM, OOS

Figure 16.3
Sample Mergers and Acquisitions Task Codes

First, the list is relatively limited, which in turn means it is easier to track and capture time for the vast majority of activities an attorney would do on a matter. (I have also seen mergers and acquisitions lists that have more detail, but not frequently more than 15–20 tasks).

Next is the use of the project management task code. After all, where else will you track and capture your time (remember you should track how much effort you spend on this, even if you choose not to charge it).

And finally, have at least one code for out of scope. What we all know is that there is likely to be work that is potentially out of scope on the matter (as we discussed during Step 3). What, typically, lawyers are less good at is tracking the effort spent on those activities. By simply having an approach that makes lawyers think whether work is "in scope" or "out of scope" is very valuable, as it makes them think about what they are being asked to do.

It is an approach we use in my current firm, and I know is also adopted in a similar manner at a number of others, including Bilzin Sumberg and Faegre Baker Daniels.[5]

Taking the example in figure 16.3, you could therefore have two task codes for due diligence depending upon what was the originally agreed scope,

5. For more information, see *How to Track Legal Work That Is out of Scope*, LegalBizDev (May 22, 2013).

and the work subsequently *agreed* (the key word here!) and conducted but that was out of scope of the original fee estimate.

This tracking improves awareness, internal management, and external communication. In addition, if you begin to see the number of hours captured in the "out of scope" task codes increasing, it quickly acts as a warning sign to confirm with the client how they want you to proceed before the number gets even higher (and you potentially have to write down time).

Some other firms (for example, Baker Donelson) have taken a more granular approach.[6] For those firms that are able to get to this level of detail consistently, this will prove extremely helpful in driving the capture of valuable matter information. For the rest of us, the simpler the better during the initial adoption stages.

Which Way Now? UTBMS or My Own?

The UTBMS codes can provide you with a great foundation to build from. Depending upon the focus of your firm, you may also find that the existing codes are sufficient.

However, I have found that they are sometimes too general in nature to be useful, especially for areas such as corporate, tax, and employment. As such, many firms (including mine) have begun to develop their own codes for key areas of work to help capture the necessary level of detail that they wish internally (for matter analysis and future matter planning), and at a level that helps when communicating matter status to their clients.

One thing we need to be mindful of is what to do when we are using our own set of codes and yet we have a client who wants to use UTBMS codes, or may even have their own defined codes (either for e-billing purposes or another).

In this instance, there are really only two approaches:

- Use the client's codes and when required "map" these to your own post-matter (so you are able to conduct "like for like" matter analysis).

6. Jim Hassett, Legal Project Management: Quick Reference Guide 52 (3d ed. 2013).

- Convince your client that your codes are more appropriate for the matter in question.

It is important to make sure that regardless of the approach taken you can review and analyze the adopted task codes later. Too often, we finish a matter and then move immediately on to the next one. If you have used the client-defined or UTBMS codes on a matter, ask someone in your finance team or similar to help do a mapping for you (they will need some legal insight from you but probably no more than 10 minutes in this instance). Depending upon which time entry system you use, you may also be able to define both sets of codes there, making future analysis much easier.

But do not forget to do the mapping—it will pay off down the road.

So I guess there are really three forks in the road. Use UTBMS, use a variant of these codes (but add some of your own to give you the necessary detail), and finally, develop your own.

Focusing on the Bigger Picture

Whatever level you decide to go to (and indeed your clients ask you for) and whatever system of codes you choose to adopt, the benefits of a task-based budgeting and management approach are numerous:

- the ability to provide more predictable costs
- the ability to identify ways of further lowering cost
- a marketing edge created by a record of better results
- better communications from the outset with clients
- improved results as all the steps are identified and the key resources are better deployed
- a reduction in cycle times for bill preparation by the firm and bill payment by the client

The benefits are there for those willing to put in the effort, and realistically, there are many ways to accomplish this coding. Where most law firms are struggling today is getting the lawyers using an approach that they are comfortable with. Therefore, don't be too prescriptive at the start. *Aim for adoption, then standardization.*

As with most things, the key to success is to keep it simple.

Step 9: Approving New Timekeepers

One area often forgotten when starting a project is the process for bringing on (and approving) new timekeepers, especially on complex and/or multi-jurisdictional matters.

You may be surprised if reviewing some of your firm's larger matters to see how many timekeepers are involved on the matter that you have no visibility of, but also the amount of time each was potentially spending on the matter. Often the number of "invisible" timekeepers can be significant, and yet the overall amount of time for each relatively small (for example, two hours or less).

Whilst there may be a need for specialist resource for expertise on the matter, more often than not this is not the case. When it comes to reviewing the bill, it is often those timekeepers who find their time is written off or not charged.

By communicating a clear process up front to your own team as to the approach reviewing and approving new timekeepers to the matter, not only can you help mitigate the amount of time written off but you will also be able to make sure that these new team members are inducted properly and have a clear sense of matter scope.

Step 10: Staffing the Core Team and Agreeing on Client Responsibilities

Think back to some of the matters you have worked on. What made the good ones good, and the bad ones bad? Chances are high that the more positive experiences were those where you had a clear sense of what you needed to accomplish, and where you were being positively challenged and stretched in your role. Now take a step back in the present day, and think of the matters that you are now responsible for. What would the lawyers on your team say if they were asked the same questions?

How we choose to staff the team at the start of the matter has a key impact on overall success, profitability, and client satisfaction. We should therefore make sure we spend time to "get it right." Luckily, there are a couple of key rules of thumb that can help you do just that.

The Rule of One: One Task, One Owner

Each task should have only one owner.

You, as the matter lead, need to know who is responsible for conducting the task. The responsible lawyer also has a better sense of ownership of the task at hand. If ownership is blurred, too much time is wasted either chasing status or coordinating responses.

Staff by Level, Not Individual

Good practice is to staff by level, not individual. Although many of us typically prefer to use those lawyers we know from previous matters, you need to resist the temptation for the "easy fix." (It is also not limited to the legal professionals. Consultants are guilty of doing the same).

This initial tendency can be counterproductive and costly (both in terms of matter profitability and also to retention if you are using overqualified resources).

The advantage of identifying the level of the resource first (rather than the individual lawyer) is that it encourages you to assign *the right activities to the right level.* You then assign the right resources based on the identified level of expertise required. Now, I appreciate that there may be some staffing constraints, which means that the ideal or preferred candidate is not available. In that case, go with the flow and use the next best fit. Do not, as many lawyers have done in the past, decide it is then easier to do the work yourself.

(A slight caveat to this statement: As discussed earlier when looking at pricing and fee approaches, it may make more sense for someone who is very qualified to do a specific activity if they can do it significantly faster than another potential member of the team. This is especially true for fixed- or capped-fee arrangements. Even in this case, though, the basic premise holds true—that is, that you *assign the right activities to the right level.*)

Be Clear on Client Responsibilities

We often forget (or are, at best, reluctant) to be clear on those areas and responsibilities our client needs to perform during the matter.

We don't need to be specific about who in the client team will actually perform each activity (unlike us, where we want that visibility and clarity). However, we do need to be explicit about what the client responsibilities in aggregate entail. These should also ideally be documented in the engagement letter. Speaking of which . . .

Share the Engagement Letter

As we mentioned earlier, the engagement letter can act as an extremely powerful communication tool. So, once you have staffed your team, make sure they actually *see* a copy of the engagement letter. It will help them understand the matter at hand, key timelines, and scope. Otherwise, we will need to rely on their hitherto unproven psychic abilities.

The key theme of this, and the previous, chapter has been to make sure we "get it right from the start."

Through application of the 10 key principles outlined, you will do just that.

Putting a strong foundation in place from the start *really does* save a lot of grief and frustration later, not to mention the positive impact on matter profit and client satisfaction. In time, it also gets a lot easier as you begin to amass your own templates and methods of doing these steps quickly.

Resist the temptation to jump straight into the matter and its detail, enticing as it may be (see the sidebar "Are Lawyers Different?"). Your partners and clients will thank you for it.

Are Lawyers Different?

Dr. Larry Richard, in an article published in *Legal Management* in July/August 2002 called "You've Got Personality," looked at what makes lawyers different from the general public in terms of personality traits.

As part of this study, he noted that lawyers typically demonstrate "higher urgency" than the broader population (with a score of 71 versus 50 out of 100), with key symptoms being "impatience and a need to get things done." He has subsequently extended this original analysis to look at what are the right traits for legal project management, presented at LawVision's Legal Project Managers roundtable (March 2012).

Don't forget *(a summary of the key points):*

- Make sure your team knows what has been agreed with the client, keep them regularly informed, and make sure they know what to do when things deviate from your agreement.
- "No surprises" should be the guiding mantra behind all client communication and reporting—communications should be clear, concise, and (for format) consistent.
- Define the *appropriate* level of phases or activities that work for you and your client on the matter—do not overcomplicate it, otherwise its effectiveness is lost.
- Staff sensibly—there are some simple rules of thumb to help you.

Chapter 17

Maintaining the Momentum: During the Matter

You will probably be relieved to know that this is a much shorter chapter, and yet may be slightly confused as this is surely where the bulk of the work is, is it not?

From a legal perspective that certainly is the case, but at a project or matter level this should be less difficult—*if* you have taken time to build the solid foundation described in the previous chapters on getting it right from the start. If you have, this is where you reap your reward.

What often happens in the rush to start the matter (remember the earlier comment about urgency?) is that the solid foundation is wobbly at best. It may not seem important at the time, but when the hard legal work starts (and remember, this is why your client is paying you the big bucks!) you will have significantly less time to devote to *managing* the matter.

Overall, this chapter is going to cover six key areas:

- your role as the project manager
- managing your client's expectations
- keeping your team on track
- managing to your deadlines
- managing to the agreed fee
- managing change

Each of these areas directly relates to the key themes of communication or verification, and can be further grouped as those activities that relate to managing the client (No. 1 and No. 2), managing the team (No. 1 and No. 3) and managing the matter (Nos. 4–6). (For those of you wondering where we are in (legal) project management "speak," we are now entering the Execution and Monitoring phases; see table 17.1.)

Table 17.1: Our Six Key Steps: Where They Sit and What They Support

Step	Step Description	Theme(s) Addressed	Traditional Project Management stage
1	Your role as the project manager	Better communication Verification	Execution Monitoring
2	Managing your client's expectations	Better communication	Execution Monitoring
3	Keeping your team on track	Better communication	Execution Monitoring
4	Managing to your deadlines	Better communication Verification	Monitoring
5	Managing to the agreed fee	Verification	Execution Monitoring
6	Managing change	Better communication Verification	Execution Monitoring

Becoming the "Two Hatted" Lawyer

Over the last couple of years, there has been the slow but steady rise of a new breed of the two-hatted lawyer. Although it may sound like something taken from the pages of Dr. Seuss, it is anything but fictitious.

It is true, the two-hatted lawyer is still rare (at least the very good specimens are), but in time this will become the norm, as Darwinian theory takes hold (for those of you who believe in it).

So what is this strange breed? In short, one who is able focus on both doing the legal work required on the matter, but is equally adept at managing the matter (and not in the traditional sense). The legal stuff you already know and the good foundation put in place earlier will make wearing the second hat much, much easier.

Why is this going to become the norm? There are now a number of key differences in client expectations of their lawyers who lead significant matters on their behalf. Clients are now looking for (and indeed, sometimes demand) greater efficiency and effective management of the matter. Most lawyers need to be much more proactive to meet this challenge. The second key area is an increasing expectation from some clients that their outside counsel adopt the same project management tools and approaches that they use themselves (for example, this has been publicly stated by companies such as DuPont).

When wearing your second hat, your role as an effective matter manager becomes quite wide ranging, and will include the following:

- driving the development of (and subsequent management to) the engagement letter, scope document, and matter plan
- monitoring the budget, progress (actuals), and any changes to the originally agreed scope
- managing any conflicts within the team and key stakeholders
- managing all the stakeholder expectations
- monitoring and managing changes throughout the matter, whether these be staffing, changes in scope, timelines, fees, etc.
- ensuring that all necessary matter communications and information are shared with those that need to have visibility of it

However, it is important to remember that you don't need to do everything outlined above yourself. It is good practice, though, to have at least someone in your team keeping an eye on each of these elements.

It is also useful to enter into this with your eyes wide open. There are a number of potential challenges that you may come across at this stage (and that relate back to two of our three themes discussed in Chapters 15 and 16, greater clarity and better communication)—for example:

- if the actual scope is different to your original (and potentially client's) understanding (that is, a need for *greater clarity*);
- when there is a need to amend your schedule (for example, work is more complex than anticipated, or there is pressure from the client to complete certain tasks very quickly) (*greater clarity*);
- actual events overtake your plan (for example, when a trial date is brought forward, or where the client's target acquisition decides to acquire another company) (*greater clarity*);
- the client is taking a lot of your time (for example, this is common currently with some Chinese clients investing overseas who are less familiar with some of the legal topics to be addressed, and want more "partner" time) (*greater clarity*);
- the client is difficult to deal with (*better communication*); and,
- the project team does not feel informed (or even worse, the client doesn't feel informed) (*better communication*).

All of these can be anticipated during the earlier stages of the matter. Each of these are also not necessarily specific to a matter, but are *more common* project management themes. Over time you will be able to swiftly address these, either at the initial stages of the matter or by having a good process in place to allow you to manage these effectively during the matter itself.

Managing Expectations

A number of books and courses on project management or legal project management often have "managing expectations" as one of the last items covered during this stage of the matter. For me, it is the crux of what good project management (legal or otherwise) is about. It is also the one theme that is very focused on our *client*, rather than ourselves, more internally.

With your matter management hat on, this should be (no, *needs* to be) your number one priority—there should be no surprises to your client *throughout the matter*.

No Surprises!

Unless you are extremely fortunate, there *will* be changes during the lifetime of the matter—to one or more of scope, cost, and timeline (schedule). First, don't panic! Second, remember the key principle—no surprises. You should always let your clients know if there are changes to any of our legal project management milk stool™ legs. Don't keep them in the dark.

Some things may be minor and have a relatively minimal impact. Others, you instinctively *know* you need to discuss. A few may be somewhere in between—if in doubt, *always* err on the side of transparency, as it helps the client feel that they are able to influence the outcome and also increases the likelihood of any additional costs being approved.

Don't Forget: Expectation Management Started at the Proposal Stage

In a recent conversation with my ex-colleague, Ori, he reminded me of something that is very easy to forget. Expectation management *starts* at the proposal stage.

As Ori mentioned, expectation management "starts with being careful and specific when making any claims or promises during the initial proposal stage. It is, therefore, extremely important to consider the long-term consequences of any claims made which are made at that time."[1]

Although I am sure no lawyer would intentionally set out to make any claims or promises that they were unable to meet, the fact is that things do change between the time of the initial proposal and eventual commencement of the matter.

For example, what happens if you have promised your internationally recognized "A Team," only to discover that the "promised" skilled resources are either fully occupied elsewhere on another matter or, worse, have since left your firm? (This is also often the case when the team presented to the client is completely different from that which turns up on day one of the matter—something that causes clients no end of frustration and sets the matter off on the wrong foot from the start).

1. Ori Weiner, High Impact Fee Negotiation and Management for Professionals 208 (2013).

Discuss the "Rhythm" of the Matter

No. I am not advocating dancing here (although it may be a good way of keeping high morale amongst the team—depending on how good a dancer you may be). What I am referring to, and is something we have mentioned previously (Step 3), is making sure that the client understands clearly any changes in potential work effort involved during the phases of the matter. During the lifetime of the matter, there are likely to be peaks and troughs throughout, rather than a smooth flow from beginning to end. By having an early discussion on this with your client, you can avoid awkward discussions and interrogation of narratives at a later (billing) stage.

Managing the "Bad News Message"

When there is bad news, a common response in the legal community is to make a form of concession at the point of billing by taking something off the bill. This hurts you in two ways: first, from a matter profitability perspective, but second (and longer term more importantly), on a client satisfaction level.

According to some research done by the LawVision group and Dr. Larry Richard, although one of the most important skills required by lawyers is the ability to have "difficult conversations," the personality characteristics of lawyers often inhibit this.[2]

This is, in part, lawyers being low on two key personality traits that directly impact this—these are the traits of resilience and sociability.

- *Resilience* (sometimes also referred to as *ego strength*)—if being low in this trait, you are more likely to be very sensitive to feedback and react badly to criticism. Lawyers who have this are those who typically do additional work on the matter but don't charge for this, as they do not wish to have the "difficult conversation" with the client. (Lawyers scored 30 percent versus 50 percent for the general public on this measure, although the spectrum was quite wide and many lawyers scored in the bottom 10th percentile.)

2. Larry Richard, *You've Got Personality*, Legal Mgmt., July/Aug. 2002. The article looked at what makes lawyers different from the general public in terms of personality traits. He has subsequently extended this original analysis to look at what are the right traits for legal project management, presented at LawVision's Legal Project Managers roundtable (March 2012).

- *Sociability*—this trait refers to the ability for someone to be open and share information about themselves, even if this may be emotionally difficult. Again, for many lawyers this can act as a further disincentive to have the "difficult conversation." (Lawyers scored only 12.8 percent versus 50 percent for the general public on this measure.)

Contrary to popular belief, admitting mistakes can often improve the degree of trust with your client and strengthen the overall relationship. But remember the earlier comparison to wine—bad news does not get better with age.

It is often how you deal with the difficult issues that informs your future relationship. As an illustration, think of how you have been treated in a restaurant when you have raised an issue—in some, you will never go back, but for those that quickly and effectively dealt with your problem you have probably returned multiple times over.

Use Your Status Reports

Apart from the regular client conversations, regular client status reporting (for example, weekly or every two weeks) also plays a pivotal role in managing client expectations. It is amazing how quickly clients get used to receiving the (weekly/biweekly) status reports. In my experience, I even had a number of clients who would query if this was delivered even an hour later than "usual," they had become so used to the receipt of these. Status reports are a *key tool* in managing client expectations, in addition to any specific discussions you may have. Just remember to make them clear, concise, and factual—otherwise they will never be read and you will mistakenly assume that "all is well" on the matter, until you discover painfully that it isn't.

The Dangers of Hidden Stakeholders

Finally, be mindful of the dangers of hidden stakeholders—these are the clients who remain in the background, but who can have a significant impact on the outcome of the matter. They could be from another business unit or department, or even in the same department and looking to advance the expense of their colleague.

Whoever they are, they may be out of sight, but they have an unnerving ability to become *front* of mind if not managed carefully. Identify these players quickly if you can, and make sure you communicate and manage them as much as you can.

Keeping Your Team on Track

Making sure that your team stays on track is sometimes one of the hardest things to do, especially if you have teams that are working in multiple jurisdictions and also across a number of different practice areas. If you then add into this mix the need to use a number of correspondent law firms where you may not have an office, this can become even more complex, as you are also now dealing with third parties.

In your role as the matter manager, it is key that you avoid being bogged down in too much detail. Remember the saying "You can't see the forest for the trees"? You need to keep a focus on the bigger picture and manage to that. Your team is in place to focus on the details.

At the Very Start

By simply communicating and making visible a number of key documents, your team will be much more able to stay on track, as they will have a much better sense of the overall context.

For example:

- sharing the matter plan (or as a minimum, key dates) with everyone creates a sense of urgency and also reminds them that they are not working in a vacuum (that is, others may be impacted by their own ability to deliver work on time)
- making sure each member of the team knows what they need to do
- making sure that your team knows where to charge their time to (and reminding them to do so *promptly*)
- reminding them of the process for flagging potential out-of-scope requests or requesting new timekeepers (as identified in *Steps 3 and 9*, respectively, in our previous chapters on "Getting it right from the start")

Addressing these "hygiene" factors up front will help.

The Importance of Regular Team Meetings

One very effective way of ensuring that the team is focused on the overall objective and upcoming tasks, milestones, and key deliverables is via regular team meetings ("regular" here will vary depending upon the duration and complexity of your matter, but at least weekly is recommended).

Standing Up Can Be Good for You

I had a boss when a consultant who every morning held a "stand up meeting" for the key members of his team. (This obviously can only be done if you are all in the same place, but the concept can also work if there are only a few needing to conference in by phone). By having all of the team stand, it helped keep people focused on delivering concise updates, but also allowed him to quickly deliver any key messages and updates. Often within five minutes the key points have been covered and key messages delivered. Then it was back to work.

Having this regular forum to exchange information cannot be highlighted enough. All too often I have come across surveys (both internal and external) in which associates (or consultants when I was one) are requesting more information on the matters that they are working on.

A suggested agenda for a team meeting is provided in Figure 17.1.

Key Topics for discussion	*Indicative Timings*

• Review current matter status, including
  • progress to plan (timeline *and* deliverables)
  • financial status: budget vs. actual costs (by phase if appropriate)
	(10 minutes)

• Review recent change requests received/approved and discuss impact	*(5 minutes)*

• Review
  • changes to client expectations/key stakeholders
  • potential risks/ mitigating approaches
  • changes to team staffing
	(10 minutes)

• Confirm and agree next steps
  • Confirm and agree next steps/actions (including any updates to project plan)
  • Agree on date/time of next meeting (if possible)
	(5 minutes)

Figure 17.1
Sample Team Meeting Agenda

If the meeting has a number of actions identified, these should be issued promptly (by which I mean within 24 hours as an absolute maximum delay) by e-mail or similar (see below about collaboration tools). Doing so promptly both allows you to then adjust your focus onto other matters and allows the "actionee" to start working on their action in a more effective manner.

Making Information Easy to Find

The easier it is to find information, the more likely your team is to refer to it. There are a number of readily available tools that we already use in our day-to-day professional (and often personal) lives that can ease this process.

You can effectively use your existing office software tools to help keep the team on track, whether you are more familiar with Microsoft Outlook, iCal, or similar programs.[3]

Each of the office tools typically has a range of calendar, to-do list, and e-mail features that you can use. These may range from having a number of shared calendars for the project team to using team distribution lists for meetings and e-mails to the ability to set up rules that "prefile" specific e-mails from named individuals or groups. You may also look to set up a number of shared folders (with or without restricted access) within your document management system. The possibilities are many. Help guides for your software application will provide more details.

You can also take advantage of instant messaging applications to quickly share appropriate information, ask questions, or get a quick status update. Applications such as Yammer are readily available and can often be downloaded for free or already come with your Microsoft Office application software suite.

Another approach that a number of firms are adopting is using collaboration tools. One of the more common examples of this is Microsoft SharePoint, although there are a number of other options available. Each

3. Jim Hassett, Legal Project Management: Quick Reference Guide 86–89 (3d ed. 2013).

has the ability to set up a central location for the project team to access, review, and edit key project documents.

This allows you to set up team calendars, contact lists, task lists, and shared folders. This can be expanded for key types of work; for example, as part of due diligence you could use this functionality to create document indexes, enable easier review, capture issues, post questions and answers, and so on, with documents grouped in a manner that makes sense on your matter.

Access to this can be restricted to your team only, or you may choose to make these available (subject to any technical constraints) to include your client and its team. As this allows you to share information in real time, workload and progress becomes much more transparent (in addition to becoming much more efficient).

Managing to Your Deadlines

The first thing you need to do here is make sure that your team is aware of the key dates, milestones, and deliverables at all times. If following the suggestions included within "keeping the team on track," this should not be too difficult.

But there will be times that you need to amend your existing plan. It happens. For example, the actual execution of the tasks in hand will overtake your plan. This could occur when the matter team initially comes on board. If it does, one good suggestion here is to have them focus on the simpler, more discrete tasks first.

Realistically, you will continue to refine your plan during the early stages of the matter as new information comes to light. For example, you may need to refine your initial phase structure based on a request from the client (about how they wish to see reporting) or due to a new work stream or sub-phase being a more sensible way to capture effort and associated cost. You should also remember to keep an eye on previously identified risks, and be on the lookout for any potentially new ones, as these may have an impact on the existing deadlines in place.

Condensing Your Plan

There will also be times when you need to *condense* the originally agreed time plan or schedule, especially when deadlines are looming and there are tasks running late.

Some of the options available to you include the following:

- look to rearrange tasks (including having the client take responsibility for some tasks, or "rebalance" work within the team)
- add resourcing (an all too common solution, either through splitting tasks between a number of resources or having the new resource focus solely on the critical tasks)—this can add significant cost, not all of which may be recouped in fees
- look to reduce scope (although that then leads to a difficult client conversation—it is, however, often the most necessary option)
- one final technique commonly used in project management is to "fast track" work, in which work normally done in series (as the subsequent activity is dependent upon the outcome of the first) is done in parallel, based on some key assumptions—the danger here is that there is a further delay if the assumptions are proved to be incorrect, so use sparingly!

Regardless of what approach you choose to take, once the change is made, make sure that those who need to know, do. *Communication is king.*

A Word to the Wise

It is useful to be aware that sometimes our clients may see the reduction of any matter timetable as a way of lowering the final bill to be paid. This is most evident if using hourly based fees. If you take a quick step back and think about it for a second, you may quickly realize the impact—the client is wanting the same ultimate value but wishing to pay less for it.

If a shorter matter duration is requested by the client, only consider reducing any agreed fee if there is an actual reduction in work effort required (due to a change of scope) rather than a compression of time. (Sometimes I have even seen lawyers argue, with good cause, that this actually *increases* the originally agreed fee).

Managing Work to the Agreed Fee (or Simply Managing to Budget)

This is sometimes referred to as managing to budget. Personally, I prefer "managing to the agreed fee" for one very simple reason: one person's budget is another person's cap (remember our discussions during our chapter on negotiation?).

A budget also implied it can be changed in time and therefore subconsciously can mean that there is less rigor of focus on meeting it. The concept of an "agreed fee" feels more absolute (even if this, too, may change due to changes in scope).

The obvious action here is to keep an eye on your original phase estimates (defined during Steps 2 and 4 of the previous chapter) and regularly monitor progress against these (as defined during Step 8 of the previous chapter). An example of a simple fee tracker is shown in table 17.1.

Table 17.1: An Example of a Simple Fee Tracker

Phase Of Matter	Original Fee Estimate	Week 1	Week 2	Week 3	Week X	Original Fee Estimate Remaining
SPA	$40,000		$8,000	$2,000		$30,000
Ancillary Documents	$10,000		$2,000	$2,000		$6,000
Due Diligence	$30,000	$5,000	$5,000	$20,000		$0
Labor & Employment advice	$10,000	$1,000	$2,000	$3,000		$4,000
Transaction Management	$40,000	$5,000	$8,000	$15,000		$12,000
Tax advice (Out of Scope)		$3,000	$2,000	$3,000		
Total in scope	*$130,000*	$11,000	$25,000	$42,000		*$52,000*
Total out of scope		$3,000	$2,000	$3,000		
Grand total		*$14,000*	*$27,000*	*$45,000*		

There are, however, a number of other techniques you can adopt that will also help. These are highlighted below.

Invoice Regularly

First, invoice frequently (for example, monthly or at agreed milestones). A good guide is to invoice monthly if the matter is two months or more in duration. I know of a number of firms that do this very successfully, even if this is not the "cultural norm" within their specific jurisdictions (for example, some of the jurisdictions in Asia). If you don't ask, you will never know—and you may get a pleasant surprise when your client agrees.

Apart from a positive impact on cash flow, this also provides another two benefits: feedback and profitability. If your client has a query on the bill, first, this is discovered during the matter (not at the end) and allows you to change course as needed. Second, rather than your client then being able to query the *total* amount of fees (with the risk that you need to take a severe "haircut"), they are able to only potentially withhold the outstanding amount of fees. (A third benefit may also be that you are in a better negotiating position if this happens during the course of the matter, as the client will also be focused on ensuring its successful conclusion.)

Using Alerts

A number of law firm client teams use internal "alerts" to notify them at key points throughout the matter when fees are being accrued. Although the ability to do this varies depending upon your time recording and billing systems, the basic principle is that these alerts are based on the level of fees accrued against the matter, which are then communicated to the appropriate matter partner (and other appointees) as required.

Specific levels of alert will vary (for example, some people prefer this to be an absolute dollar figure rather than a percentage of the total), but a good guide is to have (as a minimum) alerts issued when fees accrued reach the 50 percent, 75 percent, and 85 percent of the total mark.

Whilst many use an automated process, you can achieve the same objective by having your finance team review information and report back to you, especially for significant matters. There are also a number of software tools that are specifically designed to help you manage this type of process more effectively—for example, Thomson Reuters' Engage, or those from ERM Legal Solutions.[4]

Remember the RULES

The acronym RULES is used in many law firms today and provides an extremely useful way to help your matter team focus on the key drivers of profitability. This concept was introduced to the legal world by Robert J. Arndt in his book *Identifying Profits (or Losses) in the Law Firm* (published by the ABA in 1988).

In some respects, the concepts he went on to describe link directly back to one of our very earliest chapters.

The acronym itself stands for

- Rates
- Utilization
- Leverage
- Expenses
- Speed

Each of these drivers will help improve profitability if appropriately managed. Some have more of an impact than others. Figure 17.2 provides a summary of RULES.

Taking each of these drivers in turn:

- **Rates:** The charge appropriate for the work you're doing. Seek to avoid giving any additional discounts over and above those *initially agreed* with your client. I have always been amazed at how frequently I hear of discussions in which partners in a number of law firms automatically reduce the bill further prior to sending the client an invoice. Whereas

4. Examples of sample project management software applications include Thomas Reuters' Engage product (details available via http://engagelpm.com/offer/?gclid=CJaWn5KwobkCFQai4AodQnQA6A) and ERM Legal Solutions (details available via http://www.ermlegalsolutions.com).

in some situations this can be quite smart tactically, more often than not it is just a knee-jerk reaction.

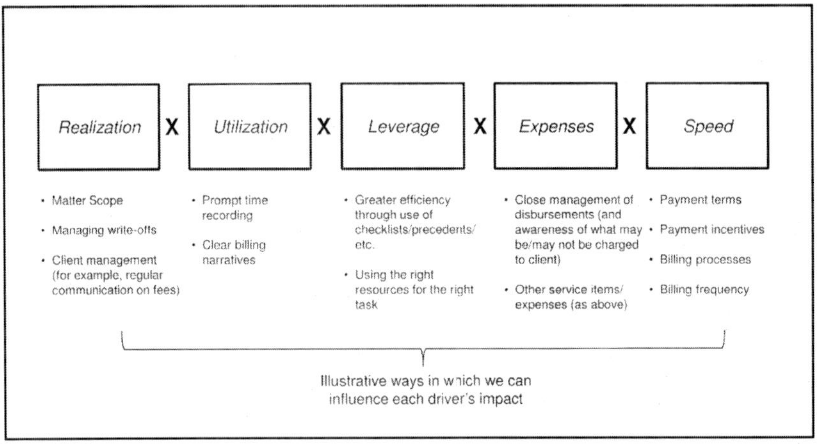

Figure 17.2
The Concept of RULES

- **Utilization:** Make sure that you are capturing *all time* spent for the client that may be charged. It is also good to periodically do a "sense check" to make sure that the work you're doing is profitable—we can all be busy, but not necessarily productive, nor profitable. If you can cast your mind back to our negotiation section, and the concept of the "best alternative" or "walk away" point, consider that we could be more productive and indeed possible to longer term by trying to attract and win new business than being busy on an unprofitable matter.
- **Leverage:** Typically, bringing more junior resources into your team is helpful both from a profitability perspective, and also, in time, in the overall effectiveness as they are further developing their skills for the next time. But leverage is not solely resource driven. One element that is useful to also consider is whether there is *technology* that can be used to improve overall efficiency. For example, one thing we use extensively with my current firm is SharePoint technology to allow greater collaboration across our client teams (and indeed with our clients), and

also any proprietary developed databases you may have. Think how you can *work smarter*.

- **Expenses:** Remember what can and cannot be charged. This will often depend on a client's outside counsel guidelines or similar, and also by jurisdiction. For example, in some jurisdictions it is appropriate to charge a flat percentage fee for expenses and disbursements, rather than provide an itemized bill. Indeed, this approach was still common in consulting a few years ago, but this figure could sometimes be 10 percent or more. If you have current expenses that cannot be charged back to the client (a situation becoming much more commonplace—for example, for secretarial overtime, printing, conference calls, etc.), it is advisable to look for ways to further reduce this cost item as it is coming out on any profit figure that you are generating. Although the figure itself will vary depending on the nature of the assignment and jurisdictions involved, when I have done some analysis on this in the past, sometimes this can become as high as 5 percent of the total fees for the overall matter itself. This, in effect, acts as a further 5 percent discount on fees but we very rarely flag this to our client, either for fear of being seen to be wasteful (not true), or for fear the client will not value this additional discount. My own advice here is that whether the client values this or not we should *make it transparent* to the client, and at the very minimum we should be including this impact in any matter analysis that we conduct for future, similar matters. It also, unsurprisingly, has a major impact on the matter profitability but is often (mistakenly) overlooked when conducting matter analysis.
- **Speed:** It sounds obvious, but get the bills out on time! As you have probably already experienced with some clients, their willingness to pay can change as the memory of a successfully completed matter fades into the distance. (See figure 17.3 for a representative client's willingness to pay cycle).

Simple, Yet Effective

One tip I recently heard of, and that I thought was great due to its simplicity, is the following.

When having a conference call internally with your team, at the end make sure you inform everyone of the following three bits of information:

- the *time* permitted to be charged on their time report (if indeed, the time is able to be charged)
- the appropriate *code* to use, and finally
- the appropriate *narrative* to use

Sounds simple, but will save you time and reduce client queries over billing.

Managing Changes to Your Matter

The final step here is managing the changes to your matter.

We talked earlier about the need to put in place a simple process to address any changes in scope (Step 3 of "Getting it right from the start"). The reason we placed so much emphasis on it at that stage is that it was removed from the "heat of battle." Now you are there, and your efforts then make managing any subsequent change so much better now. (If you didn't, you will next time.)

Top tip: When changes are made, remember to inform *all* those that need to know—there is nothing worse than having one of your key clients finding out from others (which, in turn, is likely to make them become disenchanted at best).

It Is Not Just Scope

"Scope creep" is often inevitable on a matter and is the one element that impacts fees and profitability most significantly, but it's also important to remember that things such as changing the time duration of the matter is also a change of scope.

When things change discuss this promptly—the longer it takes for you to raise the issue with the client, the more likely you will only recover part of your fee, regardless of the reasons for choosing to raise this issue later. This is a negotiation, and as in any negotiation, it is important to get the timing right.

8. Signing (and completion)
Wow – our <Law Firm> was excellent ! No one else could have done it. They are worth every cent.

7. The day before signing
We are all in 'panic' mode – except our <Law Firm> folks – they are very calm – this may just work

6. A week before signing
This is never going to fly. I am going to lose my job

5. Two weeks before signing
I am not sure this will complete on time. I will be in trouble – can our lawyers help ?

4. After a joint call
Wow! Our < Law Firm > really understood the issues and what the other party does

3. A few days later
I don't have such a good feeling about this matter after all

2. The next day
I am glad we instructed < Law Firm > - this could be more complicated that I thought!

1. The day we are confirmed
We have got some good lawyers to help us on this important deal

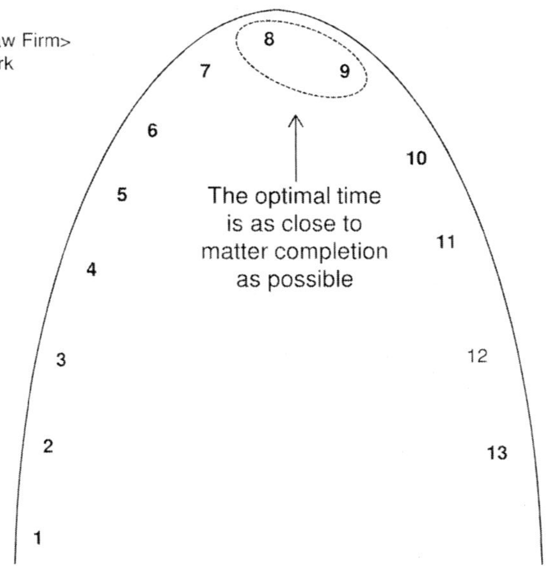

9. Ten days later
Our <Law Firm> were great – they made a straightforward deal run smoothly

10. One month later
Our <Law Firm> got it done – although the deal was never in doubt

11. Six weeks later
Which deal? Oh that one. Yes it was fine – too many lawyers though

12. Two months later
You will not believe how much our <Law Firm > says the matter cost

13. Four months later
Some random person at <Law Firm> has just sent me a reminder for the unpaid invoice for that simple deal I did a while back – they will be lucky to get any more work from me!

A Client's Willingness to Pay

The situation can also sometimes be more difficult when the matter has been won by a competitive pitching process, especially if the successful fee proposal was toward the lower end of your initially proposed range.

If there are subsequent changes of scope during the matter progressing, although difficult, you do need to reopen the fee discussion, and this should be done in a way consistent with the approach you and your client agreed to at the outset.

Make sure you fully understand your client's perspective when seeking to reopen these discussions and understand what *really* is important to them (for example, is it quality, budget, or fee?). If the relationship is valued by the client, nine times out of ten, a sensible fee discussion will always be possible.

"But It Is Only a Minor Change"

One final thing: clients can sometimes also make light of, or trivialize, a scope change (for example, "It should be very easy to do XYZ"). Often this is merely a negotiation tactic, but be wary—it has caught out many able lawyers before you.

I can remember one client, whilst recognizing that scope change may be inevitable on the matter, stated that he only wished this to be discussed for *significant* changes in scope. The challenge here is what is meant by significant, as it will mean different things to us as a law firm and to our client.

As with any statement like this, make sure you clearly understand what is being required before committing!

Don't forget *(a summary of the key points):*

- From a legal project management perspective, this stage is all about managing three critical elements: your matter, your client, and your team.
- Don't put off the difficult conversations —and remember that how you manage any "bad news message" can impact your profit through giving unintended discounts.
- Make sure that everyone who needs to know, does know—especially if there are changes agreed to scope. Never assume those who need to know do.

- Remember the RULES—effective management of these will have a significant impact on your bottom line. Small improvements to price make bigger improvements to profit.

Chapter 18

Making the Right Lasting Impression

This final stage is your opportunity to make a lasting impression. You may think, "but surely everything we've done already will convince our client we are the right folks for the job," and indeed your legal capabilities may have come to the fore frequently on the matter.

But it all counts for nothing if you make a mess of this stage. Yet, in reality, the thought of completing the matter administration is probably one that has tended to be given limited focus, if any, and typically sits very low down on the list of "must do" priorities.

During this stage there are three key themes that you should look to cover:

- the *administrative close* of the matter (including that all important final payment)
- *capturing feedback* on the matter from both your own client team and the client themselves
- the *building of institutional knowledge*—that is, the capture of lessons learned, best practice examples, and work products

We'll take a closer look at capturing feedback and building our knowledge capital when discussing our Review the Price stage in the subsequent chapters, but will also cover them very briefly here.

Don't Forget the Admin!

I confess, this bit is not exciting, and it does not matter how hard you try to dress it up. Getting it wrong, though, can build problems down the line in terms of the overall client relationship and payment of fees.

Getting Formal Sign-Off

The first thing it is important to do is to get formal sign-off of *everything* that you have delivered and that is complete.

It may sound obvious, but it's really important to get this sign-off because it is more than an acknowledgment that the project is completed (or at least substantially so), it's the opportunity to confirm with your clients that you really did meet the originally discussed "conditions of satisfaction" and that they are pleased with the outcome (or at least you are aware of where their frustration may be). Stephen Levy also goes on to point out that this also helps avoid the "one more thing" type of request, in addition to acting as a good barometer of your client's intent to use you again (also known as the "repurchase intent").[1]

Also, remember that not all things need to be *fully* completed at this time either. There may be a number of small items outstanding.

Recently, I had an extension built in my house in the United Kingdom. As is customary in these situations, we inspected the work and "signed off," subject to our "snag list" (for those maybe not aware of the term, a "snag list" is a list of minor items that need to be addressed, such as a wall needing repainting, a plug socket being attached, or similar). A snag list can work well on a matter too.

However, just like our builder friends, it is important that if there is a snag list in place, that we don't forget about it and take action *promptly*.

I also have a confession. When an inexperienced consultant (managing one of my first major projects), I was working for a global consumer products client in its European headquarters in Munich. We had completed

1. Steven B. Levy, Legal Project Management: Control Costs, Meet Schedules, Manage Risks, and Maintain Sanity 230 (2009).

and signed off all the deliverables, and the rest of the client team had left to travel back to their respective countries on a balmy Friday afternoon, when the client appeared at my shoulder and asked, "Where is this one?" (pointing to a line on the engagement letter).

One deliverable (luckily—for me—a summary of all the other deliverables and their respective folder locations) had not yet been done. A few frantic phone calls later to my team (and a delayed flight) and all was right again with the world. The moral? Learn from my mistake, and *always* keep a watchful eye on *all* deliverables—regardless of how important you think that they may be. As my experience above highlights, sometimes you *do* need to sweat the small stuff.

The Final Invoice

Less easily forgotten is the final client invoice. Hopefully, you will have been billing throughout the duration of the matter (for the reasons previously stated). The final invoice, however, creates its own challenges: after all, there is no opportunity to go back to the client with any further fees.

I am frequently told of examples where a client team has prepared the bill, they have checked to ensure that no outstanding time is yet to be entered, and yet within days of the final invoice being paid, some uncharged time is discovered and needs to be written off. Irrespective of the value of time being written off (which can sometimes be significant), this is purely down to how the matter has been managed and can be corrected—with a little effort.

The Zero-Sum Game: The Consequences of Good Delivery and Poor Time Capture

I know of a situation in one law firm where the client was extremely pleased with the quality of work done and agreed to pay the law firm in question a "success fee"—if the firm was able to send the final invoice promptly (this was to align with the client's payment cycle). The firm duly submitted the invoice. The client—as promised—paid the bill and agreed success fee immediately and all looked rosy. That was until, a few days later, unrecorded time for the value of the success fee was entered, and the "additional profit" that the partner had been able to gain evaporated. Don't make the same mistake.

Given this, it is really important that you communicate to all your client team (and also any external counsel that you may also be responsible for) the deadline for entering all remaining time and remaining costs. Time recording disciplines vary by company, but it really is key to get this right—the impression this gives if it is done badly is very, very hard to counter, and can prove costly in more terms that one.

Once you have captured all outstanding time and costs, it is also useful to discuss this with the client before sending the invoice. This allows you to set expectations, understand any concerns that they may have, and address any concerns raised appropriately. The key words here are *discuss* and *before*. Too often invoices are sent with little or no communication. The responsible lawyer then wonders why they have not been further instructed or paid for work done. Don't make that mistake either.

Gathering Feedback: The Matter Debrief—An Overview

We are going to cover this in more detail in the next chapter, but it's useful to give an overview here. The matter debrief (also sometimes referred to as an "after action review," "post-transaction review," or similar) is one of the areas most often neglected by lawyers, and yet is one of the most valuable activities that you can do on behalf of your firm.

It is here that you will gain valuable feedback from your team and your client, and identify ways in which you can become even better and how you deliver (and price) your services.

However, very few law firms currently do this. Typical responses given range from one such as "I am too busy," "It isn't chargeable," or even that "It is not something that we do in our firm." None, I repeat none, are good reasons not to do this. Clients are now beginning to expect this from their legal providers, and those not looking to address this meaningfully will differentiate themselves certainly, but not in the manner they had perhaps hoped for.

It is here that we can ask questions such as "what worked well or less well during the matter?" "what should we change the next time we conduct a similar matter?" "what did we learn?" "what can we reuse on other matters?" and so on.

Some suggested questions to ask are shown in table 18.1, but there are two that as a minimum should *always* be asked:

- What went well on the matter?
- What could we do better next time? (This one is key, as this helps identify where we need to improve and focus.)

The process itself is essentially twofold. The first is to conduct a debriefing or feedback session with your own client team, the second is to do the same with your client. There may be some debate about the order in which you should do these activities; however, my preference would always be to do the internal team first as this often provides you with more information and insight prior to meeting the client. As an aside, these may also be easier to organize.

Table 18.1: Sample Matter Debrief Questions

Questions to ask your client *and* your team	Questions to ask your client *only*	Questions to ask your team *only*
What went well?	What could we learn from some of your other legal providers?	What did we learn on the matter? For example, this could cover scoping, our assumptions, our pricing, our staffing, etc.
What could we do better next time?	How can we jointly deliver greater value on future matters?	What good assets (for example, precedents, checklists, and templates) did we develop?
Did we understand the business objectives?	Would you look to use our firm again? (If so, why? If not, why not?) (This can be extended to "Would you recommend our firm to any colleagues based on our work on this matter?")	How should we best share our "learnings" from this matter within the firm?
Did we meet [your/the client's] expectations?	How "commercial" and "pragmatic" was our advice?	If we were doing this matter again, what would/could we do differently?
Did we deliver value for money? (If so, how? If not, why not?)	On a scale of 1–10, how would we rate for this matter?	

From experience, these meetings work best in person, but do them however you can. The key thing is to *do something and do it promptly* after the matter completes and while it is all still fresh in everyone's mind.

In Chapter 19, we will go into a bit more detail about how to structure these reviews and give some hints and tips, as sometimes people may be wary about openly providing feedback into these types of meetings, especially more junior members of your client team.

Building Institutional Knowledge

Teams change, lawyers move to other firms, set up in private practice, or leave the profession entirely. What happens to all their cumulative knowledge and experience? Often nothing. At best there is a quick review of their computer's hard drive (and then nothing).

The amount of "lost" value escaping from law firms is massive.[2] All professional services firms rely on the ability of their teams to provide the level of knowledge and insight that make their clients choose them.

The old adage, "knowledge is power" is true—but in today's day and age for professional service firms, it is at the *institutional* level. Unfortunately, many in these firms also contend that it is true—perhaps even more so—at the *individual* level. This is further compounded by lawyers' traditional "fear of sharing" (at least when viewed as a single entity).

Clients now expect there to be a ready supply of checklists, precedents, and templates available for reuse on their matters. The "luxury" of being able to reinvent the wheel is long gone. Not only is there more explicit commercial pressure to quickly redeploy these types of assets, there is also a rising expectation that when firms are participating in a pitch process, that the proposal not only contains the "usual" marketing-drive messages and lawyer biographies, but also now contains greater content and substance.

2. For a refreshing perspective on this, see Ronald J. Baker, Implementing Value Pricing: A Radical Business Model for Professional Firms 206–10 (2010).

This was evident in management consulting and accountancy proposals many years ago, but is only now coming to the fore in the legal market.

What this means is the *capture and easy retrieval* of these materials is vital—in enabling you to win the work and then also deliver it cost-effectively, and for your clients, with them then benefitting from these efficiencies and leading to better results.

In this increasingly competitive marketplace, it is no longer a "nice to have." Make sure that you capture all documents and knowledge in your appropriate document management or knowledge management solutions.

Learning from the Management Consultants

Harking back to my consulting days (which faced similar challenges of potentially many work products to collate and the need to move on to the next chargeable engagement), there would always be one member of the team (typically one of the more junior members) made responsible for collating all the key work products. These would then be made available via the firm-wide knowledge base, subject to final partner review and "sensitivity" within days of the engagement finishing. This task would often be documented at the start of the engagement within the consultant's objectives and would form part of its engagement performance review. Although this may appear overkill or excessive, at the end of the day the approach worked and there is no reason it will not also work for you and your firm.

By giving just a *little more focus* when closing the matter—whether this is from an administrative perspective, taking some time to gather feedback, or by contributing to your firm's institutional knowledge—you will be able to create a lasting and positive impression from your time on the matter.

As we will see when we take a brief look at legal process improvement during the next section, the value of any feedback gathered and assets captured really can be turned into the legal equivalent of "gold dust" if done pragmatically.

A select number of firms are already a long way down this path (Seyfarth Shaw and Dechert spring to mind), and the opportunity to stay ahead of the chasing pack is closing, so let's now take a closer look in our next section, Review the Price, at what we can do.

Don't forget *(a summary of the key points):*

- Always get formal sign-off on your matter. It helps avoid the "one more thing" and can give an indication of your client's willingness to hire you again. (And if there is a follow-up request, do so *promptly*).
- Make sure your final invoice really *is* your final invoice—take time to discuss it with your client before you send it.
- Don't forget to capture client (and client team) feedback at the end of the matter. As a minimum, ask "what went well?" and "what can we do better next time?"
- Make any knowledge you capture institutional rather than solely individual knowledge—your colleagues will be grateful, and your clients will expect it.

Step Four:
Review the Price

Chapter 19

All Feedback Is Good Feedback: Getting Even Better

One of the most valuable, yet least conducted, activities when nearing the conclusion of a matter is proactively seeking feedback. This can be either internal client team feedback or from the client themselves, but the opportunity gathering *structured* feedback from either group (ideally both) presents is extremely significant.

With increasing pressure to deliver legal services at lower cost, increasing discounts against law firms' standard (or rack) rate and different resourcing options (including, in "extreme" circumstances, with lower-cost, third-party providers identified by the clients themselves), the ability to deliver *tangible* efficiency and greater value to the client through improved processes will differentiate the chosen law firm of the future. As discussed elsewhere in this book, the changes occurring in the legal marketplace are not temporary, and those that most fully embrace the changing environment will be those that succeed.

However, most articles and studies on this subject have tended to focus on conducting "after action reviews" or similar after *delivering a matter*, but very few—to date—have taken the more integrated approach proposed here, namely reviewing and gathering feedback at *each* of our three stages outlined to date: Set the Price, Get the Price, and Manage to Price.

Over the next few pages, I will provide a number of suggestions that can be used as a basis for you and your firm. These can obviously be amended to be more tailored to your specific situation and focus, but the key here is to review those key areas most important to allowing you to make a *tangible difference* in both how you choose to define and agree on commercial terms and then deliver, cost-effectively, against these (to your client's expectations).

Set the Price

Of the two things that are of utmost importance in improving pricing operations in any company, *leadership interest* in reviewing both qualitative and quantitative information together is one. (The other one, in case you are wondering, is the analytical capability that converts data into information.)[1] Therefore, we need to have some information for this group to review.

Although I am not advocating that the approaches outlined below are done for every matter (the 80–20 Pareto principle should always be front of mind here—that is, focus on the 20 percent of matters that generate 80 percent of your revenue), there will be a number of potentially significant opportunities that can be identified through this type of analysis and review at a client and/or matter level.

Reviewing each in turn will help improve your firm's ability to better manage one of the three key levels of pricing: transactional. But even that is perhaps not going far enough. The challenge of any pricing analysis is that you can only review what you *actually priced* your services at, not *what you could have potentially priced* your services at.

A number of the techniques discussed in our earlier chapter on pricing analysis (Chapter 7) will come into play here, especially if trying to conduct reviews of a similar group of matters (for example, at a client, practice area, or even lead partner level). Through the *constructive* questioning of the fee approaches adopted and initial analysis conducted, you will give yourself both a very robust baseline from which to compare the performance of future similar matters, and also gain a better understanding of

1. ManMohan S. Sodhi & Navdeep S. Sodhi, Six Sigma Pricing: Improving Pricing Operations to Increase Profits 88 (2008).

how successfully you have convinced your client of your value proposition through a *combination* of your analysis and internal (and client) team feedback.

Cross Your Bridge, Don't Build a New One

Ron Baker was one of the very first major advocates of conducting more rigorous reviews with a more appropriate focus on *both pricing and value*, his approach being rooted in the concept of the U.S. Army's "after action review" (AAR), which originated in the mid-1970s. These sought to answer a number of relatively open-ended questions after the conclusion of each combat mission (and even during[2]).

As Ron comments, "the Army has a saying that they never want to build the same bridge twice"[3] and yet when we come to price a matter and then seek to prepare the associated value proposition, we often do just that.

Indeed, taking time to ask your client a couple of questions on pricing and value can send many lawyers into a cold shiver, particularly after you have just submitted your final bill. But it shouldn't. We should want to know how we can better meet our client's requirements for value, and asking a question on price can provide useful competitive context.

Good questions to ask:

- How could we have added more value?
- How did our price compare to others they may have considered?
- Did the client feel they got value for money?
- How appropriate was the pricing/fee approach taken? (and, as a follow-up, what worked well and less well?)
- Were there other pricing/fee approaches proposed by other firms which they liked, and if so, what?

2. Ronald J. Baker, Pricing on Purpose: Creating and Capturing Value 324 (2006).

3. Emily Fisher, *Law Firm Efficient: Responsiveness, Reflection and Checklists*, HILDEBRANDT INST. (Nov. 30, 2012), http://hildebrandtblog.com/2012/11/30/law-firm-efficiency-responsiveness-reflection-and-checklists/.

Even if you were unsuccessful in winning the original pitch for the matter, it is *always* useful to ask some of the above questions for the next time and also for the potential competitive intelligence and insight that the answers may provide.

Internally, we should also be asking our client (and/or proposal) team the following:

- Did we add (or clearly articulate) value to our client?
- Could we have added more (and if so, could this have been at a higher price)?
- How would we rate our client's price sensitivity pre and post this matter (or pitch)?
- How high were the costs to serve this client (or matter)?

It is here that you can begin to probe, in a safe environment, what more you could have done to capture additional value and generate additional revenue. The more you do this, the better this information can be retained within your firm and the closer you are to building a solid foundation of a pricing capability. By spending some time *formally* going through this process, you are taking time to see what you can improve rather than be stuck in "doing" mode all the time. As Ron Baker says, "It forces firms to *reflect* on what they have learned, *capture* it, and then be able to *reuse* it when needed in the future."[4]

Imagine how you would feel if you could quickly reference not only the original pricing proposal and analysis for a similar client matter but then also be able to quickly review the client and client team feedback before preparing for a similar client pitch or matter. (I would think "pretty good" would be the answer.)

However, this all comes to nothing if the responses then sit in a drawer or are deemed "too commercially sensitive" be shared. Information is only useful if it is readily accessible and meaningful. Therefore, determine how

4. Ronald J. Baker, Implementing Value Pricing: A Radical Business Model for Professional Firms 318 (2010).

best to do this within your own organization so you can cross, rather than build, your pricing and value "bridge" next time.

Get the Price

The secret of all good negotiation (and negotiators) is preparation. Whilst that may make sense to most people, what is less known is that those who are the most successful are those who regularly review their negotiation performance—regardless of whether they are seen to have "won" or "lost" the negotiation.

This group will consistently review and assess how the negotiation was conducted, what messages they successfully (and *less* successfully) delivered, the roles played by the team, and also the roles played by the client.

Again, I am not recommending that we conduct this for every matter, but—as with most things—there will be those matters (or client relationships) that are important to you and your firm either because they are significant either in terms of the client relationship itself or volume of work that these typically generate. It is for *this* group of matters (or relationships) that the following simple approach will help.

The main reason for conducting a review at this time is not just to identify the negotiation mistakes that we wish to avoid next time but also to (more positively) identify what went well (planned or otherwise).

When looking at the concept of continuous improvement (for that is what it is) in the context of negotiations, this approach not only allows you to improve your "negotiated outcomes" (thus contributing directly to your bottom line) but also stronger client relationships, and your own negotiation capabilities within your firm (again, each contributing to a stronger bottom-line result).

The Three Key Questions: What, When, and How?

Asking yourself (and the wider team if you have one) the following three key questions for every *significant* negotiation you do is invaluable:

- **What?** (what did you ultimately *achieve* in the negotiation)
- **When?** (as soon as possible after each major negotiation)

- **How?** (follow a structured approach here and don't confuse *process* with *result*—think of what you would stop/start/continue for a future negotiation on this matter/with this client at each key negotiation step and also how well you worked in your respective client team negotiating roles)

There are also two additional questions, but in some respects these are more obvious—these are the "**why**" and the "**who.**"

- The "why" (that is, to avoid repeating mistakes and building upon successes).
- The "who" is harder, especially if doing this on your own, although ideally you should do this with the team.

Capturing this feedback, either in the form of training for your team, developing negotiation checklists of key do's and don'ts, and even a database of negotiation results all can help make you and those in your organization better prepared when next finding yourself in the negotiation hot seat.

What you may feel works better is to internally combine your pricing and negotiation reviews into a single meeting, given the overlapping themes (and recognizing the best use of everyone's time). This would then allow you to have a much more in-depth internal discussion on our third and final theme, covered next—Manage to Price.

Manage to Price

The focus on greater efficiency (often accompanied by expectation of lower cost) is becoming a constant drumbeat in discussions with law firm clients—even if recognizing that some drumbeats are louder than others.

This sometimes places lawyers in a conundrum—law firms are set up to be responsive to client demands and are pretty good at doing this on a day-to-day basis. As one of my colleagues, Toby Brown, has also acknowledged, however, is that what law firms struggle with is being proactive in response to increasing client demands, which in themselves may not amount to much more than requesting "greater efficiency" from law firms, but not specifying *where or how*.

A simple solution is, however, at hand, and one that has been used by other successful firms and organizations for over thirty years. Follow up, review, feedback—call it what you like—but the overriding concept here is taking *an objective view on how to improve* in future.

Learning from the U.S. Army

In order to improve the organizational learning, teams are required to continually assess performance and learn from their successes and failures. A simple and powerful tool for doing this is the After Action Review (AAR). Many major corporate organizations have incorporated this into the fabric of their culture, including Colgate-Palmolive, GE, Harley-Davidson, and Motorola.

Its application is also not limited to corporate or military spheres either, with an AAR being conducted in the aftermath of Hurricane Katrina, leading to new systems for communications during natural disasters to be developed. As Peter Senge identified, "The Army's After Action Review is arguably one of the most successful organizational methods yet devised."[5]

Indeed, the concept of conducting AARs has also been actively encouraged by the Association of Corporate Counsel Value Challenge Briefing Package as a means of continually improving performance,[6] leading to a number of major corporations also using these techniques within their own legal teams—for example, Pfizer and FMC Technologies.

Getting Started

So how does someone actually go about doing this?

An AAR is best done shortly after a project or matter ends (the sooner the better so that memories and recollections are still fresh within the team's

5. BAKER, *supra* note 4, at 212.

6. http://www.acc.com/valuechallenge/upload/value_challenge_brief_022510.pdf for example, as referenced in ACC's CLO THINKTANK EXECUTIVE REPORT: "LEADING IN FINANCIALLY DIFFICULT TIMES", 2010, *available at* http://www.acc.com/community/clo/thinktanks/upload/ACC-CLO-ThinkTank-Executive-Report-Leading-in-Difficult-Times-Dearborn-2010.pdf

mind), or—in some matters—in an abbreviated format midway through, especially if seeking to correct or amend a course of action.

In terms of participants, this should be as wide a group of those on the project as possible, and may also include clients, if appropriate. Don't be too restrictive as to who can participate either. It should not just be limited to those partners and associates who supported the matter, but be widened to include appropriate members of the marketing, finance, and knowledge management teams (or similar) if possible—that is, *all those* who played a part, who will be able to contribute, and who will be able to take away insight for the next time. (One benefit of doing so is that the more of your team that participate, the better the outcome will be. This is due to more of the matter activity being recalled and discussed, and consequently identifying more lessons that can be learned and (ultimately) shared.)

The Role of the Objective Facilitator

One quick observation regarding participation: Many of the guides currently available on conducting an AAR suggest the use of an objective facilitator—that is, one not directly involved in the execution of the matter. While this approach is undoubtedly helpful when soliciting client feedback (to help encourage a more open and honest client dialogue), it may not be practical for most law firms due to lack of available resource (either in terms of manpower or time).

Once key attendees have been identified, it is important that they are aware (prior to *and* at the commencement of any meeting) of the *intent* of the AAR. This is where many efforts have fallen down, with attendees feeling that this will become nothing more than an internal "finger-pointing session."

The key point here is that the AAR is *not* a critique. Its overall goal is to *guide and improve* how work is conducted on *future similar* matters.

In fact, the approach has a number of advantages over a critique, for example:

- It does not judge success or failure or grade any outcomes.

- It attempts to discover *why* things happened as they did.
- It focuses directly on the tasks and goals that were to be accomplished.
- It encourages employees to share important lessons in an honest and objective fashion.

Asking the Right Questions: Four Plus One

An AAR starts with four relatively open-ended questions:

- What was expected to happen?
- What actually occurred?
- What went well and why?
- What can be improved and how?

Based on suggested guidelines provided by the U.S. Army (and let's face it, who are we to argue), time is typically divided into 25 percent of reviewing what happened, 25 percent on why it happened, and the remaining 50 percent on what can be done to change and improve for next time.

All extremely useful, but I would add one more question to the four listed above: "where next?" Most *tangible* value from these meetings will derive from actually applying some of the suggestions made. You should therefore take the opportunity to think through (and if possible, gain a commitment) where to next *apply* associated learnings on future matters.

Don't Forget Your Client!

We mentioned that these reviews can be conducted with the client team only, with the client, or both. Whether your client is included as part of an AAR review or not (and good practice suggests that they are), it is, however, important to *review the outcome* with the client for three key reasons:

- It alerts clients that you are aware of, and are seeking to actively address, their needs.
- It allows the client a specific opportunity to provide feedback on the matter at hand.
- It can be used to help educate the client on potential issues that will improve communication and expectations for future projects.

A number of law firms have already instituted programs to help address this need. For example, Baker & McKenzie have had a very structured program in place for a number of years to capture client feedback via its post-transaction-review process, which is conducted for key matters (in addition to more regular client relationship reviews).

Focusing on the Few

Focus on a few—those handful of key matters that are most important to you when looked at from a financial impact, complexity, or volume and regularity of similar matters being conducted.

In addition, as time spent on AARs can sometimes be significant (sometimes two hours or more), and we know our clients are often extremely busy with little time to spare (as indeed are our own client teams), limiting your questions to two of the four key questions above will still give us enough information to improve.

- What went well and why?
- What can be improved and how (both from our firm's perspective and jointly)?

Whilst in many other organizations participants are encouraged to ask as many questions as possible, this may not be appropriate in our context—at least not when involving the client. Over time, you will easily identify a number of key questions and approaches that work best for you, as even a conversation as short as 10 minutes can identify opportunities for future improvements and efficiency if appropriate preparation has been done—but don't forget to also include the "where next?" question!

Finally, when doing this internally to your firm, don't forget to question whether the level of *project management* activity was appropriate to the scope of the matter. As a consultant I often felt that more time was spent "working the plan" than "working the work" on some of my engagements. Whilst it is important to have a plan and execute appropriately, some of the lessons learned may help refine what types of matters should benefit from dedicated or more formal project management support compared with more refined precedents or guidelines, and therefore allow you to use your resources much more effectively.

The real value of these reviews is not just to correct *things* but to correct *thinking*. Army experience has identified that flawed assumptions are the key factor in flawed execution.[7] How often is this also true when conducting legal matters?

Build slowly, beginning where the payoff is greatest and also, importantly, where there are team members committed to going through this process. There is no use in "trying to push water uphill" and, therefore, identifying one or two champions within your firm who are willing to try this will make any subsequent adoption and rollout much easier.

Communicating the Lessons Learned

Unfortunately, it is not sufficient just to do the review—you need to *communicate and then use the review*. Too often, the output of these types of reviews are documented and then submitted to a central knowledge base, only to be forgotten—or worse, ignored.

Good practice is to first communicate the outcome of the meeting to the key stakeholders (which may include your firm's senior management, depending upon the client or matter, and the client themselves). Then consider who else is likely to manage or perform similar matters and whether the information would be helpful to them.

Any report needs to provide a clear summary of *concrete and actionable* recommendations that will help improve the execution of future matters. It is also helpful to identify those tasks and topics that require leadership attention, so that you (and those concerned) do not lose sight of this.

Some of the learnings can be made into checklists, bringing potential "order to chaos." However, we need to fight the all-too-real danger of these becoming static (that is, developed and then put in a drawer or knowledge repository, never to be looked at again). Rather, these should become living, breathing, *dynamic* documents that are *actively* used and improved over time in the light of matter experience.

7. Marilyn Darling, Charles Parry & Joseph Moore, *Learning in the Thick of It*, HARV. BUS. REV., July–Aug. 2005, at 1.

As Marilyn Darling *et al.* emphasizes in their article on this topic, an AAR is not just a meeting, report, or postmortem. Each of these implies a one-off activity, something to be "ticked off" a list and then move on to the next item. The "AAR should be *more verb than noun*—a living, pervasive process that explicitly connects past experience with future action."[8]

Most organizations' attempts to conduct these types of reviews fail at this critical hurdle: utility. These outputs are only valuable if referred to, used, and then subsequently improved. Nowhere is this truer than in our industry at this time.

The Value of Reviews

Take a short step into the future—and imagine three scenarios for me.

- Imagine how you would feel if there were a library of easily accessible reviews available to you, covering the gamut of typical matters and internal processes that you and your firm regularly came across—ranging from those covering how we Set the Price through to how we Get the Price and, finally, to how we Manage to Price.
- Then take this to the next level; imagine, as Ron Baker notes "a culture that understands that AARs are real work, where time spent on not just doing the work but also *improving* the way work is done."[9]
- Now imagine the benefit of asking similar questions to those asked in the AAR process *before* you conduct a matter. For example, what are our intended results? What challenges or risks can we foresee (and how do we plan to mitigate these)? What will make us, and our client, successful? Thinking through these questions before the matter commences *as a client team* can help both ensure everyone is clearly aligned with a common objective and agreed tasks before in the "heat of the

8. *Id.* at 2.
9. BAKER, *supra* note 4, at 212.

matter" itself and also help set the stage for an effective review after the matter's conclusion.

Now a confession: I only gave you part of the previous quotation from Peter Senge. What the remainder goes on to say, and is important for those of us serious about doing these types of reviews to reflect on, is the following: "(Almost) every corporate effort to graft this truly innovative practice into their culture has failed because, again and again, people reduce the living practice of AAR's to a sterile technique."[10]

When conducting these reviews, regardless of which of our three areas you choose to focus on, will always be best served with a spirit of inquiry, openness, with patience, a "tolerance" for ambiguity, and encouragement of change. The good news here is the nature of these reviews capitalizes on well-known and recognized lawyer traits—those of decisiveness, reflection, and deep analysis. The bad news is that it takes time, but it will be time well spent *if* planned for appropriately.

Although blaming the client, as one commentator noted, is "much more simple, comfortable and common,"[11] we (as a profession) need to move away from this tendency and become more curious about how we can improve what we do in delivering better value for our clients at an appropriate price and in a cost-effective and efficient manner. We should also remember who the providers are of this knowledge. One thing we tend to forget is that creating, collecting, and sharing knowledge is the responsibility of those who actually apply it rather than the professional support lawyer, paralegal, or knowledge management director.

In our next chapter we are going to have a quick look at some metrics that will allow us (if used well) to demonstrate to ourselves and others just that—our respective firms' growing capabilities in pricing, negotiation, and also in legal project management.

---

10. *After Action Review (AAR)*, BIG DOG & LITTLE DOG'S PERFORMANCE JUXTAPOSITION, http://www.nwlink.com/~donclark/leader/leadaar.html. This website also contains some helpful information on the process of conducting AARs.

11. Aileen Leventon, Ellen Rosenthal & John Dougherty, Using After Action Reviews to Improve the Delivery of Legal Services (Ark Group Webinar, Feb. 12, 2013).

Don't forget *(a summary of the key points):*

- One of the most valuable, but least conducted, activities is proactively seeking matter feedback.
- Greatest value is driven when objectively assessing performance and capturing feedback across all three areas of how we Set, Get, and Manage to Price.
- Be pragmatic—focus on those matters and client relationships that make most sense. Adopt the 80–20 rule.

Chapter 20

Metrics that Matter

One of the biggest challenges in any organization is knowing whether you are on the right track.

This statement is no less true when trying to evaluate the success, or otherwise, of your pricing and legal project management initiatives. The old adage "what gets measured gets managed" in this context perhaps needs to be modified for our current law firm environment, as these metrics are typically not necessarily *managed* but are at least *looked at* once in a while.

But with the rise of appropriate fee agreements, and legal project management, the traditional metrics used to monitor law firm performance are now in danger of becoming increasingly redundant, or becoming supporting at best.

The Challenge of Traditional Metrics

Traditional law firm metrics have tended to focus on three key areas, those being the number of billable hours for a specific lawyer, the fees generated by a lawyer or by engagement, and the associated realization rate. A number of firms have also begun to monitor (and if you haven't so far, you need to) the margin or profit being generated from matters. On this basis, not only should the law firm be bringing in revenue, but it needs to be the *right* revenue.

However, all that these metrics do is merely serve to support the *existing status quo* that is being predominantly based on the billable-hour approach to pricing and in managing legal matters. Solely relying on these metrics is therefore fundamentally flawed in today's reality, as they do not seek to reward efficiency, and merely perpetuate the credo of the billable hour, and as such, continue to reward inefficient pricing practice.

Let's take the following simple example to illustrate the point:

A partner (let's call him Fred), who normally has an hourly charge out rate of $500, agrees with our client to conduct a matter on a fixed fee. Given the complexity of work involved, they agree on a fixed fee of $5,000. Fred then manages to complete the work in only seven hours (at a fee of $3,500 if charged on the basis of the billable hour).

Another partner (Bob) has the same charge out rate of $500, and conducts an *identical* piece of work for the client, this time on an hourly rate basis. Bob then spends 10 hours completing the matter, thus also billing the client a fee of $5,000.

Both have delivered the same amount of revenue, $5,000 each. However, Fred has clearly been more profitable and also more productive than Bob. The current method of recognizing contribution and monitoring performance, however, would not distinguish between either as both brought in the same amount of revenue.

Extrapolate the following example to the firm-wide level and we can begin to see the potential problem.

Add into this mix the way that law firms traditionally review and reward associates based on the level of billable hours and utilization during the year. With many law firms providing their associates with the target of 2,000 or more billable hours (regardless of how realistic this may be in today's economy), there is little incentive for them to become more efficient and deliver more value to their clients.

One of the key consequences of the move toward new pricing models and delivery models is that this requires a fundamental rethink of the law firm's compensation system—at partner level and below. However (thankfully), this is not a topic being addressed here.

Becoming More Comprehensive in Outlook

There is also another flaw in the nature of current metrics used to value performance in many firms. I'm sure many of you have already spotted it while reading this chapter. For those who haven't, it is a lack of any *client-focused* metrics.

All those discussed so far are *internally (law firm) focused*. Although we do not want to lose sight of those metrics, and indeed these remain very important overall, we need to become much *more comprehensive* in our outlook.

One useful starting point is for us to consider what general counsel are evaluated on and find important to measure, as we need to (as a minimum) measure and report on those metrics that matter to our clients. Just as general counsel need to use the same language and metrics to measure value as business leaders do, I would propose that law firms need to use the same language and metrics as our client general counsel.

(As an aside, this also provides law firms with a valuable opportunity to help support clients and how they can demonstrate greater value to their own organization, as we briefly discussed when talking about value.)

In 2009, the Association of Corporate Counsel (ACC) developed its ACC value index. As part of this exercise, general counsel were asked to evaluate the external counsel's performance against six key criteria as outlined in table 20.1.

Table 20.1: The ACC Value Index

The Association of Corporate Counsel ACC Value Index	
Understand objectives/expectations	Legal expertise
Efficiency/process management	Responsiveness/communication
Predictable cost/budgeting skills	Results delivered/execution

Although not all could be easily quantifiably measured, two key criteria stick out and are great examples of the need for law firms to change their thinking on what they measure and report. Those are "efficiency/process management" and "predictable cost/budgeting skills." Both fit squarely in our legal project management space, an area so far extremely underrepresented in how law firms measure performance.

For the former, this begins to include metrics such as the unit cost of work and unit cost to complete, but also begins to include the total matter elapsed time and also whether any matter management or process improvement techniques are being used to help make the process more efficient.

As for the latter, in a blog post by Pam Woldow, she hit the nail on the head when she said, "for in-house counsel a single metric reigns supreme: actual to budget."[1]

What she then goes on to discuss is increasing focus from general counsel on what she referred to as "the low delta firm." This is the firm where there is only a marginal difference (or delta) between the originally proposed budget and original fee. This plays clearly into the general counsel desire for greater predictability of cost as a means to manage their own budget more effectively and demonstrate cost control. The firms that can become a *recognized* low delta firm will be the ones that succeed.

Law firms and general counsel alike should also start to monitor use of appropriate fee agreements (AFAs). There are a number of very simple metrics that could be incorporated—for example, the number of fee arrangements conducted over time by type of AFA and the estimated value of money "saved" by using this approach (something of potentially greater importance to general counsel rather than law firms). These can then be further broken down by specific practice area, jurisdiction, business unit, etc.

With our client-centric hat on, picking up a theme from our previous chapter, client feedback and satisfaction needs to be brought more visibly into the mix. However, this makes the assumption that it is actually requested.

We also, however, need to be comprehensive in another way too. Many of the metrics that are being discussed naturally are financially driven. We also need to consider, though, those that are more operational in nature.

For example, this could include how many times we conduct matters with discounts that are greater than the ranges (or pricing fences) already agreed for that type of work. It could also include how many times people of an organization use the appropriate tools—for example, matter budgeting

1. Pam Woldow, *The Low Delta Firm: Demise of the Low Ball?*, PAM WOLDOW BLOG (Mar. 12, 2012), http://www.pamwoldow.com/2012/03/12/the-low-delta-firm-demise-of-the-low-ball/.

tools and matter management tools as part of delivering their matters. This may also include factors such as the percentage of attorneys completing pricing and legal project management training within your firm.

By identifying the right metrics for you, hopefully those being *comprehensive in nature*, you can quickly identify where further support and effort may be required.

Putting Metrics that Matter in Place

Regardless of which metrics you eventually decide are important for your organization (both when seen through an internal lens and a client lens), there are a number of guiding principles that you should always bear in mind.

Metrics need to

- be easy to understand (as Einstein said, "Everything should be made as simple as possible, but not simpler"[2]);
- be easy to update;
- be consistent and standard across your firm;
- include guidelines as to what "good" looks like or key targets (this allows an easy comparison of how you're tracking against firm-wide or practice group metrics); and finally,
- "less is more" (with it typically being recommended that a small number, for example, from five and seven, works best, and it is difficult to effectively monitor and manage many more).

A number of firms have also developed dashboards that allow them to report the key metrics in different views: for example, at the client level, practice group level, and firm-wide level. Depending upon your current reporting infrastructure, this may be a simple task or involve an element of manual

2. Ronald J. Baker, Implementing Value Pricing: A Radical Business Model for Professional Firms 181 (2010).

manipulation (and if so, it is key to make the capture and manipulation of data as easy as possible).

A Fantastic Start, But . . .

While working for one of my previous firms, we developed something we called simply a "Pricing Report." This was a short document that was able to be produced within minutes and provided a snapshot on client performance over a period of time (including previous financial reporting years) at a matter, relationship, and comparative client level. This information could then be further broken out to capture investment time, billings by office and practice area, and so on. (Note: I recognize that I was extremely fortunate in that we were able to capture this level of information readily all these years ago.)

At the time, the report was very helpful (and I am sure subsequent revisions made to it since my departure are even more so). However, again these measures were very much internally focused on the firm itself—this was not through any conscious bias, but rather was more reflective of what the firm were able to capture at the time (and also my perhaps more limited perspective at the time).

I would hope that any such Pricing Report today is even more comprehensive in its coverage and includes a number of measures that are more client and value focused as consulting or law firm and client understanding as to what are appropriate metrics to monitor continues to evolve.

Galileo "with a Twist"

We do, however, need to go in with our eyes open. There will be potential hurdles to implementation we will face.

These include the *availability of data* (whether driven from your financial systems, client feedback, or other external source). Although Galileo suggested that we "count what is countable, measure what is measurable . . . and . . . what is not measurable, make measurable," we need to be pragmatic in how we approach this given the potential level of analysis required when compared with capturing the more traditional metrics. Migrating toward this new world of metrics will take time.

Another factor to consider is the *frequency* with which these metrics are prepared and reviewed.

In a recent ALM survey on the adoption of AFAs,[3] when participants were asked "with what frequency does your firm monitor the profitability of loss of alternative fee arrangements?" the responses were as follows:

- 15 percent said weekly
- 31 percent said monthly
- 35 percent said quarterly
- 15 percent said annually
- 4 percent said never

In other words, more than 50 percent of respondents reviewed performance on these matters every three months or more.

But the most important hurdle is one we've already touched on. That is the nature of many law firms' *compensation systems* rewarding the level of billable hours achieved (and also in some, the level of client origination) rather than the efficient handling of matters and client feedback.

Something noted in other industries, and particularly relevant here, is the need to connect pricing-related metrics to financial incentives, as "[w]ithout tight connections to individual performance management, most metrics quickly become irrelevant."[4]

To this hurdle, I appreciate that there is no easy answer, and therefore remains a question for another day.

What Does "Good" Look Like?

Although by no means comprehensive, I have summarized some potential metrics that you may want to consider below in table 20.2. I have grouped these into those typically used, those that are slightly more progressive

3. ALM Legal Intelligence, Alternative Fee Arrangements at Legal Departments and Law Firms 32 (2013).

4. Walter L. Baker, Michael V. Marn & Craig C. Zawada, The Price Advantage 104 (2010).

and comprehensive, and then finally, those that—in my view at least—are "advanced" or leading edge. Hopefully, regardless of the classification I may have given them, these will provide you with some food for thought when determining those that may work best in your own organization. I have also sought to define where these metrics may be best applied.

Table 20.2: Sample Metrics that Matter

Applicability (Law Firm/ Client)	Typical/Basic Level Metrics	Intermediate Level Metrics	Advanced Level Metrics
Law Firm	Matter realization achieved versus firm-wide/practice group/ office/client average	Variance of actual [cost/ effort/resource/leverage] by phase or overall matter versus agreed plan (expressed as a percentage)	Percentage of similar matters managed to within X percent of agreed plan based on [cost/effort/resource leverage] (expressed as a percentage) (*this may also be further broken out to specific products or services*)
Law Firm	Matter margin (or profit) achieved versus firm-wide/ practice group/office/ client average	Average [standard/ billed/realized] rate achieved by phase or overall matter	Variance from agreed price fences or agreed discount levels for [matter type / practice group/firm]
Law Firm	Average [standard/ billed/realized] rate achieved versus firm-wide/client average	Average [standard/ billed/realized] rate achieved versus respective practice groups/ office average	Number of potential improvements identified *and* implemented (firm wide/practice group level) (*this could then be further broken out; for example, number of precedents identified, number of checklists developed, etc.*)
Law Firm	Leverage or gearing of team vs. firm wide/ practice group/office/ client average	Profit/margin variance vs. historic performance for similar matters	Speed of appropriate matter completion
Law Firm	Level of write-offs (or write-downs) vs. firm wide/similar matters average	Value/percentage of out-of-scope work recovered versus historic matters	Proportion of effort spent by phase versus historic matters

Applicability (Law Firm/ Client)	Typical/Basic Level Metrics	Intermediate Level Metrics	Advanced Level Metrics
Law Firm	Ratio of billed to work rate [*this may also be further done between billed and collected rate, or combination of the above*]	Unit cost of work	Proportion of effort spent by phase versus historic matters *based on external benchmarks available*
Law Firm		Unit time to complete	Additional matters won/ revenues achieved from client based on overall matter performance
Law Firm			Share of client's "wallet"
Law Firm/ Client		Client feedback score received on a specific matter/at relationship level	Proportion of <cost/ time> "saved" via adoption of improved processes/technology versus historic matter performance
Law Firm/ Client		Number of matters completed "on time and on budget"	Level of potential cost mitigated on behalf of your client
Law Firm/ Client		Volume/value of additional value-added services provided to your client (for example, bespoke seminars, secondments)	Level of potential value generated on behalf of your client
Law Firm/ Client		Total volume/value of matters conducted using AFAs versus hourly rate–based agreements	Total value of dollars saved versus using AFAs (when compared to standard hourly rates)
Law Firm/ Client		Total volume/value of matters conducted using different types of AFA	Level of team retention versus historic (*this metric can also be applied to the client team with some slight revision*)

In summary, the current internally driven focus of law firm pricing, profitability, and project management metrics clearly needs to change. Despite a small number of firms leading the way (particularly to those metrics related to legal project management), there is still much to do and very little to point to that is concrete and can be viewed as "best practices."

However, for those that *do* get it right, not only will they see better matter profitability, better client satisfaction, and more efficient and effective delivery of their matters, they will also steal a march on their competition in a number of ways.

As a closing thought I was reminded of an earlier quotation used (with emphasis added):

> If my suppliers all look and act the same, then I'll treat them that way. But if you can find a way to stand out, and demonstrate how this unique characteristic benefits my business, I'll certainly listen and I may spend more. *And if you can educate me on how to measure the performance of suppliers I know little about you're very likely to look good on the report card.*[5]

I know where I would rather be.

Don't forget *(a summary of the key points):*

- Traditional law firm metrics support the status quo pricing and delivery model—these need to become more comprehensive in scope to appropriately address today's new reality.
- We need to give greater focus on client-facing metrics—we should understand what makes our client general counsel successful and mirror (where appropriate) what they are measured on.
- Metrics should cover both financial and operational measures, as we seek to evaluate our financial performance, but also the success of our pricing approaches, policies, and client delivery.

5. Timothy C. Corcoran, *Why CEOs Love Procurement*, *in* BUYING LEGAL: PROCUREMENT INSIGHTS AND PRACTICE 26 (Dr. Silvia Hodges ed., 2012).

Chapter 21

The Chicken and the Egg

This last chapter of our section is perhaps the chapter that we have been working toward since the very start of our journey around how we Set, Get, Manage, (and) Review our price and drive profit.

It is here that we seek to improve on what we have already done, both in terms of delivering exceptional client service but also in terms of delivering enhanced and sustainable profit for our respective firms in improving the efficiency and effectiveness of how we deliver our legal service. It is the area of legal process improvement (LPI), which for me (at least) represents the holy grail of what we're trying to do.

When to Start

There has been much debate about *when* to do legal process improvement. Do you do this before or after embarking upon legal project management (LPM)?

There has also been some confusion about what the term actually means. For clarity, in this context I'll define legal process improvement as being the process of how we *improve the efficiency and effectiveness* of the legal service (that is, how do we do the steps better, and are these the right steps to be doing?).

Legal project management, on the other hand, (as we will be hopefully well aware of by now) is the proactive and disciplined approach to how we manage our legal matters (that is, the planning, organizing, and managing of resources to meet the agreed project goals and objectives). In summary, LPI is about "designing the process" and LPM is about "operating the process."

Despite both approaches being very different, there is also some element of overlap between them. In one of the very first blogs to address this topic, written by Susan Lambreth and Carla Landry in March 2011, they summed it up as follows: "If you do LPI, you typically deploy LPM approaches to manage the matters to the new process you have developed. On the other hand, if you use LPM before doing any LPI, you inevitably find some ways to improve some aspects of the process as you are managing work more carefully and with more tools than in the past."[1]

As the article then goes on to point out, the key difference is a level of scrutiny of each of the steps in the process. From LPI, we get a more efficient process. From LPM, we have a project that is managed on time and on budget.

When the article was first written, it was proposed that "in a perfect world" law firms would consider doing legal process improvement before they then started with legal project management, the latter to support managing these newly defined processes effectively. Indeed, this sequence is probably the optimal one.

The key thing here is finding what works best for you. Given some of the challenges of implementing legal project management within firms, to then add another layer of potential complexity with legal process improvement may feel like just too much and derail your existing (and necessary) LPM initiatives.

Perhaps given my "law firm perspective," I am more of an advocate of doing this at the end of the matter, when you are able to objectively review what can be improved based on real-life experiences. This is primarily the reason this step is the last substantive stage of the Set, Get, Manage, Review process, but in some situations it may make sense prior to conducting the matter itself—for example, if the matter is likely to be complex or when there is a significant fee pressure imposed—or even during the matter itself.

1. Susan Lambreth & Carly Landry, *Project Management or Process Improvement: Which Comes First?*, HILDEBRANDT BLOG (Mar. 2011).

Regardless of when you do it, once embarking on the LPI path, a number of other fundamental questions within your firm will come to the fore. Examples will include questions around how the revised processes you developed will impact the staffing of work, the level of fees, the career and training model currently adopted, and also the perennial lawyer fear of providing a commodity service to clients (due to the fact that there is a more standard "defined" way of executing that service).

Each certainly does need to be addressed, both from our legal process improvement perspective and more generally from how firms are seeking to properly implement non-hourly-based fee approaches. Unfortunately, many firms to date have exhibited more ostrich-like characteristics, with a tendency to stick their head in the sand and hope that these difficult questions disappear. Which they won't.

Whether addressing these issues head-on or not, it should not stop you from doing something in the "here and now" when it comes to legal process improvement. Adopt a process of "LPI-lite," with you focusing on, and resolving, the key pain points in your matters. But do something.

Worryingly, as part of the 2013 Law Firms in Transition survey conducted by Altman Weil,[2] when law firm leaders were asked about their greatest challenges in the next 24 months, improving efficiency only appeared as *11th* in importance on a list of 12, with 2.8 percent. As disturbing (if not more so) was that delivering value to clients appeared eighth (with 5.6 percent). (We have already mentioned elsewhere that the top four were more internal tactically focused issues, with the "primary purpose of protecting the status quo in law firms"—these being, in order, increasing revenue, generating new business, law firm growth, and profitability.)

When, as reported as part of the same survey, law firms and clients (in October 2012) were asked to identify how serious law firms were about changing their legal service delivery model to provide greater value to clients (rather than reducing rates), the median score was 5 out of 10 from law firms, but only 3 out of 10 from client respondents. A significant mismatch

2. Thomas S. Clay, Altman Weil, Law Firms in Transition 2013: An Altman Weil Flash Survey vi and 14, respectively (May 2012), *available at* http://www.altmanweil.com/LFiT2013/.

(at least in terms of communication) and a clear indicator perhaps that law firms need to become much more proactive in this area.

Where to Get Started

So where should you start?

Like most things in life, you will need to prioritize. It is probably best, at least in the early stages of doing this, to adopt the following guide (the "LPI-lite" approach referred to above, if you will).

Focus on those matter types that

- drive the greatest proportion of revenue (or where you are keen to mitigate the greatest loss of revenue),
- may be under most fee pressure, and
- you have had both positive and less positive client-specific feedback on.

In other words, the 80–20 rule.

Once you have identified which matters to focus on, find the time (hard, I know) to focus on how you can make the process better. Initially, you do not need to spend lots of time doing this. Just get started.

To quote Lisa Damon, a partner at Seyfarth, "If you get a group of lawyers and staff into a room to discuss how to make things more efficient, it is very easy to find savings."[3] (Lisa was one of the earliest and still one of the most passionate advocates of legal process improvement.) There is always room for improvement.

You may choose to have all the client team there, or only a number of key individuals, depending upon the size and seniority of the team. It may also be useful to have, as we discussed when conducting an after action review or equivalent, an external facilitator present to guide the discussion, ensure participation from all, and capture key points.

3. Jim Hassett, The LegalBizDev Guide to Alternative Fees 21 (2009).

Another useful approach "filter" or "lens" from which to then attack the selected matter types is through doing this in a way that specifically addresses the Seven Key Areas of Waste. These seven areas were originally identified by Toyota, when seeking to implement "lean production" principles to increase manufacturing efficiency (in sum, the goal was to "preserve value with less work"). This over time became the foundation of Lean Manufacturing, Lean Enterprise.

Table 21.1, heavily borrowed from Steven Levy's original[4] (to whom I am indebted here), helps us view these wastes within our own LPM-driven context.

As part of this approach, it is useful to classify work activities into three key themes:

- work that is deemed value-added work (that is, it has a part in changing the work product or deliverable, it does so in a way that is ultimately visible to the client, and it is something the client actually wants)
- work that is deemed non-value-added (that is, does not fulfill the three criteria listed above)
- work that is deemed non-value-added but required (for example, completing timesheets)

4. Steven B. Levy, Legal Project Management: Control Costs, Meet Schedules, Manage Risks, and Maintain Sanity 328 (2009).

Table 21.1: The Seven Key Areas of Waste

Toyota's Production System		How These May Apply to Legal Project Management	Value Characteristic	Potential Approach
1.	Excess Inventory	Work started on the matter, then put aside		Better allocation of work within the team Better scope management
2.	Extra processing	Having inefficient or extra processes May include duplicating communication/having multiple reviews of a document draft, etc.	Non value added	Better use of checklists/ precedents Development of new checklists/ precedents
3.	Overproduction	Doing more work that is required for the client (for example, producing a detailed due diligence report versus a red flag report; including additional depositions, etc.)	Non value added	A clearly defined scope of work Engagement letter Use of checklists/ precedents
4.	Transportation (*that is, moving a product that doesn't add value*)	Task or context switching (for example, being interrupted, looking at e-mails, etc.) (*Think how much time you can get back if you can reduce these*)	Non value added	Better work planning/scheduling of tasks
5.	Motion (*that is, people or equipment moving without adding value*)	Spending time identifying and then speaking with those who can respond to specific queries due to a lack of an appropriate knowledge management system	Non value added	Adoption of SharePoint or similar tools Access to firm-wide knowledge management Better use of checklists/ precedents
6.	Waiting (*that is, the products sits waiting to be worked on, creating extra inventory*)	Waiting due to a preceding task not being completed (for example, a document being reviewed) or resource constraint		Better work planning/scheduling of tasks

Toyota's Production System		How These May Apply to Legal Project Management	Value Characteristic	Potential Approach
7.	Defects	Poor work (defined as work of a lower quality than expected by the client, which then leads to rework, and the cycle repeats)		Building in appropriate review time Clearly understood and documented expectations

Not all can be easily addressed, but a number certainly can be, especially those that align to the "wastes" of extra processing, overproduction, and waiting. Sometimes it may even be purely down to better communication and clarity when on the engagement, rather than a fundamental shift in how you perform the matter (although ultimately that is where you want to get to).

When taking this to the next level, you may want to then more formally conduct an end-to-end process review. This requires a review of every process from the client perspective, and constructively challenge yourself and your team as to whether this really does add value for the client. If the step doesn't, it is either removed or amended to ensure that it does.

I remember as a consultant doing this with rolls of brown paper and sticky notes in meeting rooms with clients. As part of these meetings, we would diligently go through each step, action by action, to first identify what we thought should have happened (that is, the current *intended* process) before then adding "the reality" to the process (that is, what did happen as part of the *actual process*). Once done, we then eventually defined a process of what could happen (that is, the *improved proposed process*).

The very robust and rigorous approach to process mapping *can* take considerable time. These meetings can also sometimes be physically and emotionally draining, so it may be appropriate to look at the problem in chunks or discrete phases. What you want to avoid is trying to rush to the solution—in the spirit of efficiency, you really do want is to get this right the first time if possible.

Fortunately, there are a number of software tools, such as TaskMap (a business process-mapping tool) and MindView, that can make this process significantly easier.[5] The first is a business process-mapping tool used by an increasing number of law firms, and the second is a "mind mapping" application that could be used in brainstorming activities, creating Gantt charts, etc.

These applications, and other similar products, are relatively inexpensive, enable you to more easily capture this level of information, and also typically have good integration with other software applications you may use for managing your matters.

The Difference Between Efficient and Effective

One other key consideration is the difference between *efficiency* and *effectiveness*, as there is a *big* difference between being efficient and being effective. Certainly each on its own is important, but many firms are currently focusing on the former at the expense of the latter.

When I was a consultant, I was involved to varying degrees in discussions with potential clients about some of the emerging business themes of the 1990s, business process management (BPM) and business process outsourcing (BPO). Many of these potential clients were intrigued about the possibilities that approaches such as BPM or BPO could deliver to their organization's bottom line (primarily driven through the reduction of permanent headcount and access to improve process over time, although there are many more factors considered).

Sometimes as part of these initial discussions, potential clients were keen to "shift the problem" (however defined). It made them more efficient internally; however, there was limited long-term real value to outsource inefficient processes, and therefore they did not necessarily become more effective. Fast-forward to today's environment in our industry and a parallel may be drawn, with law firms often focused on being efficient, but being efficient doing *the wrong types of things*.

5. These tools, and similar, can be found easily on the Internet. TaskMap details are available via http://www.taskmap.com; MindView details are available via http://en.wikipedia.org/wiki/MindView.

Linking this back to the core theme of this book, that of *smarter pricing and smarter profit*, this is also evident in how firms approach pricing their work. If we take the move toward *appropriate* fee arrangements, despite many firms now adopting them successfully, they have not yet looked to find ways of *delivering the associated legal service more effectively*. Many have yet to address the challenges of more appropriate staffing—for example, using more junior resources supported by precedents and checklists or through greater use of technology, whether this is using collaboration sites such as SharePoint or other tools. (In the spirit of fairness, a number already have been very successful doing so—for example, Seyfarth Shaw, Bartlitt Beck, Borden Ladner Gervais Adroit, Valoreum, and Tucker Ellis among them.)

It is those firms that have gone beyond the state of thinking about *how to price* to *how to deliver* effectively (and in a way that is appropriate for the client) that will be most successful.

So spend a few minutes thinking about where you should best focus your valuable resources of time and effort *to be most effective*, as well as being more efficient.

Changing the Model

A number of firms have made admirable strides in improving their processes, some of which have already been mentioned above.

However, no chapter on this topic would be complete without acknowledging the role one firm in particular, Seyfarth Shaw, has had in changing the legal industry's thinking about how to approach legal process improvement.

This has been achieved through its well-publicized efforts around Six Sigma and Seyfarth*Lean*, its proprietary client-service model. The approach itself, as described by current practitioners, combines "the core principles of Lean Six Sigma with robust technology, knowledge management, process management techniques, alternative fee structures and practical tools."[6]

6. Karen Dalton & John Duggan, *Lean and Agile*, *in* MANAGING PARTNER 52 (2013).

Seyfarth has been doing this since 2006, long before legal project management and certainly legal process improvement was high on the law firm agenda.

The catalyst for this change has been credited to a dinner meeting between Seyfarth's managing partner Steven Poor and DuPont general counsel Tom Sager during which they were discussing how to increase efficiencies. It was at this meeting that Tom Sager suggested that Seyfarth consider adopting the management approach of Six Sigma, an approach to improve quality developed by Motorola in the early 1980s and since adopted by many organizations (especially those in manufacturing and high-tech industries) in their efforts to improve quality and reduce costs.

A large part of the Seyfarth*Lean* approach is built around process mapping, a topic we briefly touched on above. This technique helped them "identify inefficiencies, drive better data collection and engagement planning, and determine optimal work assignment and resource management. . . . When [Seyfarth staff] map legal service delivery from beginning to end, [they] identify steps to deliver the right results and identify where we need to modify re-engineer the process."[7]

The Seyfarth model, whilst undoubtedly successful, has three potential constraints that others should be aware of before heading down the path of a Lean or Six Sigma approach.

- A key one is cost. *American Lawyer* reported that, as of April 2010, Seyfarth had spent over $3 million administering and training workers, and budgets $200,000–$500,000 annually for such costs.[8]
- Another is time. Training teams in these techniques is not easy, making a key assumption you can find people to conduct the training and provide ongoing support in the first place, especially those who understand the legal environment.[9]
- The final one is senior sponsorship and commitment.

7. Carla Goldstein & Lisa Damon, *in* Legal Process Improvement Toolkit 101 (2012).
8. D. M. Devine, *Leap of Faith*, Am. Law., Apr. 1, 2010.
9. Dalton & Duggan, *supra* note 6, at 52.

Following Seyfarth's model is certainly not easy, and there will be bumps along the way. Don't go ahead with this unless you and your executive team are really and truly committed. As has been said elsewhere, it is not for the fainthearted.

However you choose to approach legal process improvement, don't forget or ignore the need to go through the process once you have successfully completed the matter (or perhaps even making tactical changes throughout). You do not need to spend significant amounts of money to identify ways to get better, but you do need to invest time and effort in doing so.

In an ideal world, we would do this on every single matter we conduct, but that is not realistic. Using the high-level framework outlined earlier in the chapter will help you focus on where you can begin to make the biggest immediate difference.

It also doesn't really matter *where* you start, it is making sure that you *do* actually get started . . . and then continue.

It will help improve matter efficiency *and* effectiveness through having a library of appropriate precedents, checklist, and the like and through having greater clarity of whom does what. It will help improve your overall matter profitability through minimizing waste and therefore having a positive contribution on margin. But most importantly of all, it will help improve client satisfaction and prepare you for the legal marketplace of the future.

Don't forget *(a summary of the key points):*

- All roads lead to this point—the ongoing identification and implementation of more efficient and effective legal processes, delivered at a fee that reflects the value of these services.
- Be careful not to confuse being efficient with being effective—otherwise you may become very good at doing the wrong things.
- Avoid the peril of overloading everyone—it is important to start looking for ways in which to improve, but be conscious of how this may distract from your wider LPM-related efforts.
- It takes time to do well, so have a clear focus and intent—but it is an investment worth making now and for the future.

Looking Ahead

Chapter 22

The Role of Technology and the Rise of Big Data

The Demise of "Anecdata"?

When recently reading an ABA article, I came across a word I'd not seen before, but one that I felt summed up very effectively how lawyers have typically made pricing and matter-planning decisions. That word is "anecdata,"[1] a term coined (I think!) by Mark A. Lemley, a Stanford law professor.

Although Mark was originally talking about it in a slightly different context (that of Big Data, a subject we will return to shortly in this chapter), I think it also appropriately sums up lawyers' traditional hesitation (or perhaps even downright resistance?) to embrace technology and, similarly, the strong reliance on their own judgment.

During this chapter, we will look at not only why those early attempts at bringing technology to law in the sphere of pricing and legal project management have been relatively low-key to date, but also how technology (and the providers of this technology) is now advancing to provide real and meaningful data to these areas. We will also take a brief look at one of the newly emerging themes or buzzwords, not just in the legal arena but, more generally, that of the rise of Big Data.

1. Joe Dysart, *How Lawyers Are Mining the Information Mother Lode for Pricing, Practice Tips and Predictions*, A.B.A. J., May 1, 2013, *available at* http://www.abajournal.com/magazine/article/the_dawn_of_big_data/.

The "Early Pioneers"

In many respects the term "early pioneers" can apply not only to the technology companies themselves that were quick to see the opportunities that lay in both providing pricing and, slightly more recently, legal project management software, but also to those *law firms* that quickly saw the potential of these tools.

The initial focus was very much around price-comparison software and tools that supported rate management, rate comparisons, or matter-specific data. Although there were many tools available to support pricing analysis in other industries and sectors, there was little that was relevant for those whose main focus was the practice of law, and therefore the advent of these tools was somewhat revolutionary for many of us.

Many of these early technology pioneers (including Peer Monitor, Redwood Analytics, Serengeti, and TyMetrix) were aggregating law firm billing and rate data, aggregating client-related e-billing data, or a combination of the two. Each also identified its core market, with some being focused purely on law firms, others on clients, and a number now branching out to provide differing snapshots or views to each.

Through providing this information in a *relatively* simple format, each was able to offer law firms (or law firm clients) a more dynamic snapshot of what the potential peer group was charging for different types of work, by level, by practice area, city, and even by jurisdiction. Indeed, many still are. However, whilst these products and solutions remain valuable in their own right, they in some respects will continue to be hindered in that *they can only report what they know* (or "see").

In the area of legal project management, there were also a number of firms or products seeking to make this process easier for law firms. Thomson Reuters' Engage product is perhaps the most widely known of these.

The Challenge of Adoption

However, in both the pricing and legal project management arenas, I'm not sure if any firm has really, as of today, "cracked the code."

The overall adoption of these tools has in some degree been hampered by three themes:

- These tools were typically in the hands of a select number of individuals within the law firm, typically those either in pricing and project management roles (see the next chapter on the rise of these roles) or in finance. It has therefore been difficult to make this information more widely available within the firm due purely to existing resource constraints. In some respects, adoption has been hampered by many lawyers' lack of *experience* in trying these tools. There is also another factor at play here. As both Jerry Walters and Larry Bridgesmith (of ERM Legal Solutions) commented, "the more successful a lawyer has been, the less likely they are to understand the need for change."[2]
- A number of the tools were initially not as intuitive or as user friendly as they may be now. Some of the earlier applications, through a desire to be as comprehensive as possible, sometimes appeared overly complex—once again, in effect self-selecting who in the law firm would be able to use this information.
- A final key constraint, previously discussed, is the fact (certainly for pricing- and rate-related applications) that the information is restricted to those who are willing to provide it or via clients that have mandated that firms use certain e-billing platforms. As such, gaps commonly exist in practice area and geographic coverage in many of these tools. This may not pose an issue for more regionally or nationally based law firms, but certainly comes into play for those with a more international flavor.

2. Larry Bridgesmith and Jerry Walters of ERM Legal Solutions in private e-mail correspondence with the author (July 15, 2013). The quote was taken from a broader response to the question, "What, in your opinion, has limited adoption of these tools to date?"

A Brighter Horizon?

Despite the potentially gloomy outlook painted above, we should perhaps not be too downcast. Since late 2011, there have been significant strides in both the functionality of pricing and legal project management tools.

These tools are becoming much more inclusive, and providing much stronger and more user-friendly analytical tools, whether through the form of dashboards or quickly tailored analytical models to help the user assess a matter's potential profitability and effort compared with not only internal information but also external benchmark data. These are also now becoming increasingly available on mobile devices.

Potential benefits now offered include better benchmarking intelligence on how much matters cost, how long they take to complete, and what level of resource is going to work. From clients' perspectives, these tools provide them with the ability to also review data in a more granular level (for example, by practice area, matter type, firm size, experience level, rates, etc.), therefore helping them identify where there may be further cost or improvement opportunities from their existing legal providers.

Nowhere has this technical evolution been greater than in the field of legal project management. Whereas a number of the earlier tools were very much focused on the planning and budgeting phase of a matter, there are a number of tools (such as ERM Legal Solutions' Lean4Legal product offering) that are much more comprehensive in scope, allowing the user to track progress from the beginning of the matter through to its conclusion. In addition, a number of these tools are now much more intuitive to the end user and, with this, are much more likely to be adopted by those in the "front line" of conducting legal matters rather than those who remain in the back office.

The Rise of Big Data

One of the key buzzwords of this time is "Big Data," in many respects the cloud computing buzzword or catchphrase of the 2012/2013 generation.

The term is by no means exclusive to use in the legal context, ranging from science (think how much data is produced and requires analysis for the Large Hadron Collider trying to determine the so-called God particle) to government to business, more generally. It has appeared in magazine and journal headlines as diverse as those on foreign policy to those on popular culture. So what the heck does it mean?

The term "Big Data" is "used to describe a massive volume of both structured and unstructured data that is so large that it is difficult to process using traditional database and software techniques." Although often associated with purely the *volume* of data, it can also refer to the *underlying technology* (which may include the appropriate tools and processes) organizations require to be able to handle this large volume of data and its subsequent storage.[3]

From a business perspective, it provides the ability to create, manipulate, and manage these large data sets—and, most importantly, then drive much more robust and comprehensive analysis. Given that the volume of business data worldwide, across all companies, doubles every 1.2 years, according to estimates, the challenge (and potential opportunity) will only get bigger.[4]

Why all the attention in legal circles? The first reason is closely related to some of the themes discussed above.

The Law Firm Dimension

A number of firms are already using currently available data from external sources to get a better understanding of what their competitors are charging and how they are staffing matters in an attempt to refine their own propositions to their clients. Through better and more targeted manipulation of this data, it is allowing them to make better, more "intelligent," and more analytically based commercial decisions.

3. *See What Is Big Data?*, Webopedia, http://www.webopedia.com/TERM/B/big_data.html.

4. *See Big Data*, Wikipedia, http://en.wikipedia.org/wiki/Big_data.

As Craig Raeburn, managing director of TyMetrix Legal Analytics, said of its LegalView data warehouse product (one of a number of similar products in the marketplace), "[M]any (law firms) have used our data warehouse to compare the rates and understand the best way to position themselves with clients—(whether as a) . . . low cost provider or high end value player."[5]

But that is only part of it. Some of the applications and tools available go much further, allowing firms to identify and exploit new opportunities (the "diamonds in the rough," if you will). Craig, in the same article, goes on to provide another example of how one firm used similar data to help understand its potential opportunity for market penetration based on the average legal spend of the corporations covered as a means of determining whether it should focus its expansion efforts. Other opportunities outlined in the article also included, for example, tools to help lawyers better understand and better predict case outcomes for areas such as medical malpractice through to patent litigation.

The Fear of What the Client "Knows"

Another key reason that it is garnering a lot of attention in legal circles is that there is a high possibility that our clients are not only seeing the same but *even better* data.

(One of the advantages of being a client in this context is that you get to see what other firms are charging and also how effective those firms are in delivering their matters, whereas we can only really compare on a client-by-client basis. Although much of this information had previously been available, like in law firms, it was typically the preserve of a select number of individuals (for example, chief legal officers or those within the client's procurement organization).

Given the advances in technology, our clients are now getting a much more refined and appropriate view. With legal spend often being one of the top two or three cost centers for many organizations, these types of

5. Dysart, *supra* note 1.

analytical tools provide them with a powerful advantage to be able to manage their own internal budgets effectively. Some tools, such as Sky Analytics Right Rate Advisor tool, can even suggest to in-house counsel whether they should approve, reject, or reduce increases in hourly rates requested by their outside law firms. These tools are providing our clients with the ability to benchmark against their peers how much they are spending on legal services and even which firms are successfully winning pertinent mandates for them.

What Does the Future Hold?

As Michael Lipps, a vice president at LexisNexis (a key provider in this space) noted: "[W]ith big data, virtually every aspect of the law is open to detailed analysis. That technology is already there. And the data is most certainly already there. It is simply a matter of imagining what you want to look for."[6] Of course, you then need to make it happen.

Some law firms, the "new wave" of pioneers, if you like, are already beginning to embrace the opportunities that Big Data may provide. Most of those that are, are doing so with little publicity (after all, why give away your competitive advantage?), while others more visibly (such as Olswang's revelation that it was looking to hire a team of "pricing boffins" to build a stronger analytical capability in-house to help analyze this new source of data[7]).

The impact of the evolving technology in our field is certainly something we should be keeping a watchful eye on. It has much potential, but, as noted, there are some limitations—such as the current quality and coverage of data, coupled with the willingness of law firm partners to get stuck into the detail rather than having a select few reviewing then synthesizing and communicating the key messages (as many respects the value of this information is through its immediacy).

---

6. Id.

7. Matt Byrne, *Olswang Targets Pricing Boffins to Gain Market Advantage*, Lawyer, June 6, 2013, *available at* http://www.thelawyer.com/analysis/the-lawyer-management/olswang-targets-pricing-boffins-to-gain-market-advantage/3005706.article.

Fee and rate information provided by these tools will continue to be helpful in guiding both matter proposals and the establishing of timekeeper rates on an annual basis, with the benefit of some external corroboration.

However, in my mind, the greatest opportunity in the mid- and longer term is the information that will be available around how we can improve our current processes in certain matters, not just from the perspective of the law firm but also how we can do so *collaboratively* with our clients. There are currently very few tools available in the marketplace that allow you to do *elements* of this (at time of writing, one being TyMetrix Matter Analyzer), but I'm confident that this will be a fast-growing area in the near term. The technology that maintains a clear focus on ease of adoption (and the corresponding implementation) can lay claim to the "high ground."

When we talked about competitive intelligence earlier on in the book, I highlighted that this can become costly both in terms of time expended and in terms of finance (although the latter is becoming less so over time). It is therefore advisable to have a clear plan of what the key data is that you're looking for, what you are looking to accomplish, and who is actually going to be using this in the "real world" before embarking down this path, as it could be expensive—in more ways than one.

As Paul Lippe, one of the most insightful of commentators in this field, commented that "in every large-scale human endeavor (whether armies, sports teams, businesses, universities, professions like law or medicine, or name-your-institution) technology changes first, then techniques and tactics, and then culture."[8]

He and I are both agreed that law is now very visibly going through this change.

It may be too soon for us to predict the demise of *anecdata* in pricing and budgeting decisions, but perhaps that day is not too far in the future after all.

8. Paul Lippe, *Expert Analysis 5: Emerging Trends That Are Changing How Lawyers and Law Firms Work*, *in* THE FUTURE OF LEGAL SERVICES: EXPERT ANALYSIS 29 (Kate Clifton ed., 2011).

Don't forget *(a summary of the key points):*

- Technology is now having an increasing role to play in how firms manage their pricing and legal project management capabilities—many of the initial challenges to adoption have been removed, although some still remain (for example, around practice area and jurisdictional coverage).
- Some progressive clients are increasingly adopting many of the newly emerging tools, especially those allowing price or rate analysis—law firms need to make sure that, as a minimum, they are familiar with what these tools are, and what they can do.
- Most law firms will be best served by utilizing a number of technology-based resources—but need to do so in a more holistic manner and with a clear roadmap in place (otherwise this may become time-consuming and expensive, with limited results).
- Pricing and legal project management decisions being increasingly driven from fact rather than perception (or "anecdata") will become the norm—but with the exception of the "new pioneers," not quite yet.

Chapter 23

The Corporate Mentality: The Changing Nature of Practice Management and the Business of Law

Over the last few years, an interesting trend has been noticed within legal firms. With overall levels of law firm hiring either flat or slightly up, coupled with the overcapacity within the legal marketplace, the question posed is, what positions are therefore being filled?

Although there continues to be lateral recruitment within firms seeking to capture a "rainmaker" who can help drive additional business or further develop a practice area, the most interesting phenomenon has been the rise of previously unheard-of practice management functions.

Practice management positions such as pricing directors, client value managers, and dedicated legal project managers now vie for attention alongside the more traditional business development and marketing roles, often competing within the marketplace for similar resources and skills. Rewind 20 or so years ago, and the roles being talked about then were probably related to those that worked in now well-established functions, such as information technology, practice management, business development, and marketing.

This chapter will look at three of these newer positions in a bit more detail, specifically those roles that relate to pricing, legal project management (LPM), and knowledge management. Whilst the last is certainly not new to the practice of law, it is becoming increasingly important in its more *explicit* contribution to law firm profitability.

Even in late 2009, some commentators had grasped the importance of these emerging roles. Mark Sirkin (of Hildebrandt Baker Robbins) wrote in a blog post of three such functions. You guessed it. These were (in his words) "project managers," "pricing specialists," and "information stewards."[1] (Mark also had a fourth role, that of "firm counselor"—that is, those roles to support a firm's leadership function.)

Let's now have a look in turn at each of our three roles, starting with pricing.

Pricing as a Career Track

First, a confession: I got into this whole area and profession by accident (note: I am very glad I did).

As a career management consultant (specializing primarily in procurement strategy, operations, and negotiation), I had not considered pricing as a possible career option, certainly not within a law firm, until a fortuitous discussion with a colleague.

However, discussions progressed swiftly, leading me to accept a position within Linklaters as its first Global Head of Pricing. The role, at the time (late 2007), was thought to be unique among major international law firms, and was a clear demonstration of intent from Linklaters that this was a role that was important both internally within the organization and also externally when engaging with clients. A number of other progressively minded firms were not too far behind either, including Baker & McKenzie, Arthur Allens Robinson (now Allens), and Vinson & Elkins, to name but a few.

I asked Ori Weiner, at the time Linklaters' global head of business development, and the key initiator of bringing pricing to the forefront within

---

1. Blog, Mark Sirkin, *New Roles in the Law Firm of the Future*, A.B.A. J., Nov. 11, 2009, *available at* http://www.abajournal.com/magazine/article/the_dawn_of_big_data/.

Linklaters, what was behind the decision to focus on this area. This is what he said:

> One of my key objectives as Global Head of Business Development was to improve the firm's quality of earnings, a concept I had learned to appreciate as an investment banker involved in company valuations and financings.
>
> The firm had excellent lawyers, a great network and was delivering premium work. As an insider however it was apparent that most lawyers were struggling to price and negotiate fees reflective of the premium and the value they delivered to clients. I therefore lobbied for a "strategic pricing initiative" to look at the root causes. This initiative quickly identified a number of measures that the firm could engage in to help individual partners perform better economically. One of the most important and potentially most effective approaches was to provide partners with support on the pricing and negotiation fronts by offering additional training and expertise available to support partners in specific negotiations and to help keep the embers glowing once partners had undergone the negotiation training. The impact of these two measures was significant, rapid, and exceeded our "best case scenario" by a large margin.[2]

Fast-forward to today (at least in the United States), and there is probably no new role in a firm's structure that is growing as quickly as that of a pricing officer. Whereas in 2008 there were a handful of us in these positions, there are probably upward of 100 or more in the United States alone (and this being a conservative estimate.)

An ALM survey specifically on this topic (and issued in May 2013) painted quite a positive picture of how many law firms had a pricing-related department, with two-thirds of the firms surveyed (out of a total of 67) saying they had pricing officers, and of the 13 firms that didn't, more than half had plans to have such a position within the next few years.

2. Ori Weiner in private e-mail correspondence with the author (July 26, 2013).

What Is Driving This Change?

While part of the increasing popularity of this role may be "me too-ism" (that is, the fear of not doing something that your competitors are), a more rational and, indeed, more likely reason is the recognition that pricing is not merely a mindless administration-type function but one that requires an element of skill. But there's another reason, excellently summed up by Richard Burcher in one of his blog posts on pricing,[3] that means having to concede that it is a skill most lawyers don't possess. John Frisch, chairman and CEO of Miles and Stockbridge, within the same ALM survey mentioned above, was quoted as saying, "in the practice management and pricing areas, we find that many lawyers didn't have the aptitude or, frankly, the interest to dig deep enough into the data that would let them in the firm make appropriate pricing decisions,"[4] further echoing Richard's comment above.

Add into this mix the concept of (commercial) negotiation, and the rationale becomes even stronger. (As we've touched on previously, I am continuously amazed at how little focus the legal profession in general has given to training its partners in the fundamentals of negotiation.)

Scoping the Role

One of the biggest challenges when trying to define a pricing role is what the scope should actually be. In many companies, there is a difference between what the role of pricing is stated to be and what it actually is.

Potential scope can cover areas such as providing guidance and financial analysis, it can focus on training and skills development within the firm in new pricing techniques, and it can be involved in negotiation (although this is less common currently) both directly with the client and in terms of delivering training to the fee earners themselves.

---

3. RICHARD BURCHER, "My Precious," Law Firm Pricing Control, (27 Oct. 2013), *available at* http://www.validatum.com/blog/my-precious-law-firm-pricing-control.

4. ALM Legal Intelligence, Alternative Fee Arrangements at Legal Departments and Law Firms 9 (2013).

Add into this legal project management (discussed in a few moments), and you can potentially begin to see how this can become quite large in scope. Ultimately, the key question is, is your intent to have someone who's a change agent driving change within your own firm in this role, or are you looking for some back-office support?

Another consideration is what the potential objective of the role is. For example, the role may be to provide "control" and ensure compliance to the agreed policies and procedures put in place around pricing. The role could be seeking to ensure appropriate consistency in how the firm goes to market and how the fee owners adopt pricing principles. And finally, it could also include an element of influencing a change in behavior (which links back to the question on whether the role is acting as a "change agent").

Organizational Fit

I am sometimes asked when attending conferences where I think, based on my experience, the role best sits. My honest answer is that it needs to be driven by your own organization.

Many of these roles are currently in finance, some are in marketing (my two roles in this area have both been here), but it can be in knowledge management, strategy, or any other. There really is no right answer (although I do have a strong preference for it to sit in marketing, as it is one of the four Ps and it's also more clearly linked into the value proposition for clients. If so, however, there needs to be a very strong link with finance at the very minimum).

What is clear, and something that has many parallels with legal project management roles, is that there should be very strong and visible executive sponsorship. In addition, this role acts in many respects as a facilitator or conduit to get things done, and as such, integration across all the business support functions mentioned above is critical.

Recommended Characteristics

A while ago, while preparing to give a conference presentation on the rise of the pricing function, I spoke with a number of my fellow colleagues to try to determine what the key characteristics, skills, and traits we believed were required to be successful in such a role. (This list is also recently reproduced in the ALM survey on this topic as appendix 1[5]).

We identified six key areas or dimensions. These were (in some rough order):

- *Excellent communication and stakeholder management skills.* Much of what we do is join the dots within an organization that is seeking to change behavior. Above all else, we felt that this was the key requirement.
- *Commerciality* was also something we saw being extremely desirable. This meant considering the impact of any proposed pricing agreement on the current (or desired) commercial nature of the client relationship in question, but can also be extended to include (commercial) negotiation.
- Strong *analytical skills* are a must (or at least, the ability to understand and direct any analysis).
- *Entrepreneurship* was another, but perhaps less obvious, criteria. This is based on the desire to find a better way to do something, which links directly to the fifth dimension.
- *Intellectual curiosity.* This was encouraging people in these roles not just to look at what is done in the practice of law but also in other professional services companies and industries (indeed, a growing number of us in these positions are either Certified Pricing Professionals or a member of the Professional Pricing Society).
- The final area was a *comfort with technology.* As we saw in the previous chapter, technology is evolving at an extremely fast pace in this area, and therefore an awareness of (if not necessarily expertise in)

5. *Id.* at 17.

these evolving tools and technologies is key. This can also be extended to include expertise and knowledge management systems or similar.

Although not a definitive list, each of the areas outlined above should be in the mix when you are looking to assess who would make a strong candidate.

There are now many more people who are becoming familiar with pricing in a legal environment. However, there is still relatively little supply for the current levels of demand. Therefore, one potential hunting ground, if you're looking to recruit in this area, is from other professional services firms, particularly consulting, for many of the characteristics outlined above are required. I'm also aware of a number of firms that have looked to other industries' pricing experts to fulfill this role.

Legal Project Management[6]

The comment John Frisch made above on pricing is potentially equally applicable to legal project management. However, to date, firms have tended to focus on the pricing dimension, both in terms of capability and hiring—but now the focus is shifting to the other key part of the equation, efficient matter delivery.

It is this that is now driving the rise of the role of the dedicated legal project manager. Although still not too widespread in the legal profession (on which, more below), this is beginning to change, driven by the twin pressures of client expectations and the quest for greater internal efficiency (read "profitability" in the first instance for many firms).

So, for the firms that have already recognized the importance of legal project management and are seeking to address it, what are they doing?

This can be neatly summarized in two different though not mutually exclusive approaches. One approach taken by a number of firms (including mine) has sought to certify lawyers themselves in legal project management.

6. Part of this chapter has previously appeared in an article written by the author for ILTA's *Peer to Peer* magazine, *Legal Project Managers Gain a Strong Foothold*, 29 PEER TO PEER 74–77 (2013).

Second, there is an increasing role being played by nonlawyer project managers, many of whom have either come from similar roles elsewhere or are certified by the Project Management Institution. For example, Baker & McKenzie hired its first dedicated legal project manager in January 2010, and were by no means the first law firm to do so.

Although the first approach outlined above is undoubtedly an interesting and necessary development, it is the latter where there is the emergence of a developing professional career track for the "expert practitioner."

There Is No Cookie-Cutter Approach

Who is this new breed of project manager? While researching this chapter, and in discussion with fellow colleagues, one thing was clear: those who are doing these roles, or are responsible for managing teams doing this, come from an extremely wide variety of backgrounds.

This, in part, is due to the evolving nature of the role and definition of legal project management within the legal industry itself, but it is also indicative of something else—the widespread diversity of appropriate existing skills within the current organizations.

Some practitioners have moved from a more internal project management role, supporting major internal projects, prior to extending—or changing—their remit to support legal project management initiatives.

One of the first to see the potential importance of this area was Kim Craig. Kim started Seyfarth Shaw's internal Legal Project Management Office in 2004, having conducted a number of operationally facing roles prior to this. As the current director of Seyfarth Shaw's Legal Project Management Office, Kim is now responsible for overseeing 17 individuals who (at time of writing) are partnering with attorneys on the efficient and successful delivery of legal services to Seyfarth's clients.

Other key exponents of the function, such as Sheri Palomaki (director of Practice Management at Sutherland, Absill & Brennan), Christopher Zust (legal project attorney within the Practice Economics Group of Bryan Cave), and Andrew Terrett (coleader of Borden Ladner Gervais Adroit), are qualified lawyers and have obtained either a JD, MBA, PMP (Project

Management Professional, the most important industry-recognized certification for project managers) qualification, or a combination.

Having an understanding of law (formal or not), coupled with strong project management skills, is a desirable requirement. As many of those who support legal project management initiatives on a daily basis are only too fully aware, legal project management is *not* the same as project management (a common misconception), with key differences including the frequency of scope changes and potential volume of stakeholders. Having that legal understanding can prove invaluable—both in understanding the content and "rhythm" of legal matters, and in also being able to "speak the language" of a matter.

Reporting lines vary too. For example, a number report to the firm's knowledge management director or equivalent (for example, at Reed Smith and Borden Ladner Gervais Adroit, where Andrew is the director of knowledge management) in client service and marketing-related (such as in my case), practice management, or finance. One common theme, however, is the access, and often direct reporting line, to a member of the law firm's executive committee or senior management.

The primary areas of responsibility supported are typically focused on enhancing the client's experience in engaging with the law firm, through providing greater efficiency, transparency, and predictability throughout the lifetime of the matter. Indeed, when participating firms were asked as part of an ALM survey on the topic of LPM[7] what key benefits they had realized as part of their LPM-related initiatives, the most popular answer (with 62 percent) indicated that the main benefit was in the strengthening of the client relationship.

However, there is also a very strong internal dimension, as borne out in the second-most popular benefit identified—improvements to internal efficiency and productivity within the law firm (with 56 percent). Through the proper application of LPM disciplines, firms are able to ensure that the LPM "hygiene factors" are suitably in place. This extends to having clear visibility

7. ALM Legal Intelligence, Legal Project Management: Much Promise, Many Hurdles 8 (2012).

of budgets, updates on fee estimates, and regular client communication, all of which help to minimize potential write-offs through poor communication and scope creep that can occur during the lifetime of a matter.

This can then be further extended to the development of process maps in an effort to drive greater process efficiency for both law firm and client—in many respects, the ultimate goal of LPM. For example, it has been stated publicly that Seyfarth Shaw has developed over 300 such process maps, many of which have been developed in collaboration with its clients.

Defining and implementing the necessary infrastructure is also key—for example, developing tools for data analysis and generation of custom reports, defining appropriate matter specific processes and procedures, through to the development and delivery of training. Consequently, many legal project managers are often also using this information and now crossing into the realm of pricing, becoming integral to a firm's development of appropriate fee arrangements.

Finally, some of these teams also have a clear revenue-generating focus. Indeed a number of law firm clients are also beginning to recognize the value that a firm's legal project managers can provide and have explicitly stated via panel tenders or requests for proposals their willingness to compensate law firms appropriately for these resources.

With a remit so broad, one of the biggest challenges this group of individuals face is therefore prioritizing where best to provide support given the relatively small, focused teams in place and growing demand for services.

This applies not only when providing "direct" support to client matters and when to say no, but also when trying to "up skill" fee earners in legal project management. Given the diverse legal practices typically represented within a law firm, it can be difficult to define and deliver a message that is both tangible and immediately relevant to each practice. As Andrew acutely observed: "[T]raditional instructor-led training on PM principles has limited utility. PM is best learned by experiencing it." This may require ongoing Legal Project Manager support and the "coaching" of appropriate fee earners throughout a matter.

Making a Clear Contribution

The majority of law firm LPM initiatives are currently, therefore, primarily focused internally, working with in-house teams to either help manage client engagements and corresponding budgeting, planning and tracking, or developing more efficient means of delivering matters through use of appropriate resources, technology, and best practices, all of which help contribute to greater client satisfaction.

However, the role is also becoming increasingly visible to clients, in part driven by providing support when responding to client requests for proposals. There are a growing number of client-driven requests either to have a firm's LPM resources dedicated to clients or to work collaboratively with them to improve an existing process, as evidenced in a number of major law firm panel requests issued during early 2013.

For those law firms at the forefront of LPM, there is a very powerful (and differentiating) external message to their current and potential client base—in summary, "we are a firm focused on providing you with the most efficient service, to the highest quality, and delivering as much value to you as possible." Which client is not going to be attracted to this? Some firms have taken this even further, proactively marketing their legal project management expertise to their clients and training client legal teams in LPM approaches and techniques (note that this is very distinct from the impressive marketing messages some firms include on their firm-wide websites!).

Measuring the actual contribution of the function for many, though, is still in its infancy. There are a number of metrics that can be used, some of which are quantifiable, others more subjective.

The level of fees and margin generated is perhaps the most obvious and easiest to manage—especially if focusing on the contribution of out-of-scope work on a matter. What is harder to measure is the impact of improved processes and delegation within the in-house legal team. Whilst intellectually this is relatively easy (indeed, as an ex–management consultant, this was something that was a consultant's "bread and butter"), where it falls down is having a concrete baseline to measure against. A few (very few!) firms have some data that they can benchmark against.

There are other indicators, however, such as the level of client demand and the number of internal requests for support received. The critical one is client feedback. Given LPM's potential in strengthening the client relationship and improving overall client satisfaction, feedback received either as part of a regular client relationship feedback process or specific to the matter (the optimum being both) is invaluable, and for many acts as the true test of LPM's contribution to the firm.

In nearly every other industry, project management has become an established and necessary discipline, one that continues to evolve (Agile, anyone?). Other professional services industries have for many years trained their staff in the importance of applying rigorous project management on their engagements (think of the management consulting and accountancy firms, to name but two), this training often started at the most junior levels and continued throughout one's career at the firm.

It is true that the legal profession has been slow, so far, to recognize the value of such approaches to both a law firm's bottom line and overall client satisfaction, but these approaches are now gaining traction and are clearly here to stay.

The Time Has Come (Again): The Growing Importance of Knowledge Management

One of the more "traditional" newer functions within law firms (if I can get away with saying that slightly strange turn of phrase), knowledge management (KM), is, in my view, at a defining moment, one almost as significant as when the earliest KM efforts "broke free" from their IT-based roots and became a recognized discrete function.

Although approaches to KM can vary widely in the legal profession, the contribution that effective KM can play in supporting the more efficient and effective delivery of projects and matters is crystal clear.

Whether it be the more U.S.-driven focus on viewing KM through a primarily technology-focused lens, the United Kingdom firms' tendency to be more people focused (as seen in the level of professional support lawyers), or the Canadian firms' efforts to obtain a blend between both, KM has a key seat at the table, and one that is of growing importance.

For those law firms where the remit is for KM to focus more on content (for example, research, analysis, document drafting, and review), in many respects the role of professional support lawyers, the potential value is also clear. Similarly, for those firms where KM is perhaps viewed as being more "strategic" (that is, not solely focused on content, but also encompassing the "bigger picture" of processes, workflow, efficiency, and quality), the potential opportunity may be even greater.

Technology, although a key part of KM, is third in the recognized sequence of addressing KM challenges. These are typically addressed in the following order: (1) Processes, (2) People, and (3) Technology.

The increasingly closer alignment between a firm's KM function and the broader one of professional development (or talent management), due to its focus on lawyer training and development, is now strengthening and playing a key role in a firms' goal of delivering their legal services more efficiently and at a lower overall cost to the client and the firm.[8]

The focus on LPM is now providing KM an opportunity to become much more closely involved with, and aligned to, a firm's client relationships through the use of its existing project management processes and tools.

The skills and capabilities brought by this group are critical during the Manage to Price phase we discussed earlier in terms of effective delivery during the project or matter. But I also see the role of KM being probably the most critical element when we are conducting the Review the Price phase. Here lies, within the existing organizational structure, a team of skilled individuals who are tasked with making processes more efficient.

If we view the stages of LPM development as (1) addressing the "hygiene factors," (2) implementing deeper project management skills, and finally, (3) identifying opportunities available through legal process improvement, KM is ideally positioned to help shape the last two *as a minimum*. KM has a shared goal and objective to those supporting project management and process improvement efforts, with each constituency focused on more efficient work approaches, enhanced quality, and subsequent reduction of risk.

8. Deborah McMurray, *Improve Client Service and Satisfaction Through Global Project and Knowledge Management*, *in* BRIGHT IDEAS INSIGHTS FROM LEGAL LUMINARIES WORLDWIDE (E. Leigh Dance ed., 2009).

KM needs to take the opportunity to realign itself away from the more inward, introspective function of the past, to one that is more externally focused.

The rise of legal project management provides those in KM with such an opportunity. As Andrew Terret of Borden Ladner Gervais Adroit acutely observed a few years ago, "KM needs to provide the underpinning of LPM, providing a just in time approach." And that "(m)oving forward, KM professionals need to not merely align themselves, but be joined at the hip with project management and process improvement initiatives."[9]

Over time, if not explicitly being done so already, those in knowledge management (especially those who fulfill professional support lawyer roles) will begin to play an extremely active role in legal project management, not just at the end of the matter when looking to identify process improvement initiatives but also by playing a key role from the outset, becoming "pseudo" project managers.

Finding Your Résumé

A few months ago, I was contacted by a 35-year-plus career lawyer who was looking for his next challenge, having previously been a successful partner in a couple of firms. He understood the potential of legal project management and had a keen desire to improve how legal services are delivered. He wanted to identify which appropriate skills, familiarity with software tools, and qualifications he would need to be successful at in addition to his years of practical legal experience. In sum, all excellent questions.

At a conference on law firm pricing and legal project management I attended (in itself, a concept unthinkable even three years ago), I was also struck by the number of law firms seeking to determine how best to implement and sustain legal project management initiatives, and associated impact on recruitment and retention. Firms represented were across a wide spectrum

9. Andrew Terret, *KM Struggles to Survive While Legal Project Management Thrives*, *in* KNOWLEDGE MANAGEMENT: WHITE PAPER 46–53 (2011), *available at* http://epubs.iltanet.org/i/34417/44.

of size, expertise, and locations. Whether this be increasing interest in pricing, legal project management, and the changing role of knowledge management or not, this is certainly something that is not being "Big Law" driven.

The level of demand for pricing specialists and legal project management services is outstripping supply—a trend likely to continue for the foreseeable future. Yet those firms that are still to fully acknowledge the need for pricing specialists and LPM will find it increasingly more difficult to compete in the evolving market, one in which heightened client expectations and commercial pressure are the norm. Those firms that have only "dabbled" in pricing will be found out, and those firms that do not bring this altogether with knowledge management will also be hindered in the capture, communication, and continual improvement of knowledge and good practice.

Gazing into the Crystal Ball

Darwinian theory where only the strongest survive is likely to quickly come to pass (unlikely to be more than 10 more years).

As clients continue to embrace the new, emerging way of legal services being delivered, law firms are going to require a larger pool of service-oriented professionals. These individuals will be tasked with focusing more on improving matter delivery processes and operational management to help support the increasing demands law departments will face. They will be required to have familiarity across a number of previously discrete skills—the most obvious of which include recognized project management expertise, strong commercial and analytical skills, and change management. However, they may also now require training and facilitation skills and a strong awareness of (if not deep skills in) evolving technologies (with advances in technology and associated transparency of matter management having the potential to fundamentally change the traditional law firm/client dynamic).

That means having the *right and appropriately skilled resources* in place that can help drive change in each of these three capabilities outlined above and provide frontline support to those who have the technical "smarts" to focus on the practice of law, but also become more commercial and value orientated in their approach.

Don't forget *(a summary of the key points):*

- The global financial crisis led to the rise of previously unheard-of practice management functions—including those of pricing and legal project management.
- Pricing has been viewed as one of the "top hot hires" over recent years, with many positions being filled by U.S. and international law firms, and legal project management is now quickly following suit.
- Knowledge management—the third of the triumvirate—is at a (re)defining moment, now having a clear, explicit role to play in the delivery of better client service and profitability.
- Having the *right and appropriately skilled resources* in situ for these three positions will become key for the law firm of the (near) future.

Chapter 24

Closing Reflections

I was fortunate enough to attend the Legal Marketing Association's inaugural "P3" conference, held in Chicago during October 2013. (In case you are wondering, "P3" stands for pricing, practice innovation, and project management). Indeed, some of you may have also been there.

This got me thinking.

During the conference, I met a colleague, Pier D'Angelo, from Australia. Pier and I had spoken by videoconference for the first time about six years previously. At the time, we were each one of perhaps *five* people globally doing similar pricing roles. It felt, at the time, like a very lonely road we were traveling down.

Fast-forward to the P3 conference, and there were over 200 people in attendance (most of whom were now doing similar pricing- and project-management-related roles). If proof were needed that pricing and project management is—and will continue to be—a "hot topic" with the legal community, here it was being demonstrated in clear and physical form. No longer was it a lonely road; it felt like a bustling freeway!

The experience merely reinforced to me the need for law firms to take a much more comprehensive approach in how to collectively price and deliver our legal services to our clients. We should all strive to be in a position to be able to provide our clients excellent client service at the appropriate quality, and deliver appropriate value for an appropriate fee.

To do so, many of us may need to change and also to challenge some long-established behaviors—either our own or our partners' and attorneys'. Undoubtedly, there will be bumps along the way, but the good news is that none of these is insurmountable with a little effort and focus.

Whether you are working in a large law firm, midsize firm, or small, whether your firm is global, regional, national, or local, the principles outlined within this book will stand you in good stead—but do not delay in your efforts.

Technology in this field will continue to move on apace, becoming more user friendly and "crunching" ever-increasing volumes of data in the search for information "gold dust." The debate about professional support staff versus attorneys in these roles will also continue, with valid perspectives being debated on each side.

But don't let any of this distract you from the key message. Law firms need to change how we price and deliver. *Even the smallest of steps can make a big difference.* When you bring all these together, we truly can develop more mutually beneficial relationships between law firm and law firm client.

Finally, all that remains is for me to wish each and every one of you good luck on your path toward "smarter pricing, smarter profit." Thanks for joining me on the freeway.

Bibliography

ACRITAS, PROCUREMENT WEB SURVEY (2012).

ALM LEGAL INTELLIGENCE, THINKING LIKE YOUR CLIENT: LAW FIRM STRATEGIC PLANNING (2012).

ALM LEGAL INTELLIGENCE, ALTERNATIVE FEE ARRANGEMENTS AT LEGAL DEPARTMENTS AND LAW FIRMS (2013).

ALM LEGAL INTELLIGENCE, HERE FOR GOOD—PRICING PROFESSIONALS IN LAW FIRMS AND THEIR IMPACT ON CLIENTS AND FIRM BUSINESS (2013).

ALM LEGAL INTELLIGENCE, LEGAL PROJECT MANAGEMENT: MUCH PROMISE, MANY HURDLES (2012).

THE AMERICAN LAWYER, Various.

AM LAW DAILY, Various.

A.B.A. J., Various.

ASS'N OF CORPORATE COUNSEL, ACC 2011 CHIEF LEGAL OFFICERS SURVEY (2011).

ASS'N OF CORPORATE COUNSEL, LEGAL PROJECT MANAGEMENT PRIMER (2011).

RONALD J. BAKER, PRICING ON PURPOSE: CREATING AND CAPTURING VALUE (2006).

RONALD J. BAKER, IMPLEMENTING VALUE PRICING: A RADICAL BUSINESS MODEL FOR PROFESSIONAL FIRMS (2010).

WALTER L. BAKER, MICHAEL V. MARN & CRAIG C. ZAWADA, THE PRICE ADVANTAGE (2010).

Harry Beckwith, *Selling the Invisible: A Field Guide to Modern Marketing*, BUSINESS PLUS (reprint ed. 2012).

BARBARA BOAKE & RICK KATHURIA, PROJECT MANAGEMENT FOR LAWYERS (2011).

ROBERT BOLTON & DOROTHY GROVER BOLTON, PEOPLE STYLES AT WORK . . . AND BEYOND: MAKING BAD RELATIONSHIPS GOOD AND GOOD RELATIONSHIPS BETTER (2009).

Toby Brown, THREE GEEKS & A LAW BLOG, Various.

COREY BRANDON, RUSS SCHMIDT & MARCOS RAMIREZ, PEER MONITOR: MONTHLY CLIENT REPORT (Thomson Reuters, Dec. 2012).

BRIGHT IDEAS: INSIGHTS FROM LEGAL LUMINARIES WORLDWIDE (E. Leigh Dance ed., 2009).

CHRIS BULL, LEGAL PROCESS IMPROVEMENT TOOLKIT (2012).

ROBERT B. CIALDINI, INFLUENCE: SCIENCE AND PRACTICE (Allyn & Bacon, 4th ed. 2000).

THOMAS S. CLAY & ERIC A. SEEGER, ALTMAN WEIL, LAW FIRMS IN TRANSITION 2012: AN ALTMAN WEIL FLASH SURVEY (May 2012).

THOMAS S. CLAY, ALTMAN WEIL, LAW FIRMS IN TRANSITION 2013: AN ALTMAN WEIL FLASH SURVEY (May 2013).

THE FUTURE OF LEGAL SERVICES: EXPERT ANALYSIS (Kate Clifton ed., 2011).

PATRICK COLLINS, TALKING YOUR WAY TO WHAT YOU WANT: NEGOTIATE TO WIN! (2009).

Timothy B. Corcoran, *Why CEOs Love Procurement*, *in* BUYING LEGAL: PROCUREMENT INSIGHTS AND PRACTICE (Dr. Silvia Hodges ed., 2012).

JAMES D. COTTERMAN, ALTMAN WEIL, ISSUES IN REALIZATION (2012).

FIONA CZERNIAWSKA & PETER SMITH, BUYING PROFESSIONAL SERVICES (2010).

Marilyn Darling, Charles Parry & Joseph Moore, *Learning in the Thick of It*, HARV. BUS. REV., July–Aug. 2005.

Proposed by ROGER DAWSON, SECRETS OF POWER NEGOTIATING (1999).

Dan DiPietro & Gretta Rusanow, *Citi: Firms Posted 4.3% Rise in 2012 Profits*, AM LAW DAILY, Feb. 7, 2013.

ROBERT J. DOLAN & HERMANN SIMON, POWER PRICING: HOW MANAGING PRICE TRANSFORMS THE BOTTOM LINE (1996).

Jordan Furlong, *Rise of Pricing Risk in the Legal Process*, LAWYERS WEEKLY (June 24, 2011), http://www.lawyersweekly.ca/index.php?section=article&articleid=1444.

Jordan Furlong, *Law 21*.

STEVE GATES, THE NEGOTIATION BOOK: YOUR DEFINITIVE GUIDE TO SUCCESSFUL NEGOTIATING (Wiley, 2011).

Julie Goldberg, *The Evolution of Law Firm Risk*, RISK MGMT. MAG., Aug. 2008.

HARVARD BUSINESS ESSENTIALS, NEGOTIATION (2003).

HARVARD BUSINESS REVIEW ON PRICING (2008).

JIM HASSETT, THE LEGALBIZDEV GUIDE TO ALTERNATIVE FEES (2009).

JIM HASSETT, LEGAL PROJECT MANAGEMENT, PRICING, AND ALTERNATIVE FEE ARRANGEMENTS (2013).

JIM HASSETT, LEGAL PROJECT MANAGEMENT: QUICK REFERENCE GUIDE (2d ed. 2011).

JIM HASSETT, LEGAL PROJECT MANAGEMENT: QUICK REFERENCE GUIDE (3d ed. 2013).

BUYING LEGAL: PROCUREMENT INSIGHTS AND PRACTICE (Dr. Silvia Hodges ed., 2012).

REED HOLDEN & MARK BURTON, PRICING WITH CONFIDENCE: 10 WAYS TO STOP LEAVING MONEY ON THE TABLE (2008).

DAVID KEAN, HOW NOT TO COME SECOND: THE ART OF WINNING BUSINESS PITCHES (2006).

PATRICK LAMB, ALTERNATIVE FEE ARRANGEMENTS: VALUE FEES AND THE CHANGING LEGAL MARKET (2010).

SUSAN RARIDON LAMBRETH, LEGAL PROJECT MANAGEMENT: TRANSFORMING LEGAL SERVICES (2011).

Susan Lambreth & Carly Landry, *Project Management or Process Improvement: Which Comes First?*, HILDEBRANDT BLOG (March 2011).

Law Firm Efficient: Responsiveness, Reflection and Checklists, HILDEBRANDT INST. (Nov. 30, 2012), http://hildebrandtblog.com/2012/11/30/law-firm-effi ciency-responsiveness-reflection-and-checklists/.

THE LAWYER, Various.

STEVEN A. LAUER, VALUE-RELATED FEE ARRANGEMENTS (2012).

LEGAL WEEK, Various.

Aileen Leventon, Ellen Rosenthal & John Dougherty, Using After Action Reviews to Improve the Delivery of Legal Services (Ark Group Webinar, Feb. 12, 2013).

STEVEN B. LEVY, LEGAL PROJECT MANAGEMENT: CONTROL COSTS, MEET SCHEDULES, MANAGE RISKS, AND MAINTAIN SANITY (2009).

Paul Lippe, *Welcome to the Future: Embracing the New Normal*, AM LAW DAILY, Mar. 19, 2010.

Paul Lippe, *Expert Analysis 5: Emerging Trends That Are Changing How Lawyers and Law Firms Work*, *in* THE FUTURE OF LEGAL SERVICES: EXPERT ANALYSIS (Kate Clifton ed., 2011).

BRUCE MACEWEN, GROWTH IS DEAD: NOW WHAT?: LAW FIRMS ON THE BRINK (2013).

DAVID H. MAISTER, MANAGING THE PROFESSIONAL SERVICES FIRM (2003).

DAVID H. MAISTER, CHARLES H. GREEN & ROBERT M. GALFORD, THE TRUSTED ADVISOR (2001).

MANAGING PARTNER, Various.

Michael V. Marn & Robert L. Rosiello, *Managing Price, Gaining Profit*, HARV. BUS. REV., Sept.–Oct. 1992.

Deborah McMurray, *Improve Client Service and Satisfaction Through Global Project and Knowledge Management*, *in* BRIGHT IDEAS—INSIGHTS FROM LEGAL LUMINARIES WORLDWIDE (E. Leigh Dance ed., 2009).

KENT B. MONROE, PRICING: MAKING PROFITABLE DECISIONS (McGraw-Hill, 3d ed. 2003).

NABARRO, GENERAL COUNSEL: VAGUE ABOUT VALUE (2011).

THOMAS T. NAGLE, JOHN E. HOGAN & JOSEPH ZALE, THE STRATEGY AND TACTICS OF PRICING: A GUIDE TO GROWING MORE PROFITABLY (Prentice Hall, 5th ed. 2010).

Professional Pricing Society, PRICING ADVISOR, Various.

Professional Pricing Society, QUARTERLY JOURNAL, Various.

PROJECT MGMT. INST., A GUIDE TO THE PROJECT MANAGEMENT BODY OF KNOWLEDGE (PMBOK GUIDE) (5th ed. 2013).

Dr. Larry Richard, *You've Got Personality*, LEGAL MGMT., July/Aug. 2002.

MICHAEL ROCH, PRICING AND PROFITABILITY FOR LAW FIRMS (2010).

G. RICHARD SHELL, BARGAINING FOR ADVANTAGE (1999).

Hermann Simon, *The Magic Word: Pretium*, PRICING ADVISOR, Sept. 2012.

Mark Sirkin, *New Roles in the Law Firm of the Future*, HILDEBRANDT BAKER ROBBINS (Nov. 11, 2009).

MANMOHAN S. SODHI & NAVDEEP S. SODHI, SIX SIGMA PRICING: IMPROVING PRICING OPERATIONS TO INCREASE PROFITS (2008).

TARGETING PROFITABILITY: STRATEGIES TO IMPROVE LAW FIRM PERFORMANCE (Helen Roche ed., 2013).

Andrew Terret, *KM Struggles to Survive While Legal Project Management Thrives*, *in* KNOWLEDGE MANAGEMENT: WHITE PAPER (2011).

THOMSON REUTERS PEER MONITOR/GEORGETOWN LAW CTR. FOR THE STUDY OF THE LEGAL PROFESSION, 2013: REPORT ON THE STATE OF THE LEGAL MARKET (2013).

ORI WEINER, HIGH IMPACT FEE NEGOTIATION AND MANAGEMENT FOR PROFESSIONALS (2013).

ALAN WEISS, VALUE-BASED FEES: HOW TO CHARGE—AND GET—WHAT YOU'RE WORTH (Pfeiffer, 2d ed. 2008).

Melania Wenstrup, *Putting Your Best Foot Forward: Bidding to Procurement*, *in* BUYING LEGAL: PROCUREMENT INSIGHTS AND PRACTICE (Dr. Silvia Hodges ed., 2012).

Pamela Woldow, PAM WOLDOW BLOG, Various.

Acknowledgments

First, I would like to express a very big thank-you to everyone who has helped shape (and challenge) my thinking during my professional life (to date) and to those who will in the future. It goes without saying that the views expressed in this book are mine and mine alone and should not be seen as reflecting those of both my current and previous employers, who I am sure would express them much more clearly if they were.

I would also like to thank a number of contemporaries, especially Toby Brown for agreeing to write the forward to this book, but also for his invaluable and infectious enthusiasm for this field, and similarly to Chris Emerson, both of whom in particular have made my transition from the United Kingdom to the United States an extremely pleasant adjustment. Similarly, there are a number of others who have provided me with great insight and have been extremely generous with their time—for example (and in no particular order), Colin Jasper, Ori Weiner, Jim Hassett, and Susan Raridon Lambreth.

I would like to express my thanks to all those at Baker & McKenzie who allowed me to write this book, especially Laurie Robertson and Winston Zee, and also to Jon Malysiak, my editor at the ABA who has worked wonders with my initial draft and who was generous enough to approach me initially about writing this book.

Finally, a huge thank-you to my wife, Ophelia, and daughter, Isla, who have had to keep themselves busy while I continued to do "just one more chapter," have been extremely patient and understanding, and encouraged me to embark on this in the first place.

Stuart J. T. Dodds

April 2014

Index